IMAGES
of America

Bayfield and the Pine River Valley 1880–1960

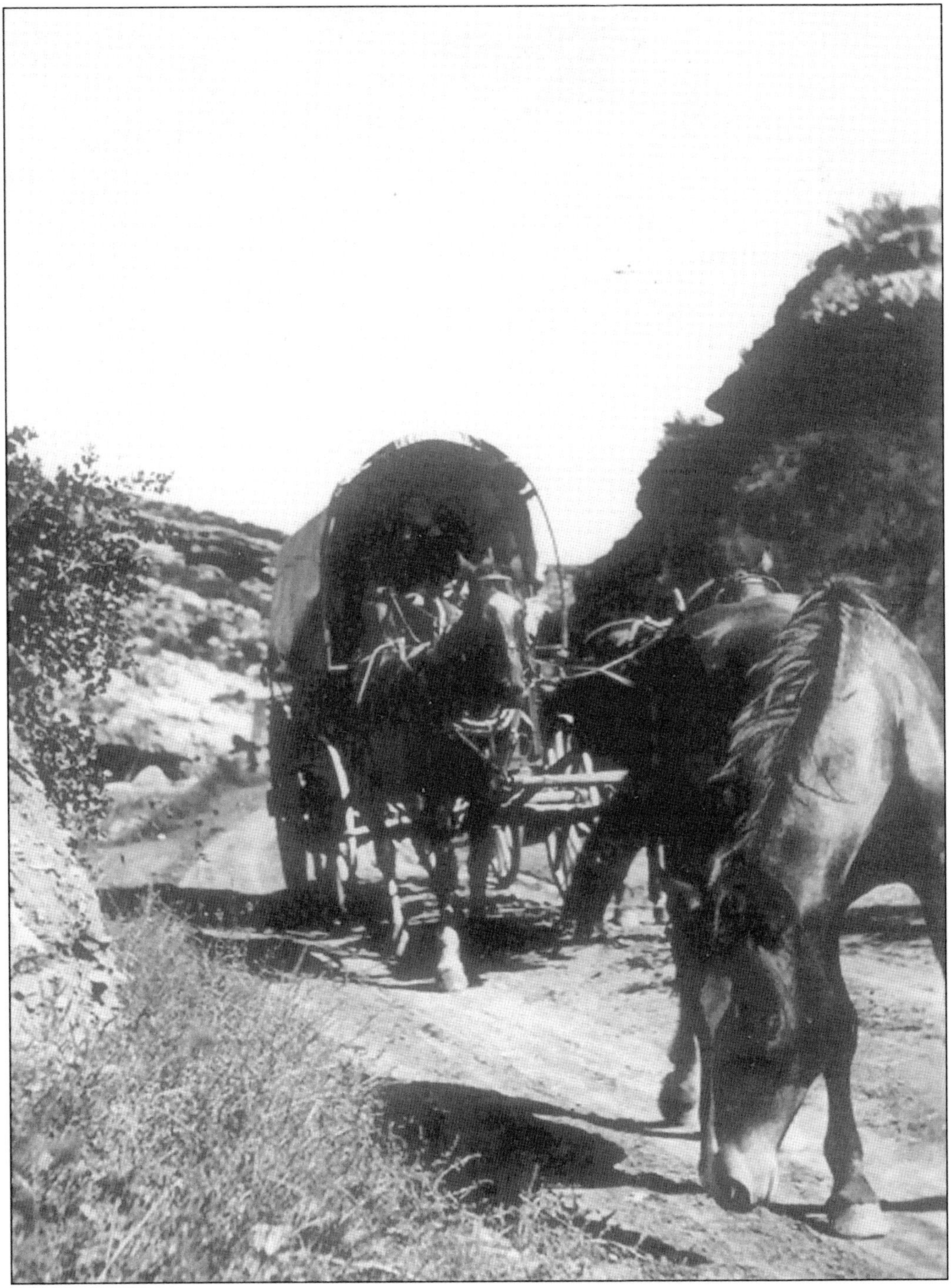

James and Susan McKenny arrived in the Pine River Valley after the town of Bayfield had been established. However, the early European settlers that crossed the Continental Divide, as early as 1877, had to lower their wagons down cliffs as they came across. Roads were later built over the mountains and the road over the Divide became know as Wolf Creek Pass. (Courtesy of Barb Fjerstad.)

IMAGES
of America

BAYFIELD AND THE PINE RIVER VALLEY 1880–1960

Laddie E. John

ARCADIA
PUBLISHING

ISBN 978-0-7385-2052-2

Published by Arcadia Publishing,
Charleston, South Carolina

Printed in the United States of America

Library of Congress Catalog Card Number: 2001098615

For all general information contact Arcadia Publishing at:
Telephone 843-853-2070
Fax 843-853-0044
E-mail sales@arcadiapublishing.com
For customer service and orders:
Toll-Free 1-888-313-2665

Visit us on the Internet at www.arcadiapublishing.com

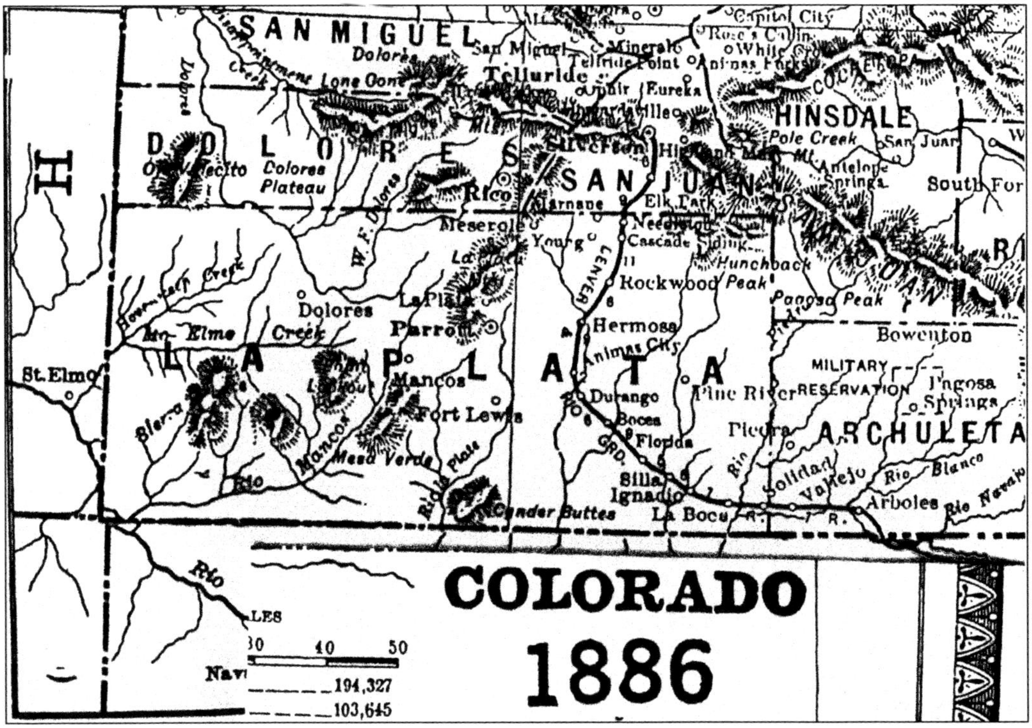

This 1886 Colorado map shows the San Juan Mountains where many of the rivers in Southwestern Colorado originate, including the Rio de Los Pinos (Pine River) and the Vallecito River. It also shows the early settlement of Pine River. This settlement was one of the first in the Pine River Valley (the other being Los Pinos) before the town of Bayfield was laid out. (Courtesy of K. B. Slocum Books, Austin, Texas.)

Contents

ACKNOWLEDGMENTS

The author would like to thank the following for sharing their photos in compiling this collection of views of the Pine River Valley and Bayfield:

The Denver Museum, Western History Department
La Plata Historical Society
Center of Southwest Studies, Fort Lewis College: Todd Ellison and Catherine Conrad
The Telecommunications History Group, Inc., Denver
Pine River Irrigation: Warren Joe Brown

Jo Griffin
Fred McIntyre
Freda Brown
Glade Stowell
Delmar Jenkins
Ralph Martinez
Roberta Barr Collection
Poncho McNew Collection
Michele Teriot
Danny Rodman
Bob McCoy
Barb Fjerstad
Tom Moga Shoreline Collection
Mrs. Alfred E. Shelhamer
Harold Wilmer
Jess Newman
Dobin Shupe
Bea Bartholomew
Cecil Sower
Earl Jack
Hanna Cundiff
Tim Walters
Deana Wright
LaVina Mars
Merle Harrison
Henry Parks Collection
Merle James
Kenny Montgomery Collection
Mart Huchins
Betty Fahrion
Grace Sassaman Schirard
Hugh Purcell
Gene Basset
Mrs. Orrel Brewer Collection
L.T. Ostwald Collection

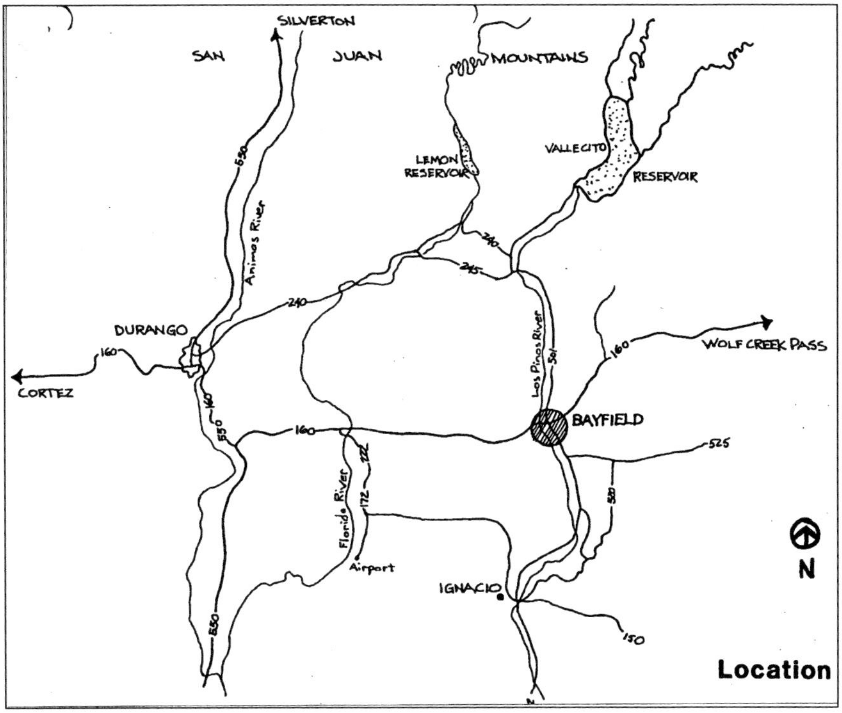

A special thanks goes out to anyone that I might have missed. If anyone has information regarding identification of any people shown, please contact the author, 970-884-2199.

Introduction

The Pine River Valley in southwestern Colorado is the first valley of any consequence west of the Continental Divide. The average elevation of the valley is 6,500 feet. This has much to do with the climactic conditions; this elevation makes a month difference in the length of the growing season compared to other mountain valleys that may be higher in elevation and have much colder winters.

With the climate, elevation, and abundance of water, the Pine River Valley has been ideal for the planting of fruit trees, wheat, oats, hay, and potatoes. Farmers would have rushed into the area much sooner if it had not been Indian land owned and defended by Ute bands. Many of the old nineteenth century orchards introduced by Scotch-Irish pioneers are still producing fruit today. Not only are there agricultural possibilities in the valley, but there are many other resources. Geologists discovered coal under the hillsides, and nearby there are huge quantities of gas and oil.

Many lumber mills sprang up in the 1890s because most of the forests had not been touched, and with the coming of the Denver and Rio Grande Railroad, lumber could be shipped to distant markets. Locally, settlers selected the best logs for their homes and supplied their cooking and heating fuel needs with thick stands of ponderosa pine.

When the settlers moved into the Pine River Valley and Bayfield, they settled in the valley proper and also along small tributaries such as Wallace Gulch, North and South Texas Creek, Beaver Creek, Dry Creek, and Bear Creek. Most days are sunny and dry, but heavy snows come in the winter. Spring can happen as early as February, although the valley has been known to get its heaviest snowfalls in March and April. In the spring the land is usually ready for cultivation, and alfalfa hay remains the major crop.

The Pine River supplies abundant water for irrigating almost every acre of this fertile valley, and the Southern Ute tribe has the senior water rights. Because the Pine River sometimes flooded the valley due to too much rain rather than the spring snow melt run-off, settlers sought to contain the river's flow. The Newlands Reclamation Act (1904), advocated by explorer John Wesley Powell and signed into law by President Theodore Roosevelt, created the Bureau of Reclamation to build dams to harness rivers and conserve western water. Environmental issues were not yet understood and neither were principles of ecology. Instead, the act promoted conservation for the benefit of settlers and small farmers, with no thought to environmental impacts for other species. After the tremendous flood of 1927, the government stepped in and built the Pine River Dam.

The name was later changed to Vallecito Dam, which impounds the Pine River and has created magnificent Vallecito Lake, which lies east to west between high ridges of the San Juan Mountains. Now the valley is assured sufficient water for the summer crops; however, in 1957 the valley flooded again. It rained too much, and the lake filled, and the floodgates opened. When Bureau of Reclamation staff went to close the gates, they saw they were filled with debris and could not be shut.

I have lived in the Pine River Valley for twenty-five years. I was born in Kline, Colorado, which is on the west side of La Plata County, but my family moved to Animas City (now part of Durango) when I was two. Our family moved from Animas City in 1942, and I returned to the area in 1967, to finish my college education at Fort Lewis College. After I graduated I taught school in Durango for twenty-seven years, and I have been retired for six years. Much of that time I have been researching photographs and anecdotes for this book.

Hopefully this publication will express some of that local southwestern Colorado history, because the stories of the pioneers need to be told. We live in a pristine mountain valley, and agriculture and cattle ranching has long been associated with tourism, superb elk hunting, and excellent trout fishing. Now houses are cropping up in former hayfields, and pioneer log cabins have given way to summer homes. The Pine River Valley and Vallecito Lake has become an important summer tourist destination for travelers driving north from Texas and New Mexico, but many local residents prefer the valley in the fall and spring when there is less traffic.

To the first settlers, the Utes and the pioneer families who homesteaded the valley bottom and up the side creeks, this book is dedicated. They worked hard so that the rest of us can enjoy the stunning mountain views and breathe that clear alpine air.

Prologue

I am long (fifty miles). I am narrow (just a few miles across), but further down I am wide (twenty miles). I am very beautiful. Glacial movement many, many, years ago formed me. I have an excellent lifeline and numerous smaller lifelines feed me. I am covered by beautiful foliage such as majestic pines, colorful oak, flowering shrubs, and a variety of flowers. Wild deer and elk roam throughout my beautiful forests, and the upper reaches of my arms touch the sky. In the winter, all is white and buried under many feet of snow.

My skin is very fertile, as evidenced by the lush growth that covers it. For centuries native people moved upon my skin, hunted my wild animals, and gathered the abundant berries that I produce. However, they did me no harm. We lived in harmony with each other. The Utes named one of my larger lifelines *Shu-ah-gauche* (Vallecito Creek), which translates as "crooked water."

Other men, different from the ones that roamed freely upon my skin, gave my main lifeline a name. Spanish explorers in the 18th century called me "Rio de Los Pinos" (River of Pines) because of the abundant pine trees that grow along my main lifeline. Thus, I became known as the Beautiful Pine River Valley.

Soon settlers came and started digging into my skin. They began taking dirt and rock away that they believed to be valuable to them. This digging was short lived, but still the scars remain and can be seen today on my beautiful upper arms. In the lower valley, men were clearing some of the beautiful pines, tilling my fertile skin, and planting various plants, not native to me. They also dug small lifelines to get water to the crops they had planted. This did seem to enhance my beauty.

In the springtime, I can get quite wild. The cold, white covering I have in the winter season melts and my smaller lifelines run over their banks. As they all come together, my final lifeline becomes a large, raging river. I have flooded the valley savagely a couple of times after the settlers arrived. It was after the Vallecito Lake. However, I am still the Beautiful Pine River Valley.

One

UTE INDIANS AND JOHN TAYLOR

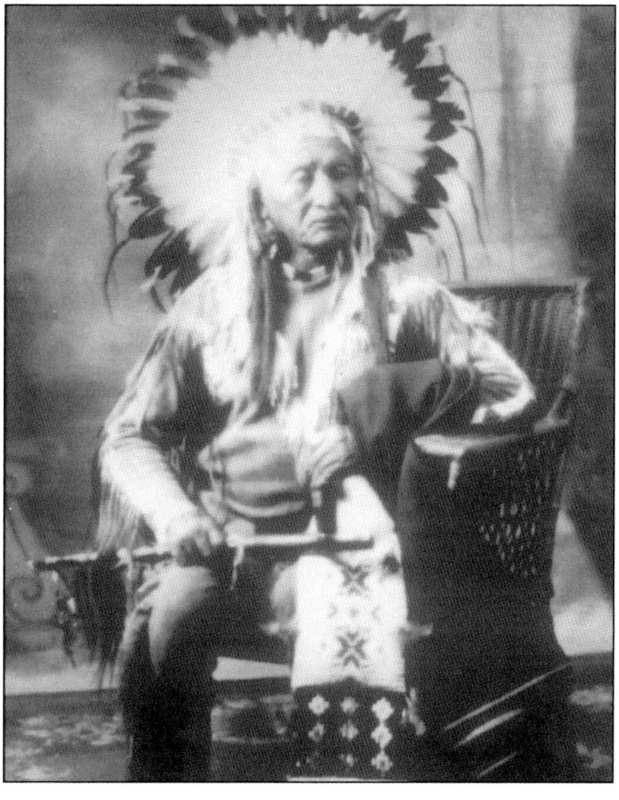

Buckskin Charley, born in 1840, became a prominent chief c.1870. He was recognized as Chief of the Mauche and Servero Bands and Principal Chief of the Capote. When Chief Ouray died in 1880, Buckskin Charley became principal chief of the Southern Utes at Ignacio, Colorado. He served as chief for 56 years and died in 1936 at the age of 96. (Courtesy of Jo Griffin.)

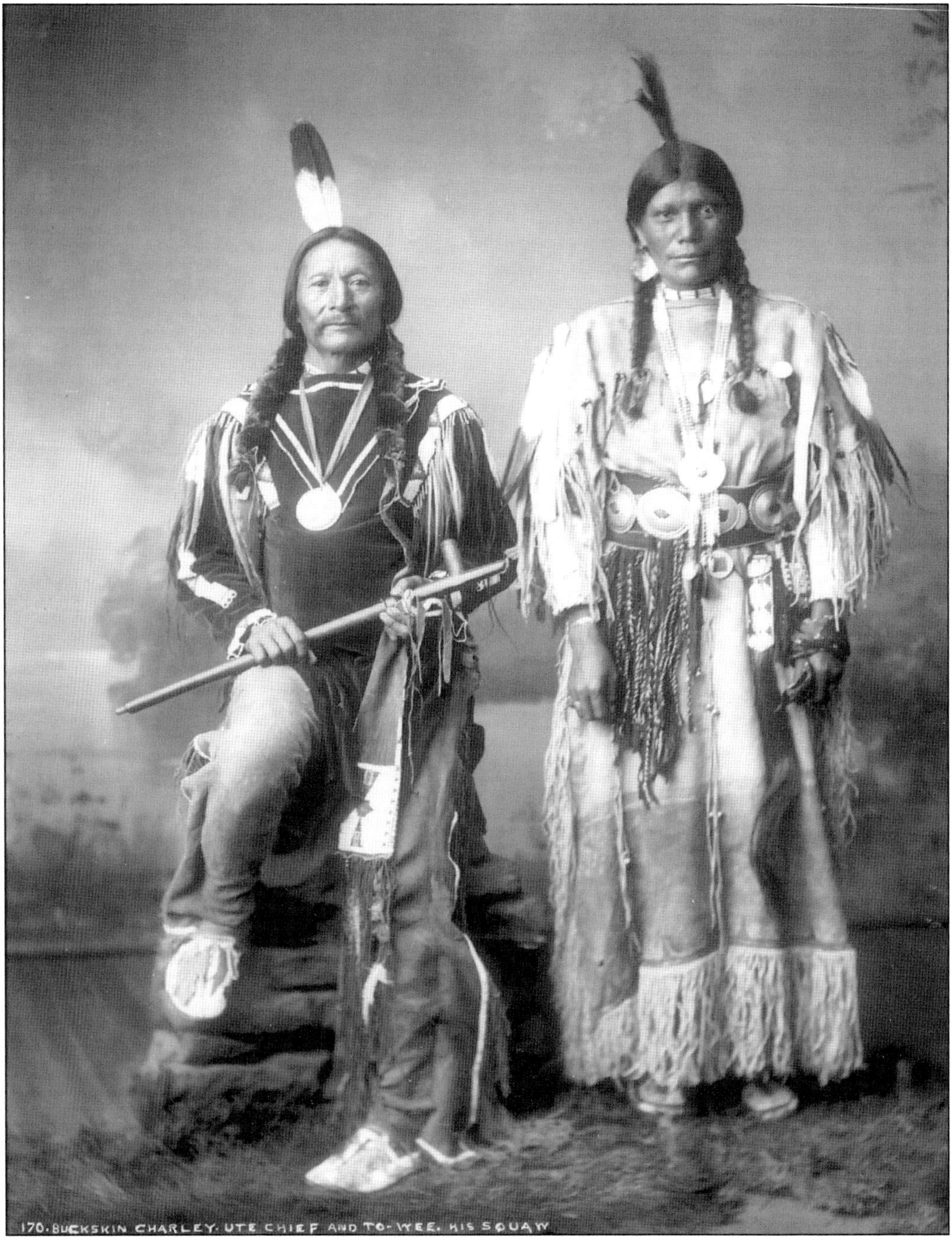

Buckskin Charley, Chief of the Southern Utes, poses with his squaw, Te-Wee, in this 1899 photo by Rose and Hokins, Denver. (Courtesy of Denver Public Library, Western History Department.)

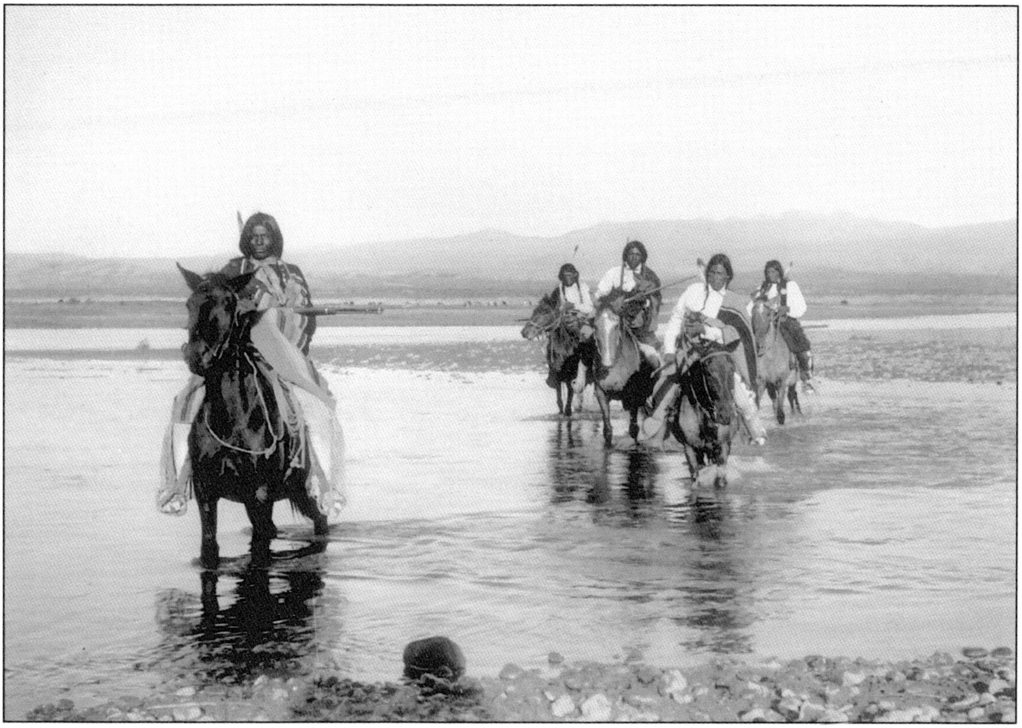

Pictured here are Ute horsemen crossing the Rio de Los Pinos (Pine River) on the Southern Ute Reservation below Bayfield in 1899. (Courtesy of Denver Public Library, Western History Department.)

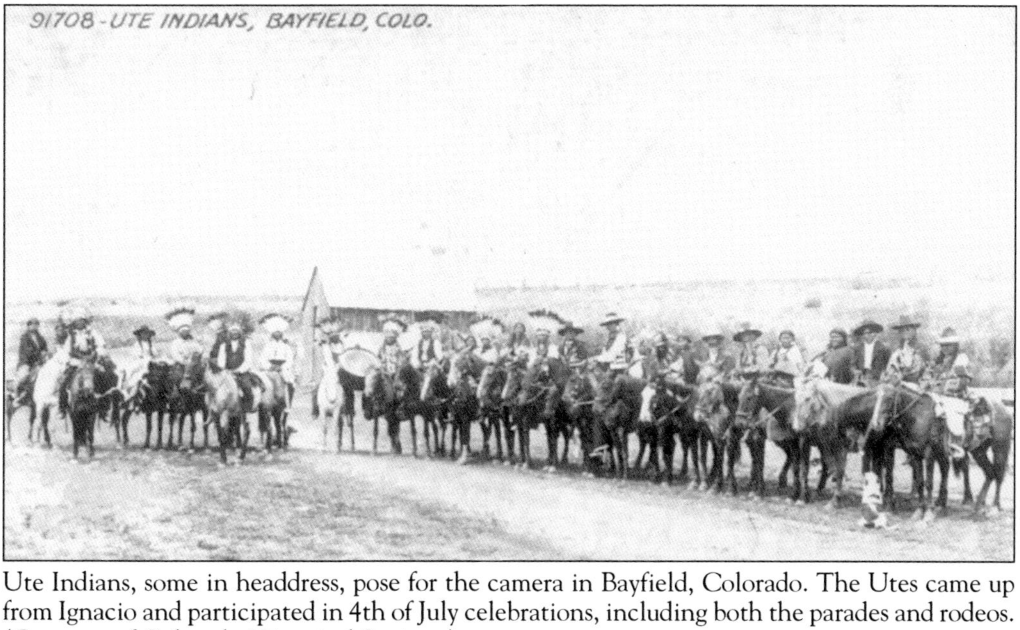

Ute Indians, some in headdress, pose for the camera in Bayfield, Colorado. The Utes came up from Ignacio and participated in 4th of July celebrations, including both the parades and rodeos. (Courtesy of Colorado Historical Society.)

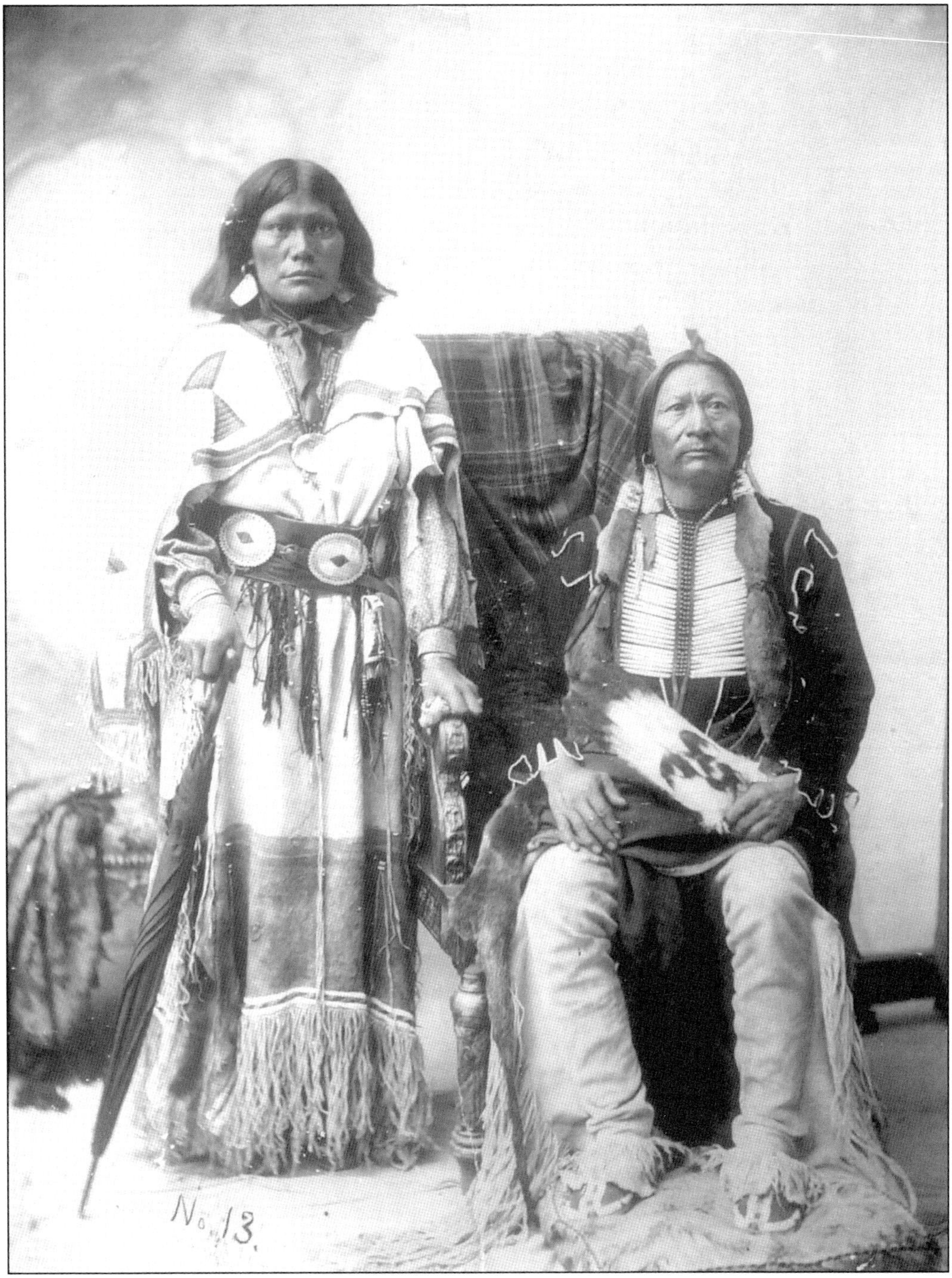

Posing here for a later photo in native dress are Buckskin Charley and squaw Te-Wee. Buckskin Charley, after the Utes were established on the Southern Ute Reservation, was instrumental in getting his tribe to follow his example in becoming farmers. (Courtesy of Denver Public Library, Western History Department.)

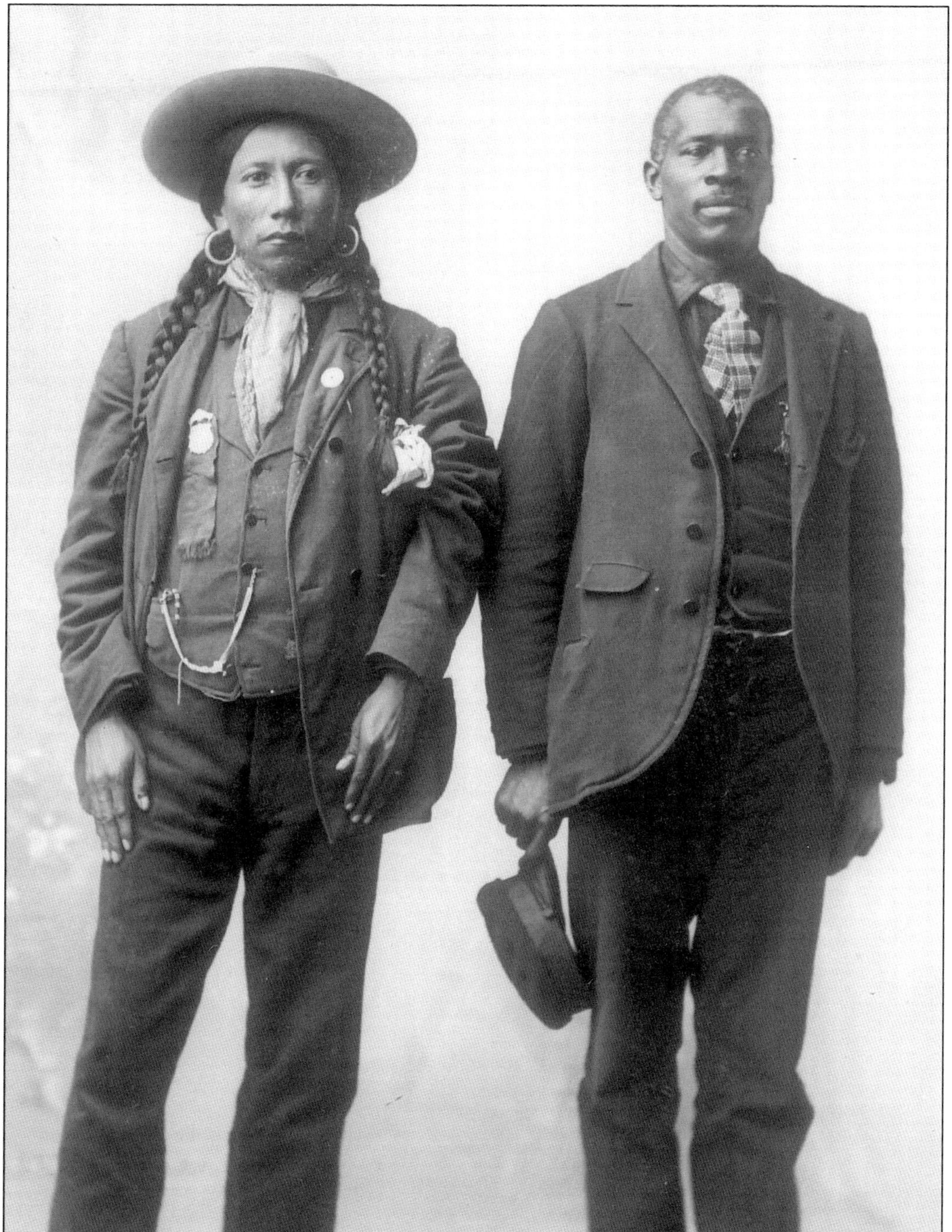

A Ute friend (left) poses with John Taylor. Taylor was the son of slave parents, fought in the Civil War, and later became a Buffalo soldier. He first came to the Pine River Valley as a trapper-settler in 1871–72, but missing the renegade life with the Indians, he left and joined with a Navajo band. He returned to the valley in the mid 1870s after joining with a band of Utes. He always said he was the first white man to settle in the Pine River Valley of Southwestern Colorado. (Courtesy of Denver Public Library, Western Department.)

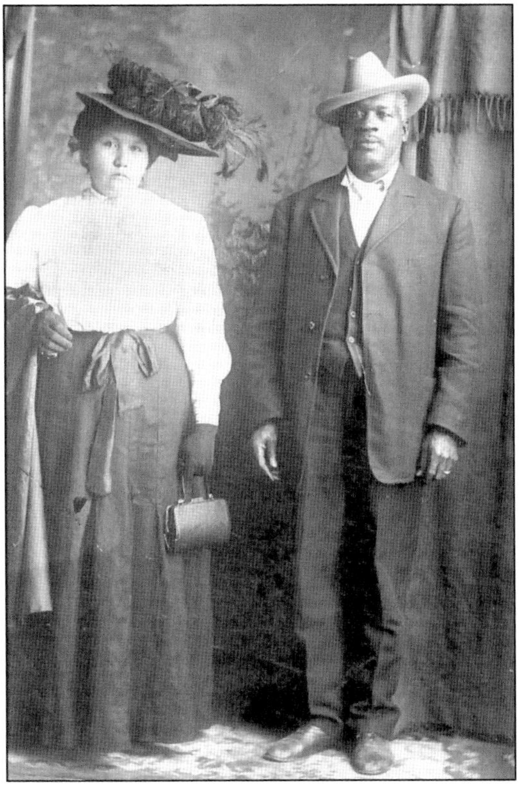

Kitty Cloud and John Taylor pose for their wedding photo in Durango, Colorado, in 1907. (Courtesy of La Plata County Historical Society Animas Museum Photo Archives.)

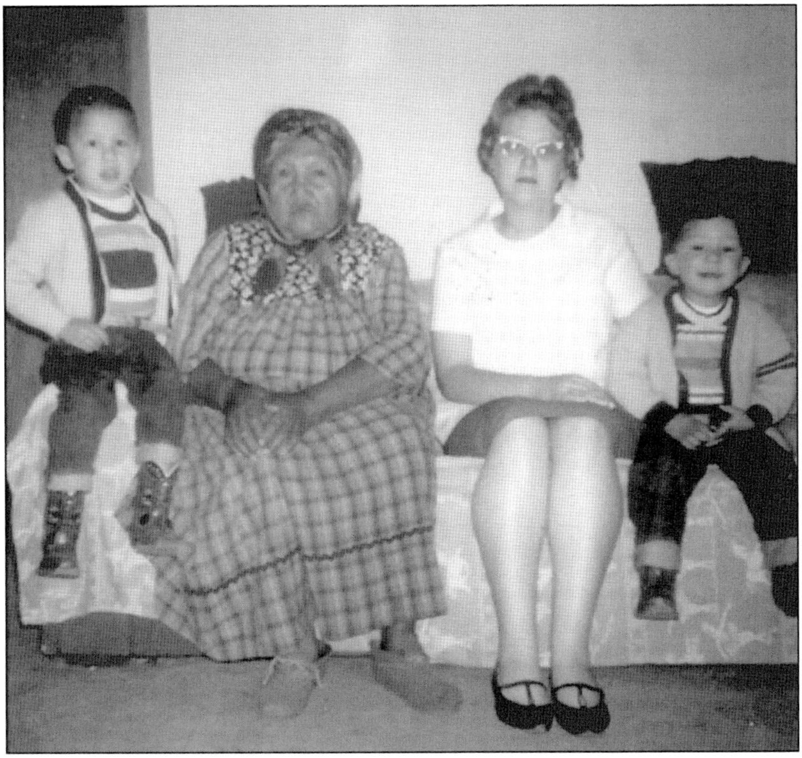

Kitty Cloud sits with her grandson Erwin's wife and two great grandchildren. Pictured from left to right are Trent Taylor, Kitty Cloud, Carolynne McIntyre Taylor, and Lance Taylor. (Courtesy of Carolynne McIntyre Taylor.)

Two

HOMESTEADS

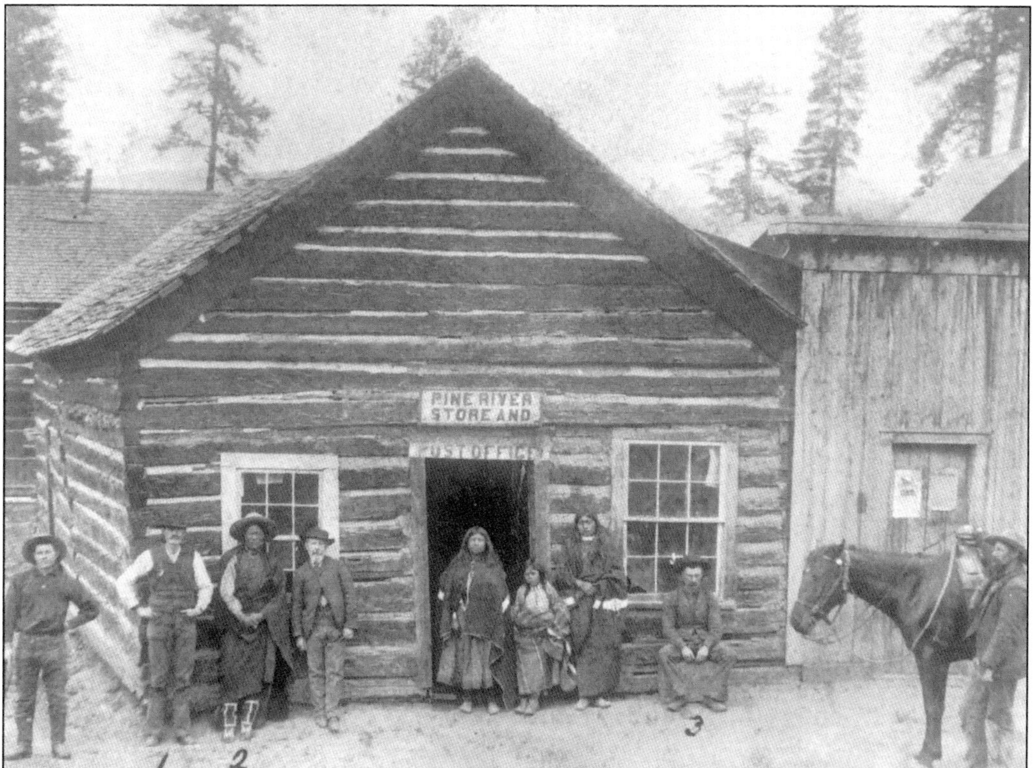

Pictured is the Pine River Store and Post Office at Pine River, Colorado, opened in 1887. The settlement consisted of about 100 residents. Pictured, from left to right, are W. T. Helm (#1, father of Mrs. Gradyshelm McPherson), Buckskin Charley (#2), and Charles F. Wood (#3, postmaster in 1890). The group of Ute Indians by the door and the other three men are unidentified. (Courtesy of Jo Griffin. Number identification by Todd Ellison, Center of Southwest Studies, Fort Lewis College.)

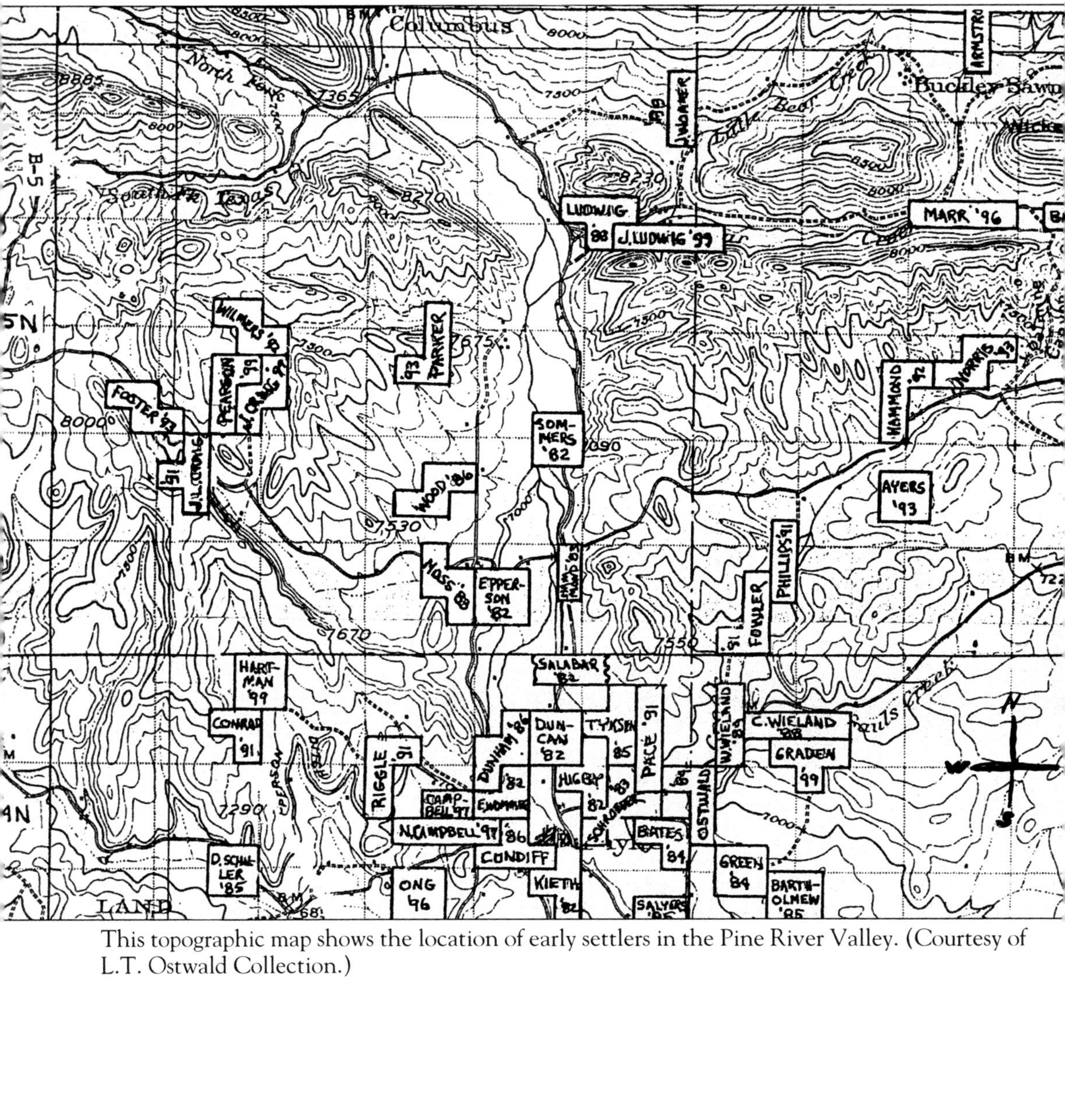

This topographic map shows the location of early settlers in the Pine River Valley. (Courtesy of L.T. Ostwald Collection.)

ADJUDICATED DECREES 1934 & 1966

Ditch	Priority Number	Amount Priority S. F.	Cumilative River	Total Ditch	Remarks	Year
U. S. (Indians)	P-1	212.0 *				1868
Bean	P-2	3.25	3.25	3.25		1877
Thompson-Epperson	P-3	4.75	8.00	4.75		1877
Los Pinos	P-4	11.50	19.50	11.50		1878
Wommer Irrig.	P-5	6.25	24.75	5.25		1878
Bear Creek & Pine River	P-6	14.00	38.75	14.00		1878
Citizens	P-7	3.50	42.25	3.50		1878
Higbee	P-8	1.00	43.25	1.00		1879
Myers-Asher	P-9	3.33	46.58	3.33		1881
King Consolidated	P-10	0.30	46.88	0.30		1881
Taylor	V-1	4.0			B. of R.	
Taylor	P-11	9.0			B. of R.	
Schroder Irrig.	P-12	27.12	74.00	27.12		1881
Farrell	P-13	2.00	76.00	2.00		1881
Grimes (Decker)	V-2	11.25			B. of R.	
Hensly Spring	V-3	1.00			-1.00-	1882
Island	P-14	0.50	76.50	0.50		1882
Bennett-Myers	P-15	4.00	80.50	4.00		1882
Bennett-Myers	P-16	1.00	81.50	5.00		1882
Newell-Asher		1.5			B. of R.	
Huntington ranck	P-17	0.125	81.625	0.125		1883
Kirpatrick	P-18	6.0			-7.00-	1884
Graham Ck. #1	E-1	1.0			-8.00-	1884
Thompson-Epperson	P-18	0.625	82.250	5.375		1884
Graham Ck. #2	E-1	0.375			-8.375-	1884
Patrick	V-4	1.0			-9.375-	1885
Highland	P-19	5.5			B. of R.	
McLoyd	V-5	8.0			-17.375-	1889
Bobeson #2	V-6	1.0			-18.375-	1889
Catlin	P-20	0.53	82.780	0.53		1890
Foster	V-7	2.0	in Vallecito		-19.375- B.R. 1.0	
Robt. Morrison Cons.	P-21	0.375	83.155	0.375		1890
Bean	P-22	40.0			Power	
Dunham	P-23	1.0	84.155	1.00		1894
Thompson-Epperson	P-24	4.55	88.705	9.925		1894
Thompson-Epperson	P-25	12.0	100.705	21.925		1896
P.-R. Canal & Sp. Ck.	P-26	203.9		203.9		1900
Thompson-Epperson		12.75		34.675		
Dr. Morrison		7.8				
Robt. Morrison Cons.		40.13		40.505		
McBride	P-27	1.25	441.235	1.25		1901
Wommer Irrig.	P-28	1.0	442.235	6.25		1901
Farrell	P-29	2.5	444.735	4.50		1901
North Side (M. Safley)	V-9	1.0			-20.375	1901
Rhodes (Dale)	V-10	2.5			-22.875-	1901
Martin Springs	V-11	0.5			B. of R.	
Moore	V-11	7.0			B. of R.	
Boyle	P-30	1.0			B. of R.	
Kirkpatrick	P-31	0.5			-23.375-	1902
Meadow Brook	V-12	3.0			B. of R.	
Thompson-Epperson	P-32	1.75	446.485	36.425		1902
Bean	P-33	0.38	446.365	3.63		1903
Robt. Morrison Cons.	P-34	5.65	452.515	46.155		1909
Robt. Morrison Cons.	P-35	12.61	465.125	58.765		1910
Sullivan	P-36	7.08	472.205	7.08		1910

This document shows adjudicated water decreed in 1934 and 1966. The Ute Indians of the Southern Ute Reservation had water rights in 1868. They still have priority water from Vallecito Lake. When the early settlers came they begin digging ditches to irrigate their land. (Courtesy of Ted Sparks.)

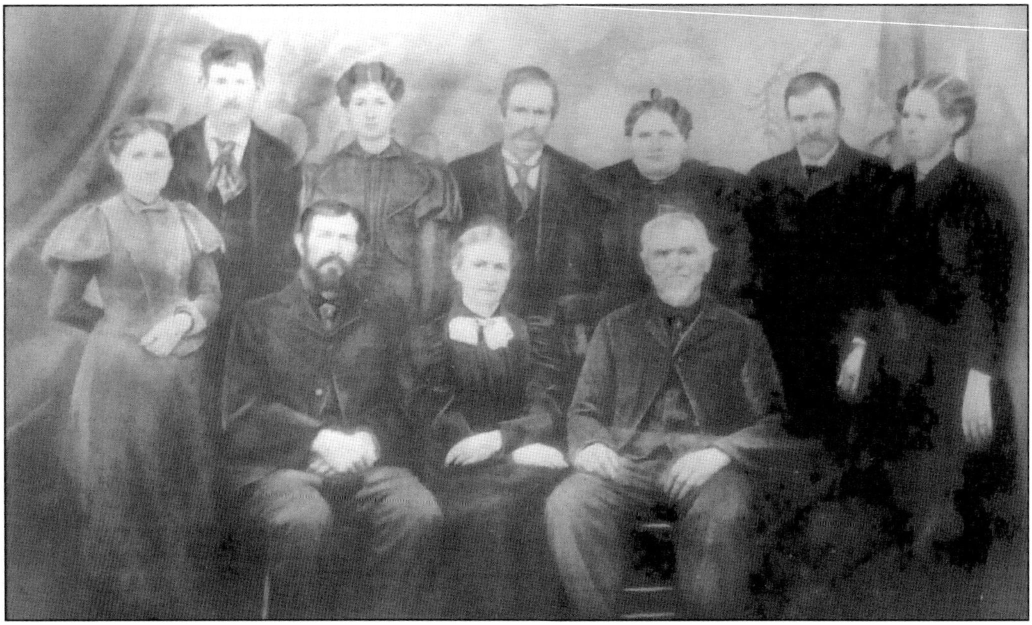

The Spencer family poses in this early photo. The Spencers were related to the Montgomery family of Bayfield. Pictured, from left to right, are (front row) Laura Spencer; Will Spencer, great uncle; Sarah Spencer, great grandmother; Appolis Spencer, great grandfather; (back row) Seneca Spencer; Cecila Spencer, great aunt; Perry Spencer, great uncle; and three unidentified people. (Courtesy of Kenny Montgomery Collection.)

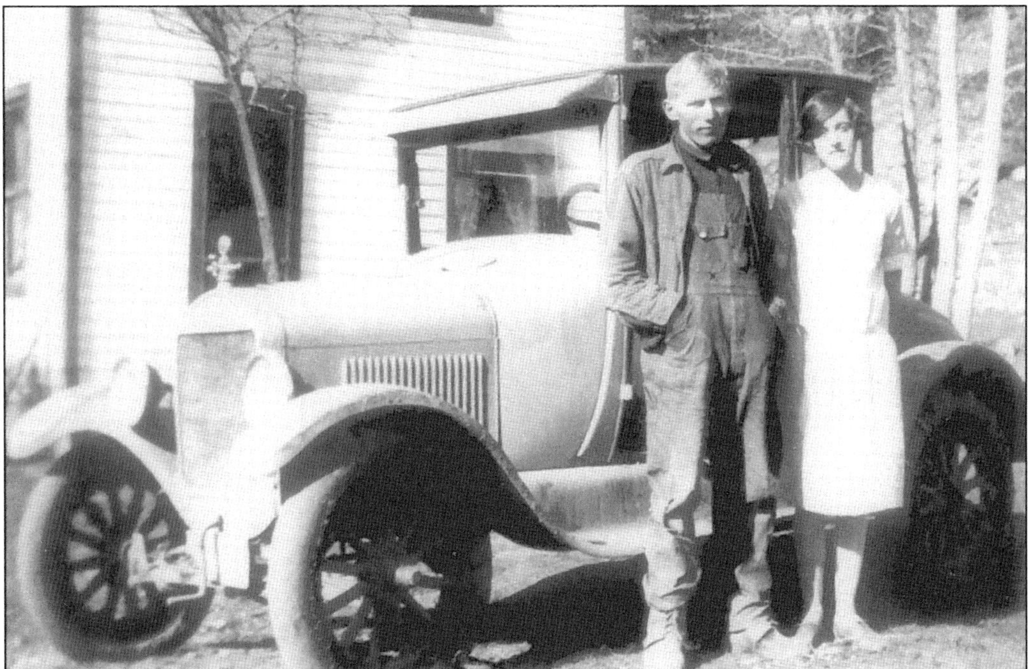

Frank Wommer Jr. and wife Jessie stand by their car and home in the Pine River Valley. (Courtesy of LeVina Mars.)

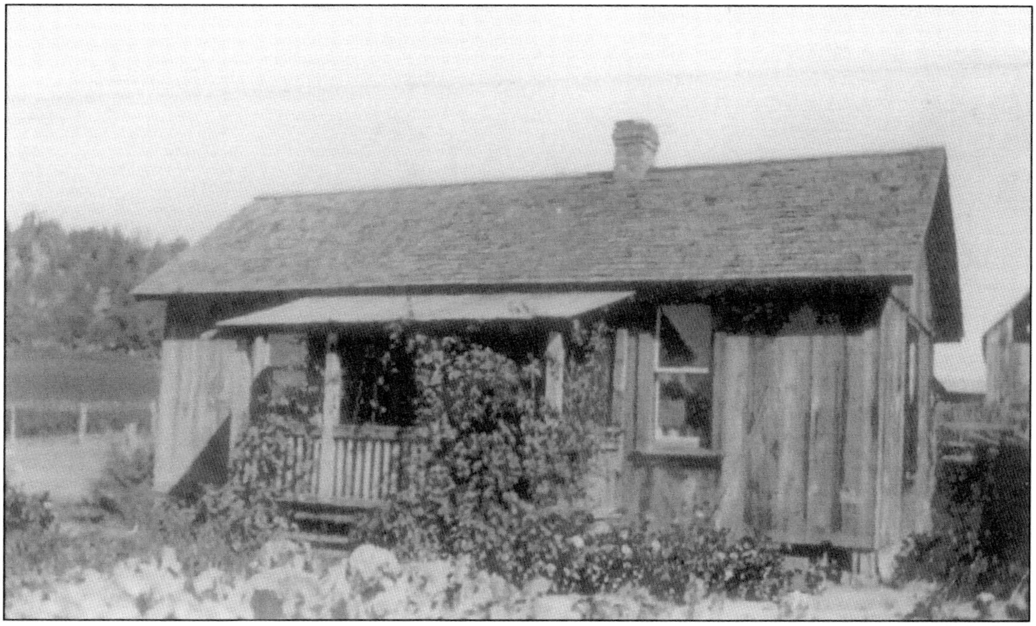

This view is of the Armour Gearhart homestead, homesteaded in the late 1880s on Dry Creek. Some of the original homestead land is still under cultivation and some has been subdivided for other development. (Courtesy of Orrel Brewer Collection.)

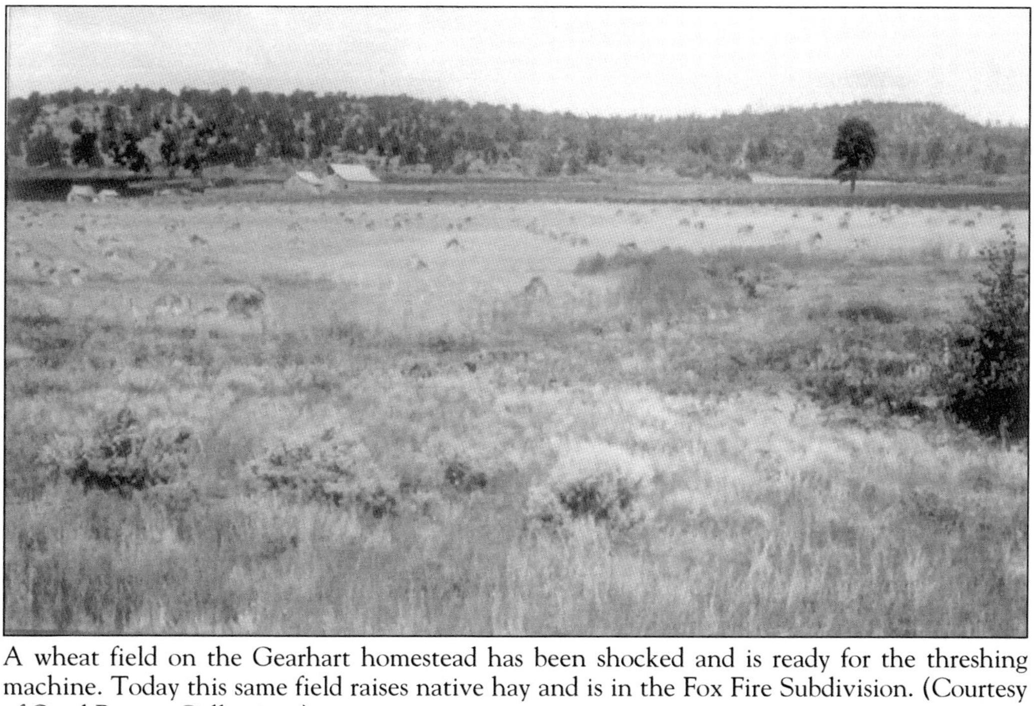

A wheat field on the Gearhart homestead has been shocked and is ready for the threshing machine. Today this same field raises native hay and is in the Fox Fire Subdivision. (Courtesy of Orrel Brewer Collection.)

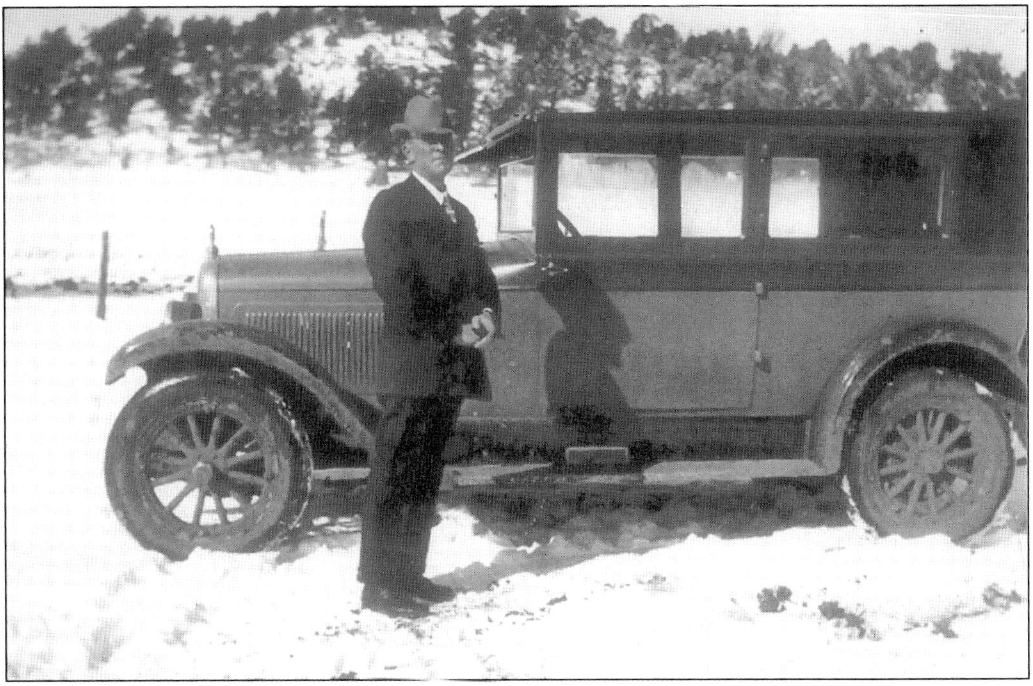

Armour Gearhart is pictured standing by his new "touring" car at the Gearhart homestead on Dry Creek. (Courtesy of Poncho McNew Collection.)

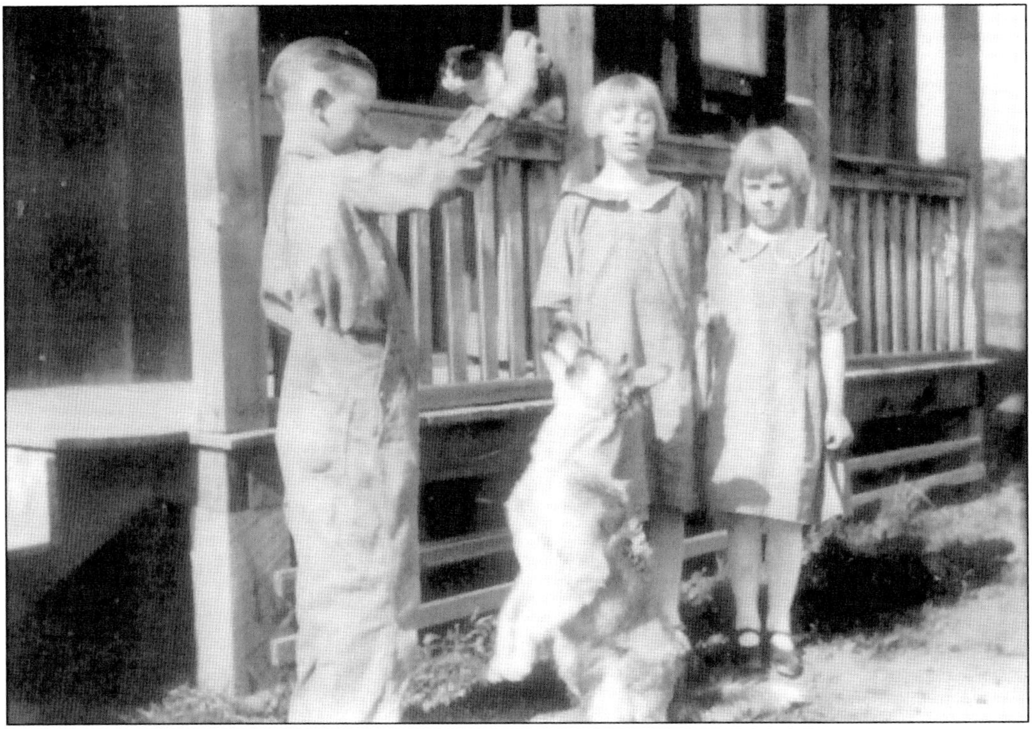

Kenneth Gearhart teaches his dog "Tillie" to sit up as Dorthy and Ernestine watch. Note the cat sitting on the porch rail ignoring the whole scene. (Courtesy of Orrell Brewer Collection.)

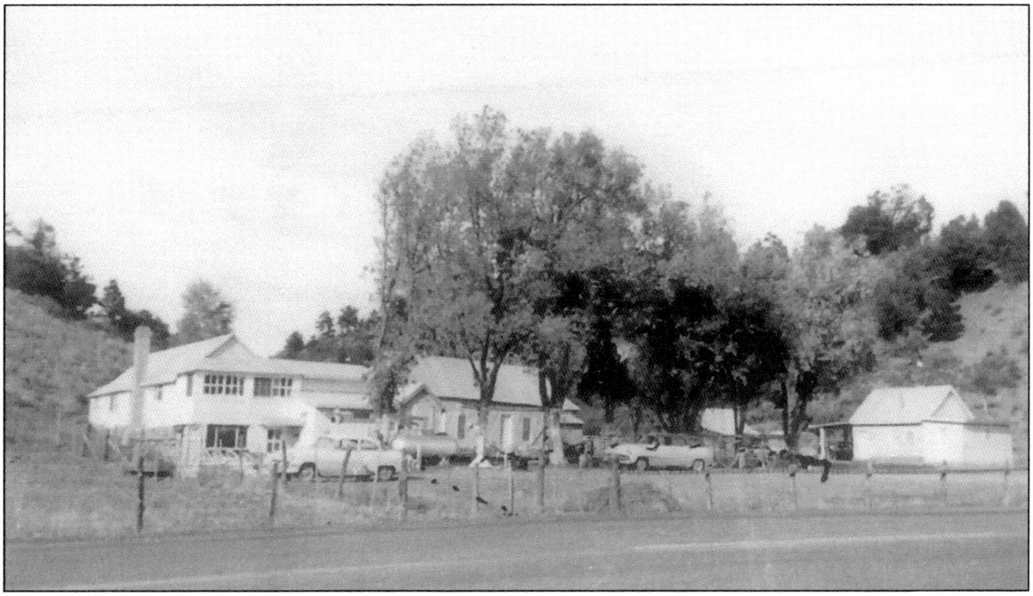

The John Williams homestead on Dry Creek has had some additions put on the original log house. The small building on the right was the bunkhouse. The barn and other out building cannot be seen. The house, barn, and outbuildings were burned as a controlled burn in the fall of 2001. (Courtesy of Janet Neilegh.)

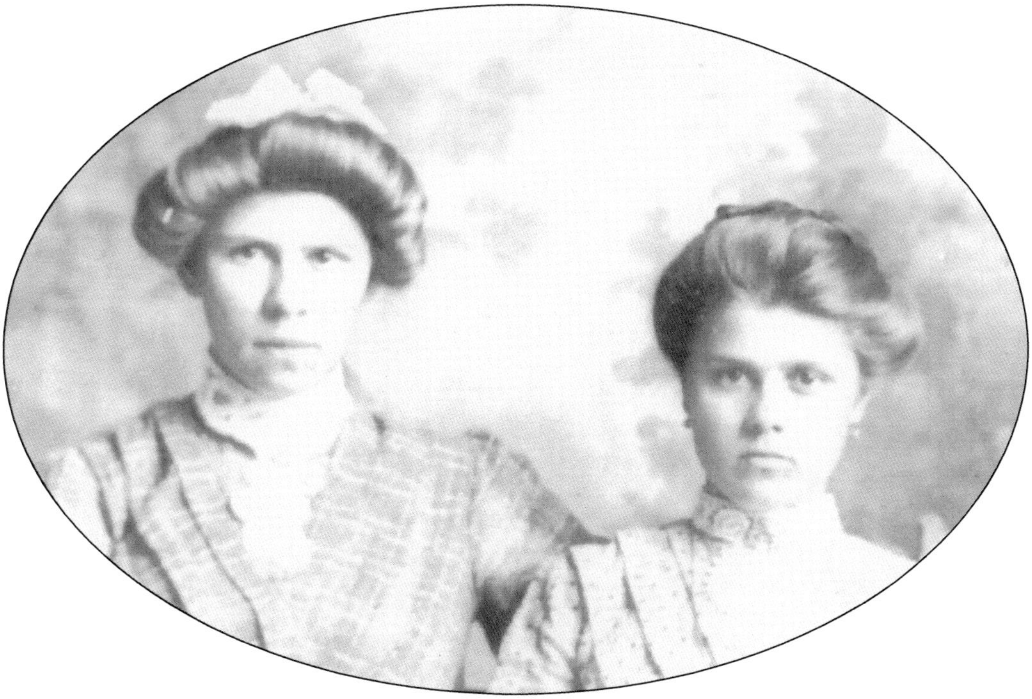

Posing for this picture are Hattie and Rosa Ludwig. (Courtesy of Jewell LePlatt.)

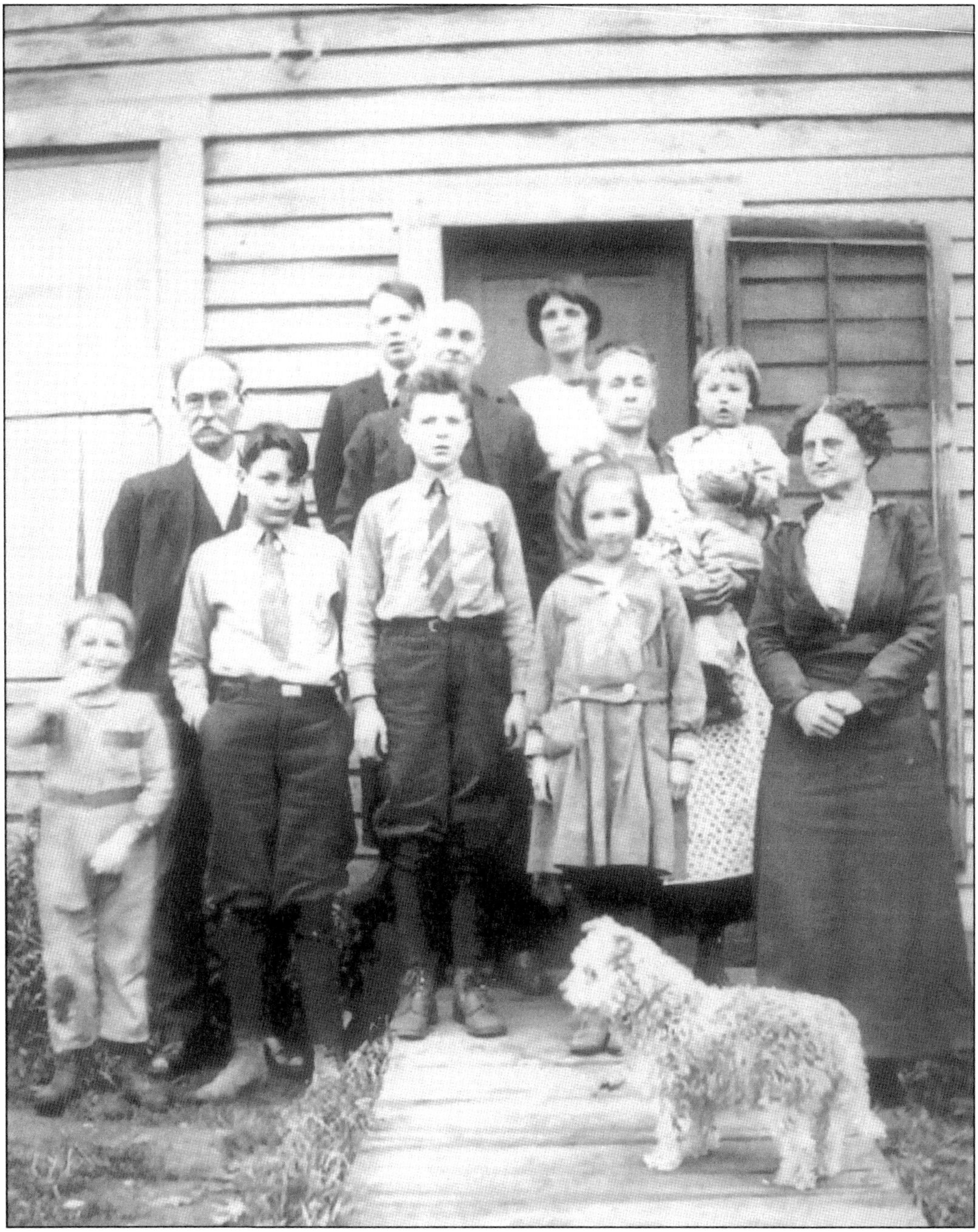

Posing here are the Bill McCaleb family and relations. Pictured, from left to right, are, (front row) four unidentified McCaleb children, Elsie McCaleb with dog in front; (middle row) Bill McCaleb, Grandpa Brown, Grandma Brown holding one unidentified McCaleb child; (back row) unidentified son, and Aunt Grace Brown Lewis. (Courtesy of Melba McCoy.)

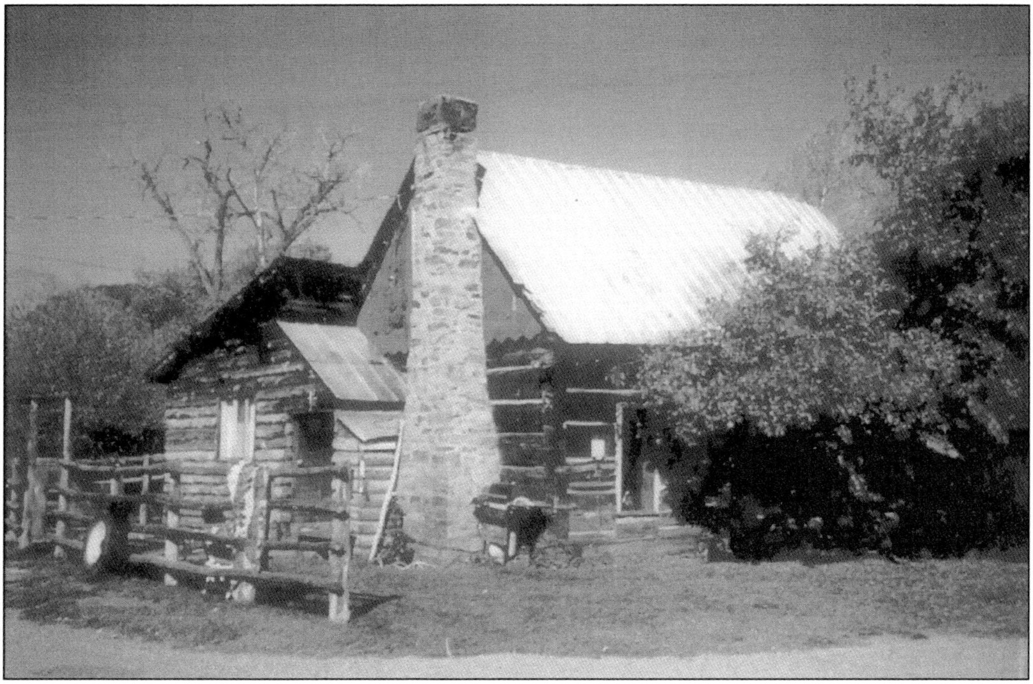

This cabin was part of the Susan Dunham homestead and is located in bottom land below the Jack LePlatt home. This cabin withstood the 1909, 1911, 1927, and the 1957 floods that raged through the Pine River Valley. The flood of 1957 occurred after the building of the dam. (Courtesy of the author.)

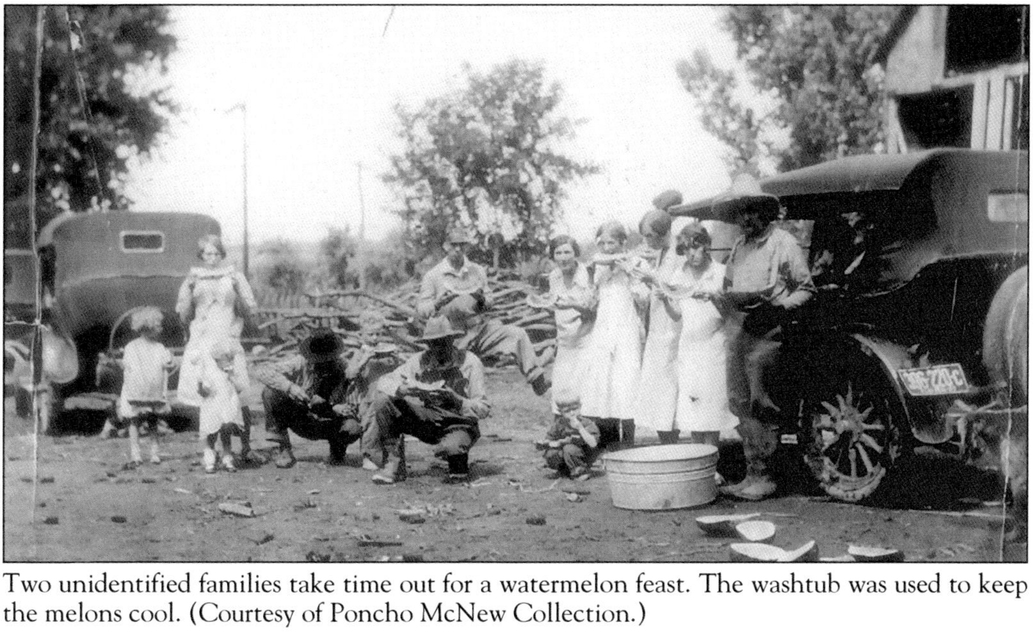

Two unidentified families take time out for a watermelon feast. The washtub was used to keep the melons cool. (Courtesy of Poncho McNew Collection.)

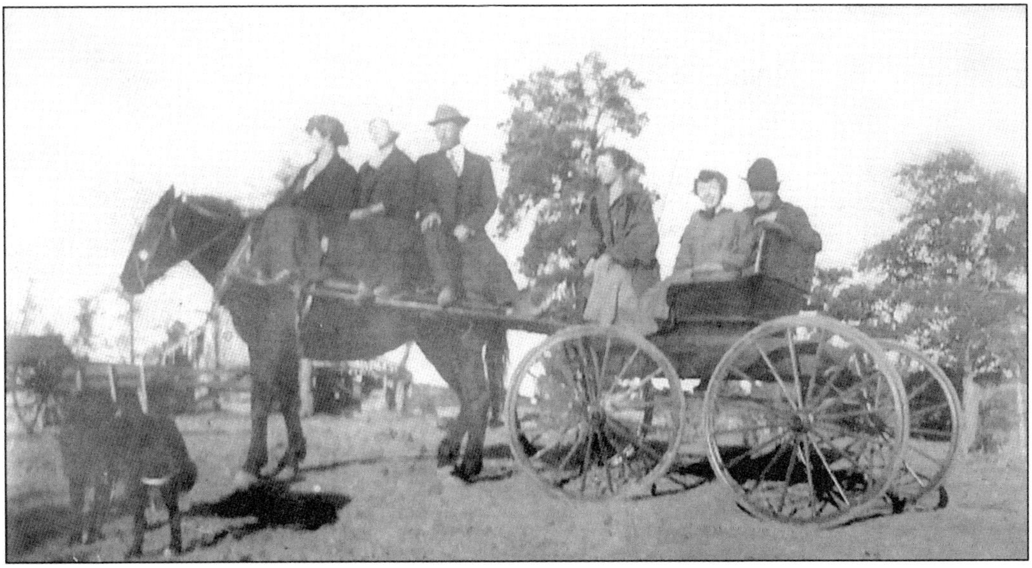

William Wiser (third from left) and an unidentified group of friends take a buggy ride on the Wiser homestead on Beaver Creek. Due to the lack of room in the buggy, some had to ride on the horse. (Courtesy of Poncho McNew.)

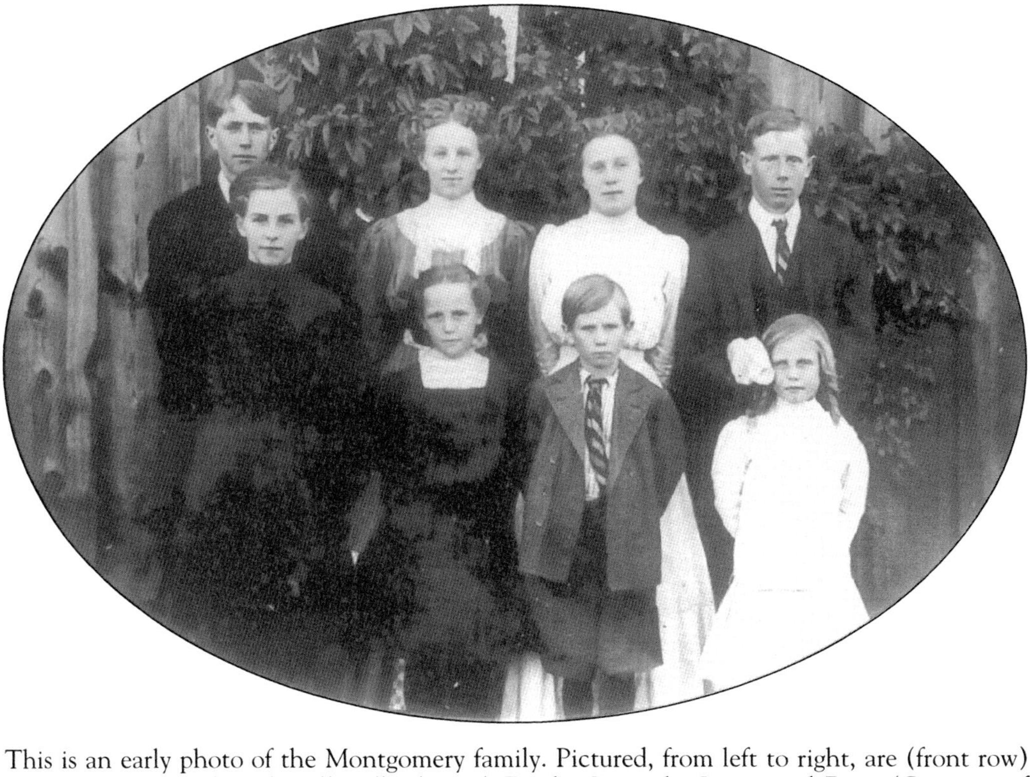

This is an early photo of the Montgomery family. Pictured, from left to right, are (front row) Monte, Metta, Ted, and Nellie; (back row) Frank, Gertrude, Irene, and Burt. (Courtesy of Kenny Montgomery Collection.)

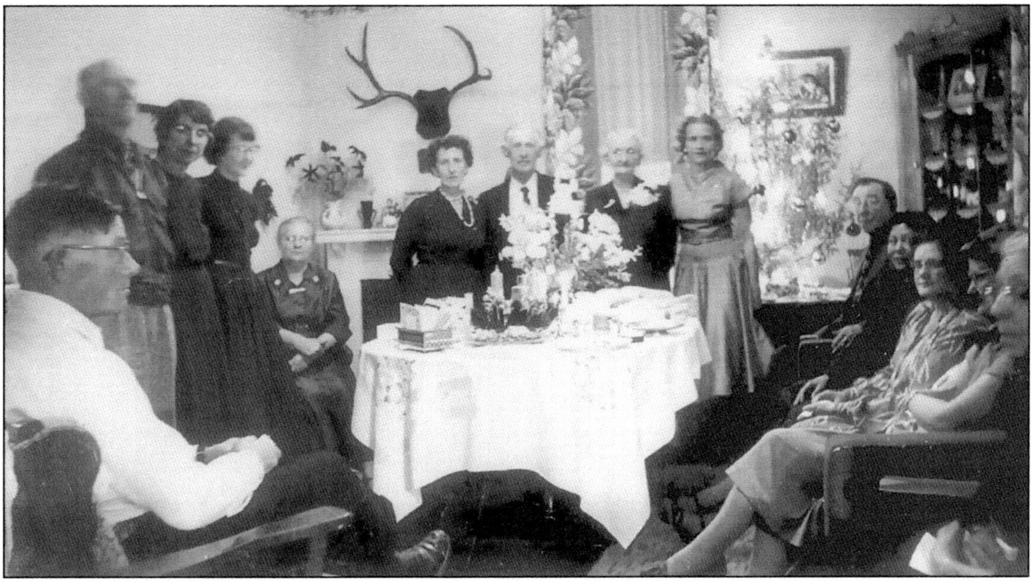

Mr. and Mrs. Bill Carr celebrate their 50th wedding anniversary with friends in their Bayfield home. Pictured, from left to right, are Harold Kingsley (seated), Clyde Petersen, Mrs. Petersen, Kylda Petersen, Vols Norris (seated), Golden Perkins, Mr. Bill Carr, Mrs. Carr, Hazell Carmack, the rest unidentified. (Identification by Jack Carmack.)

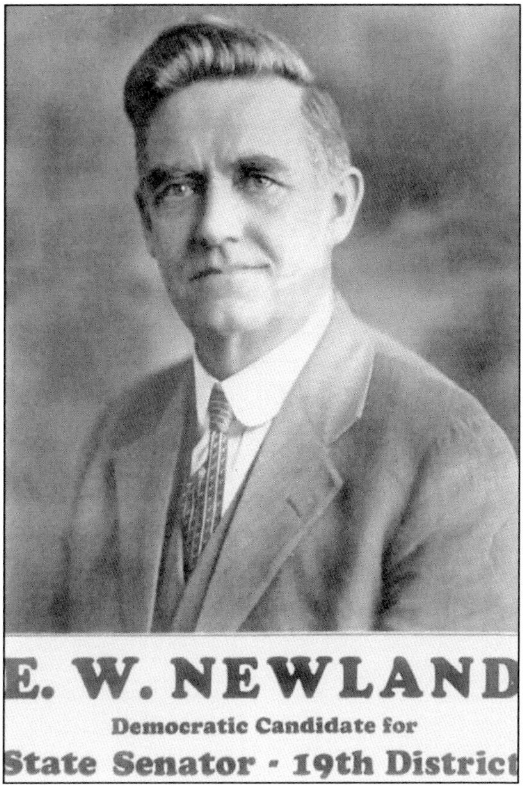

This portrait of E. W. Newland was taken when he was the Democratic candidate for the 19th District State Senator's office. (Courtesy of Jess Newland.)

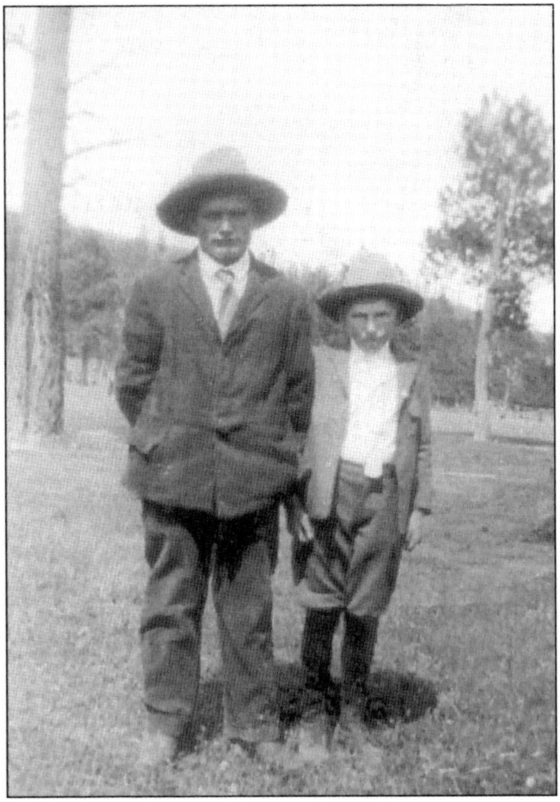

Frank Wommer Sr. and his son, Frank Jr., stand in the yard of the Wommer homestead in the Pine River Valley. (Courtesy of Poncho McNew Collection.)

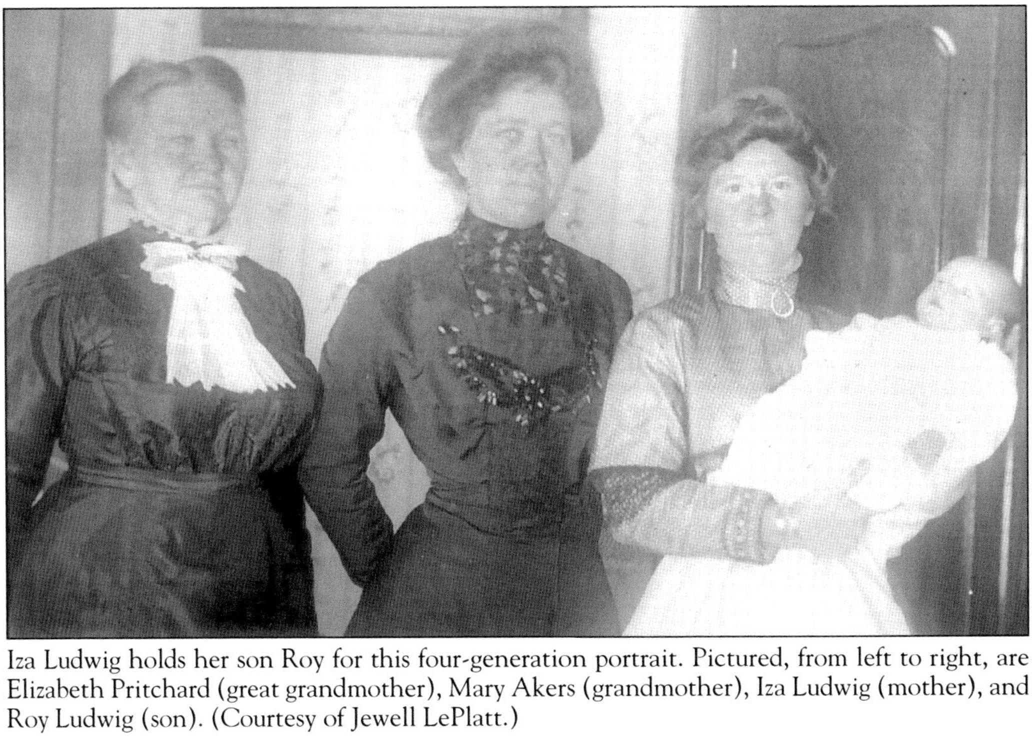

Iza Ludwig holds her son Roy for this four-generation portrait. Pictured, from left to right, are Elizabeth Pritchard (great grandmother), Mary Akers (grandmother), Iza Ludwig (mother), and Roy Ludwig (son). (Courtesy of Jewell LePlatt.)

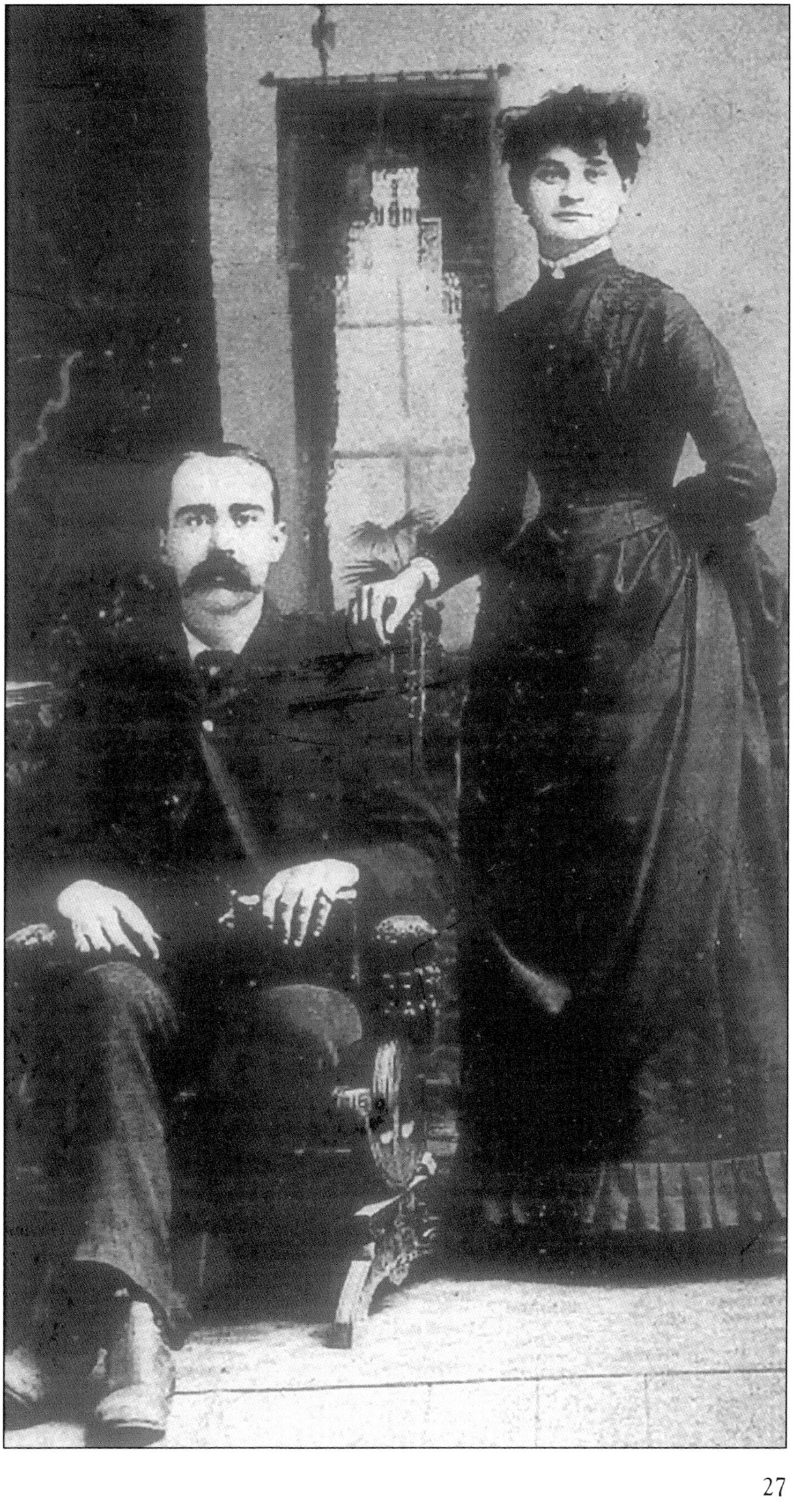

George Wheeler and Mary Ellen Corrigan Wheeler are pictured here in this photo dated 1888. George Wheeler was the first mayor of Bayfield when it was incorporated in 1906. (Courtesy of Debra Janus.)

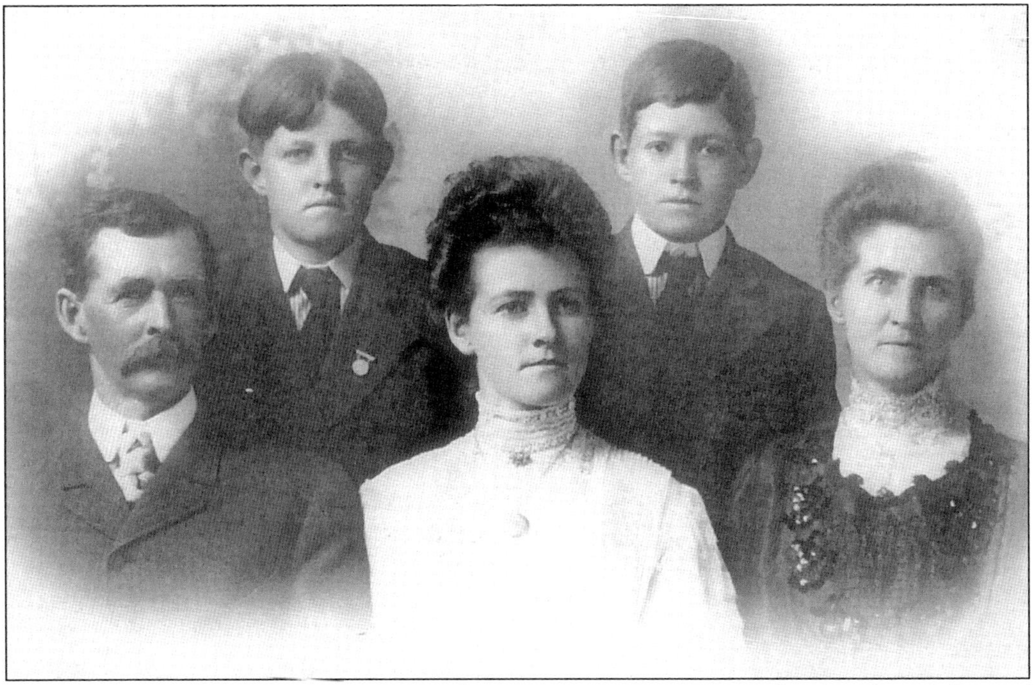

The William A. Bay family is pictured here. Mr. Bay was one of the founding fathers of Bayfield, and instrumental in naming the town. Pictured are, from left to right, (front row) William A. Bay, wife Pearl Bay, and Aunt Laura; (back row) Willie Bay and Carl Bay. (Courtesy of Grace Schirard.)

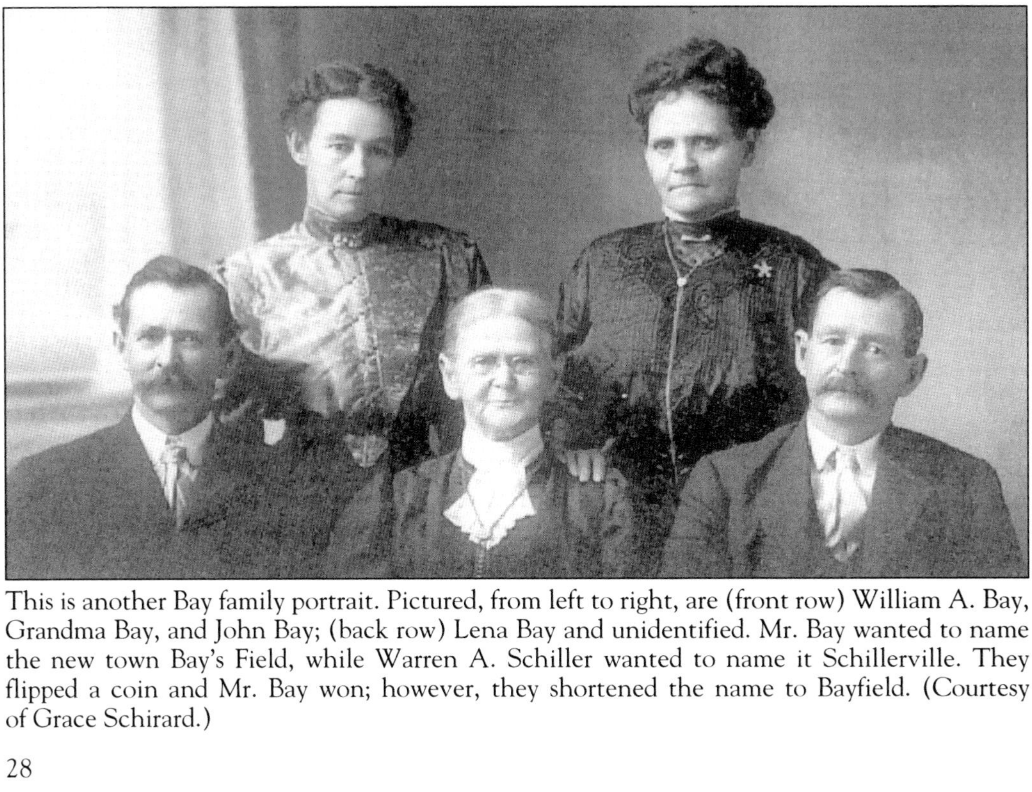

This is another Bay family portrait. Pictured, from left to right, are (front row) William A. Bay, Grandma Bay, and John Bay; (back row) Lena Bay and unidentified. Mr. Bay wanted to name the new town Bay's Field, while Warren A. Schiller wanted to name it Schillerville. They flipped a coin and Mr. Bay won; however, they shortened the name to Bayfield. (Courtesy of Grace Schirard.)

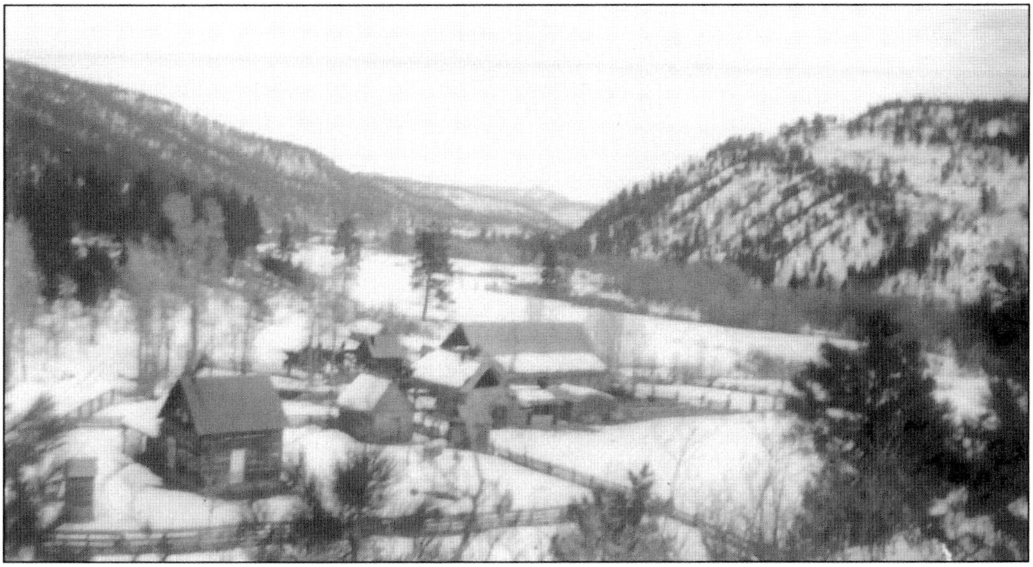

Pictured is a winter view of the Sam Parks homestead on the Pine River. Sam Parks settled in the Pine River Valley in 1894, and raised potatoes and hay. They took these products to Silverton and sold them to the miners. Parks also had a mine claim in Cave Basin, which is between the Pine and Vallecito Rivers in the San Juan Mountains. Notice the small shed in the lower left side of the photo. It could be a cover over the well, but looks like an outhouse. (Courtesy of Henry Parks.)

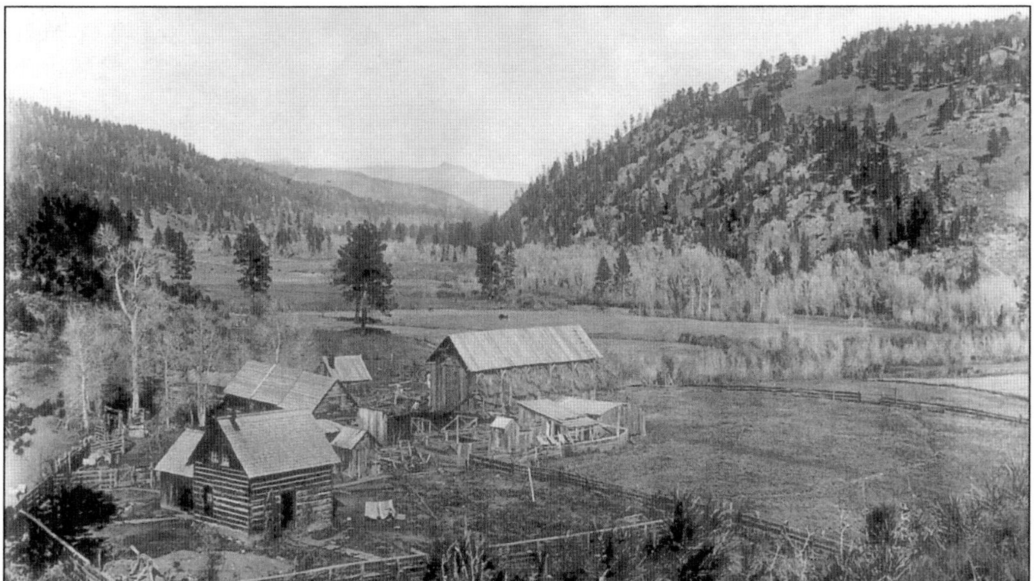

This is a spring or summer view of the Sam Parks homestead. Notice in the lower left corner of the photo, the well with the wheel structure to lift the water from the well. Today the well has been covered and an ash pit built on top. The house has been remodeled and other rooms added on the north end of the log house. The house burned in the mid 1980s, and another house was built. The ranch is now called the Pine River Cattle Company. (Courtesy of Henry Parks Collection.)

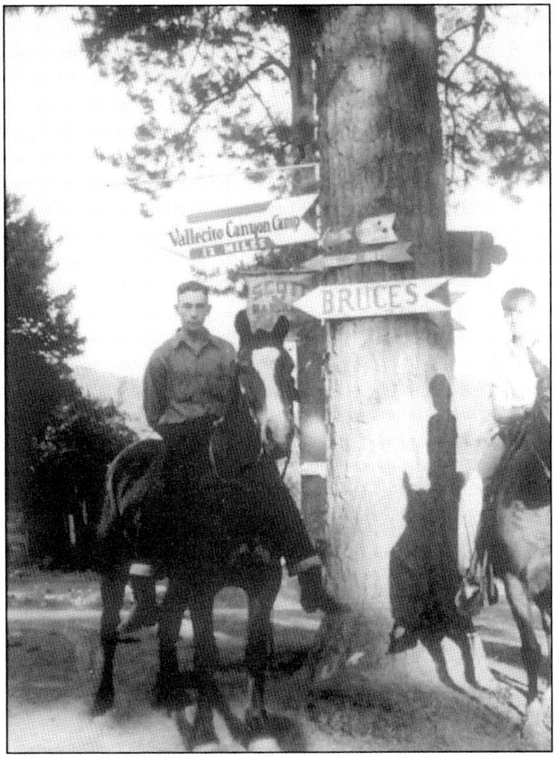

Unidentified riders pause by a large Ponderosa pine tree that used to stand in the middle of the road that goes up to Vallecito Lake. The road at this point in time ran right in front of the Parks Ranch. This photo was taken sometime in the early 1940s, as the lake was completed in 1940. The pine tree was cut down when they realigned the road, which is now County Road 501. The businesses advertised were all at the lake. (Courtesy of Henry Parks Collection.)

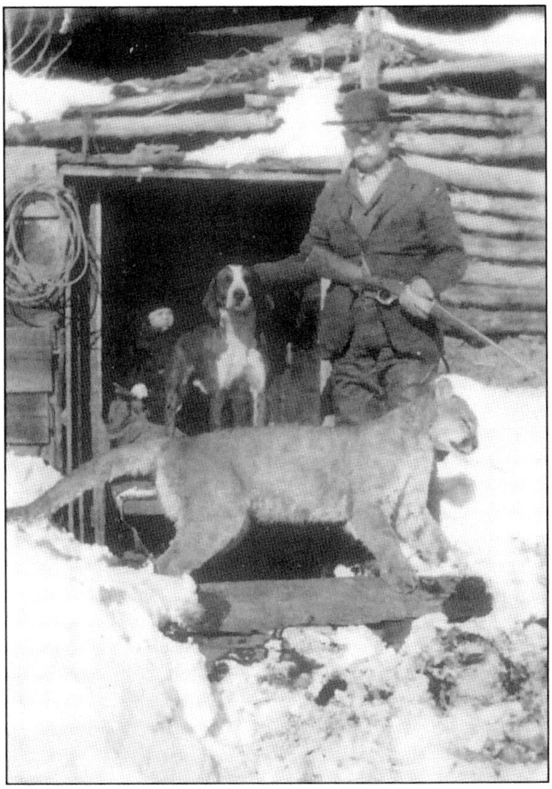

Sam Parks, pictured on the Parks homestead, stands in front of the potato cellar with a mountain lion he had just killed. Mr. Parks, known to be a good lion hunter, killed 12 lions in a single day. (Courtesy of Henry Parks Collection.)

This is a portrait of Samuel (Sam) Parks. (Courtesy of Henry Parks Collection.)

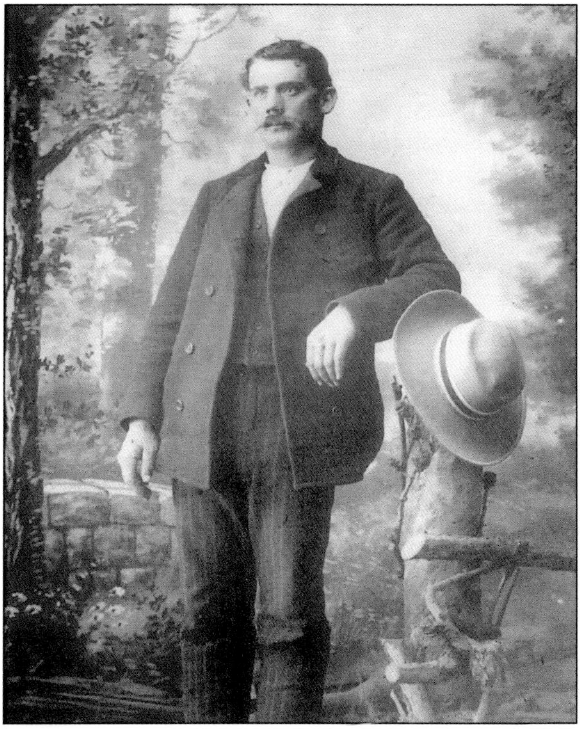

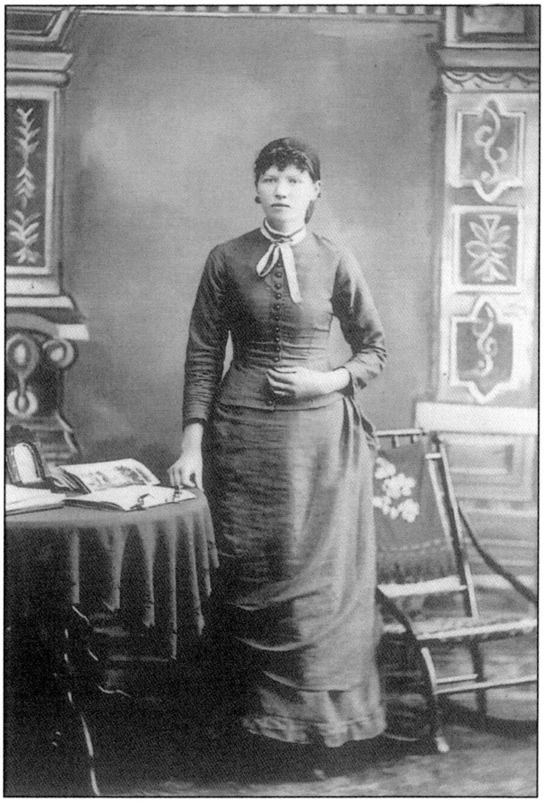

This is a portrait of Lydia Ann Bishop Parks. Mrs. Parks raised four boys. Her grandson, Henry, owns the Parks Collection. (Courtesy of Henry Parks Collection.)

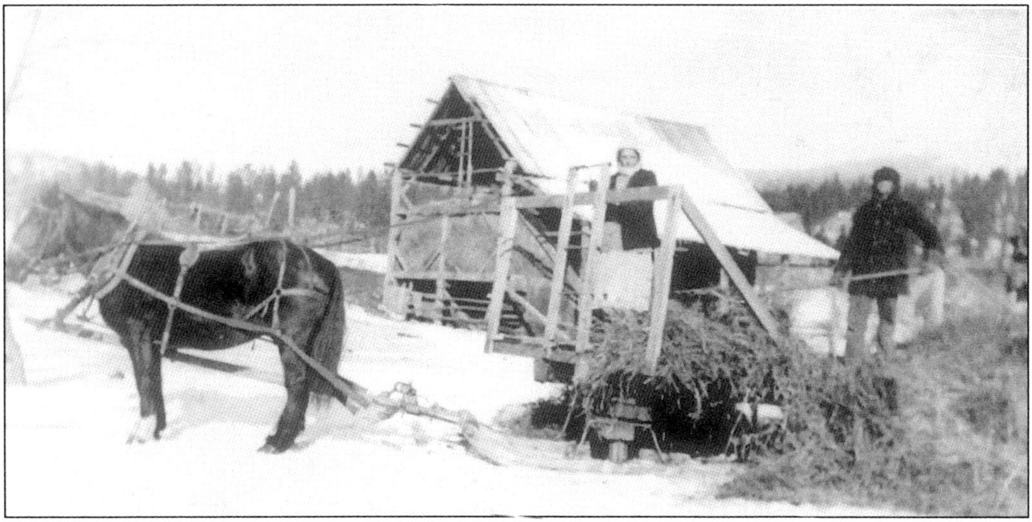

Lydia Parks drives the team while Sam, her husband, feeds their cows. (Courtesy of Henry Parks Collection.)

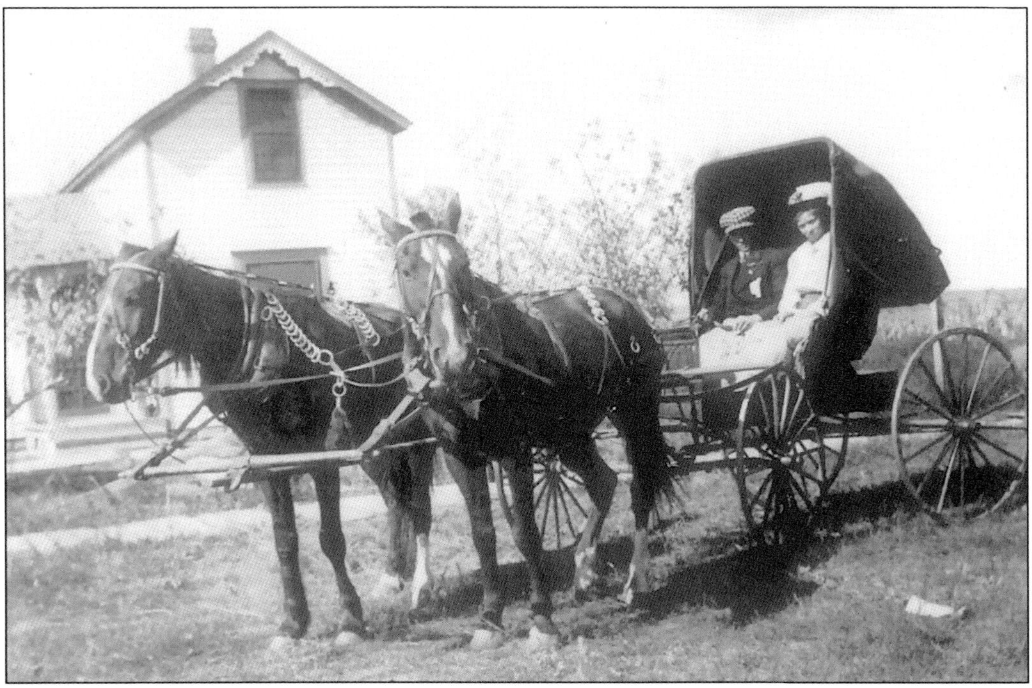

Calvin Parks, son of Sam Parks, courts Pearl Knight, his wife to be, in the family buggy. (Courtesy of the Henry Parks Collection.)

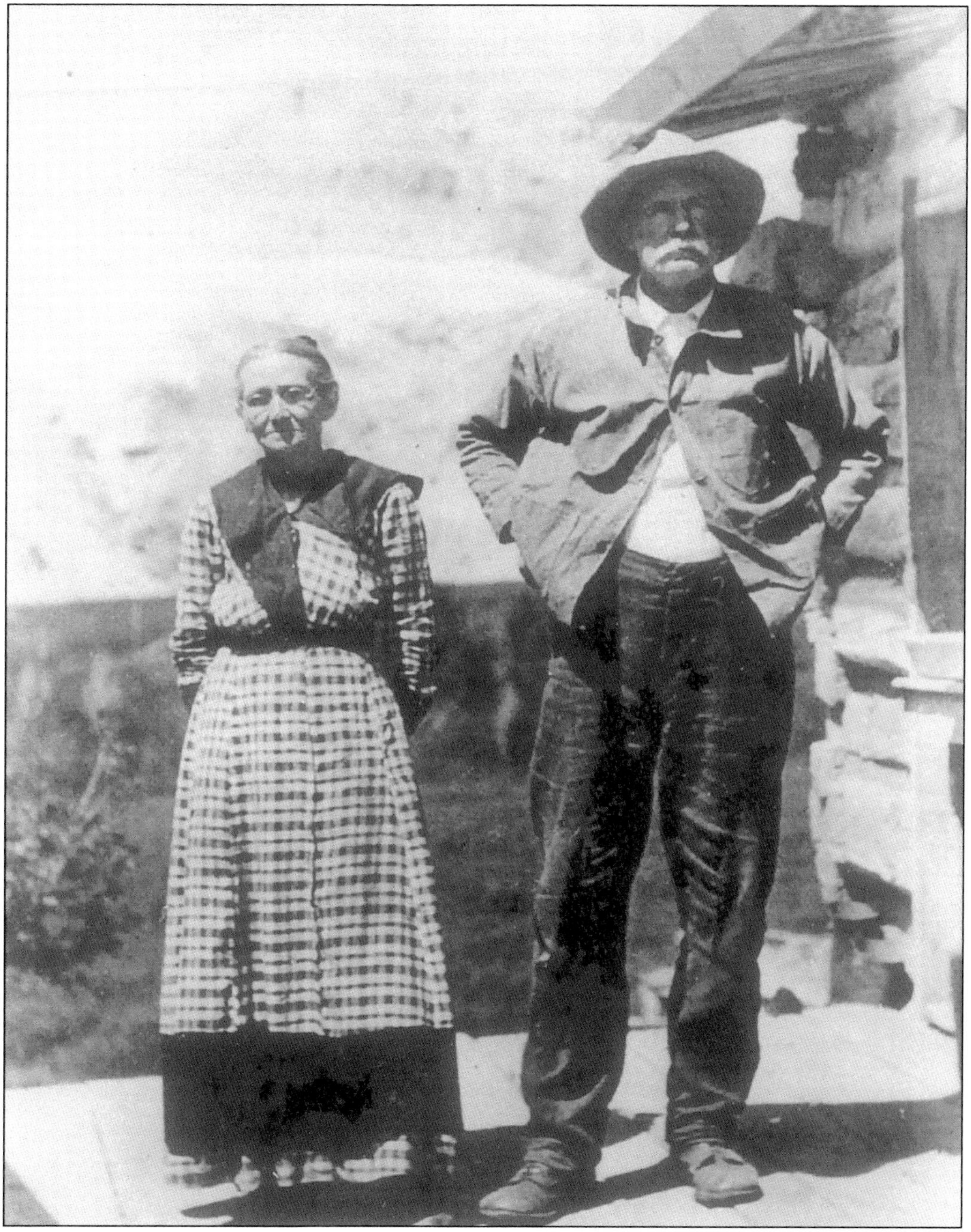

James and Susan McKinney stand outside their home in Bayfield. (Courtesy of Barb Fjerstad.)

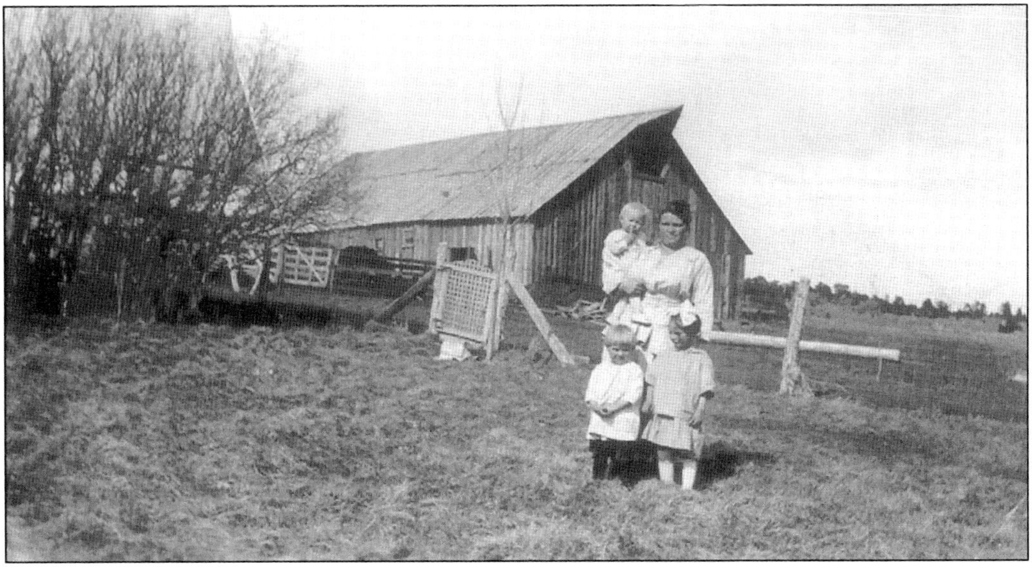

Mrs. Shelhamer stops with three of her children in front of their barn on their Beaver Creek homestead. (Courtesy of Poncho McNew Collection.)

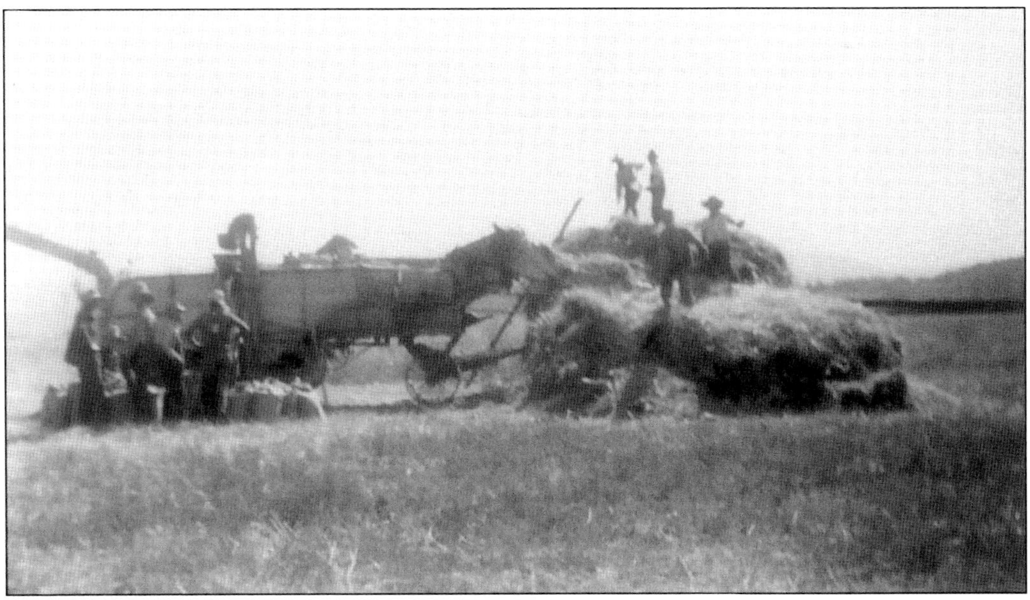

A group of farmers thresh the Shelhamer grain on their Dry Creek homestead. A threshing machine would come into the area and go from farm to farm doing each farmer's grain. The farmers would also go help their neighbor with his threshing. (Courtesy of Poncho McNew Collection.)

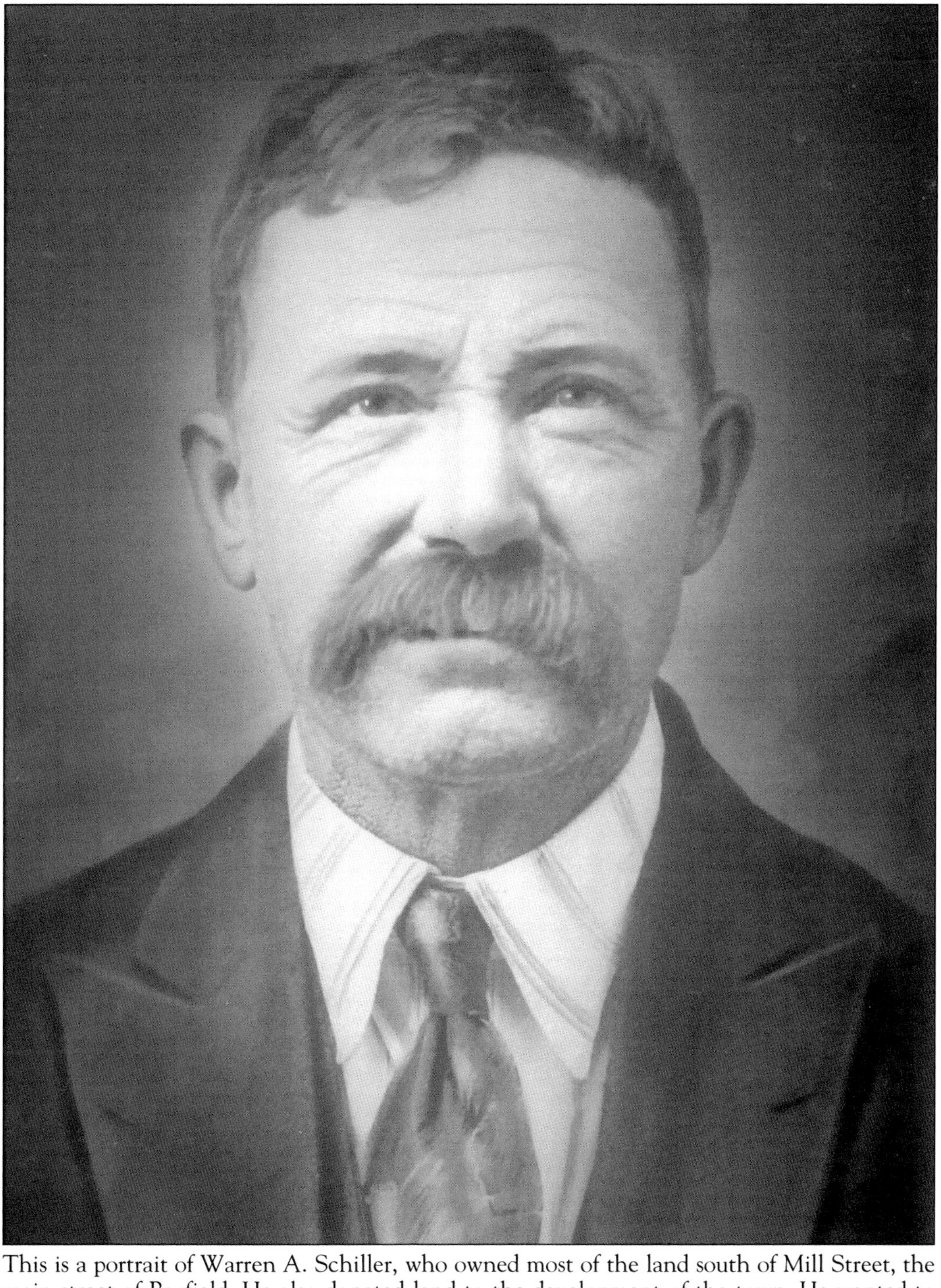

This is a portrait of Warren A. Schiller, who owned most of the land south of Mill Street, the main street of Bayfield. He also donated land to the development of the town. He wanted to name the town Schillerville and Mr. Bay, who owned land on the north side of main street, wanted to name it Bay's Field. Attempts were made to incorporate both names, but failed, and a coin was flipped and Mr. Bay won. They shortened the name to Bayfield. (Courtesy of Danny Rodman.)

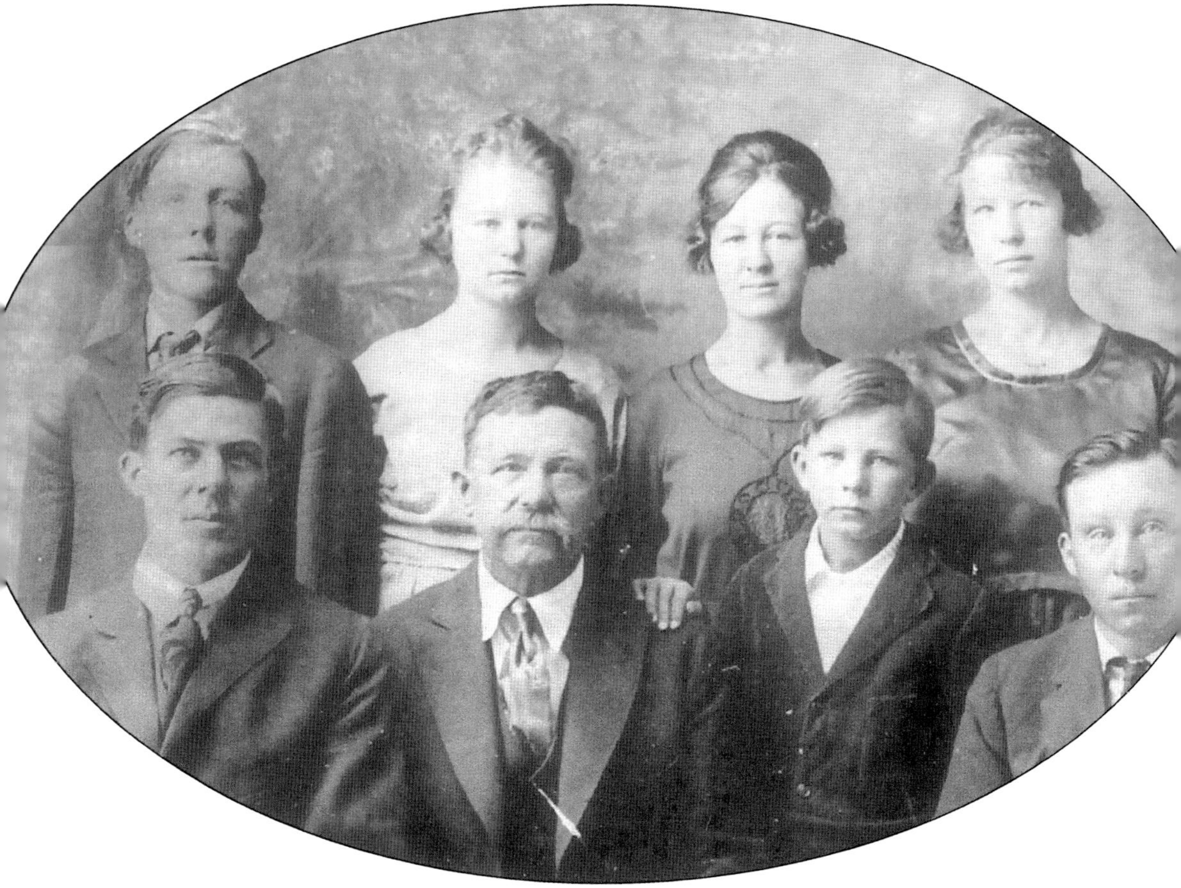

Pictured is a family portrait of Warren A. Schiller and his children. Pictured are, from left to right, (front row) Christopher, Warren, Charles, and Wesley; (back row) Walter, Freda, Emma, and Josephine. (Courtesy of Danny Rodman.)

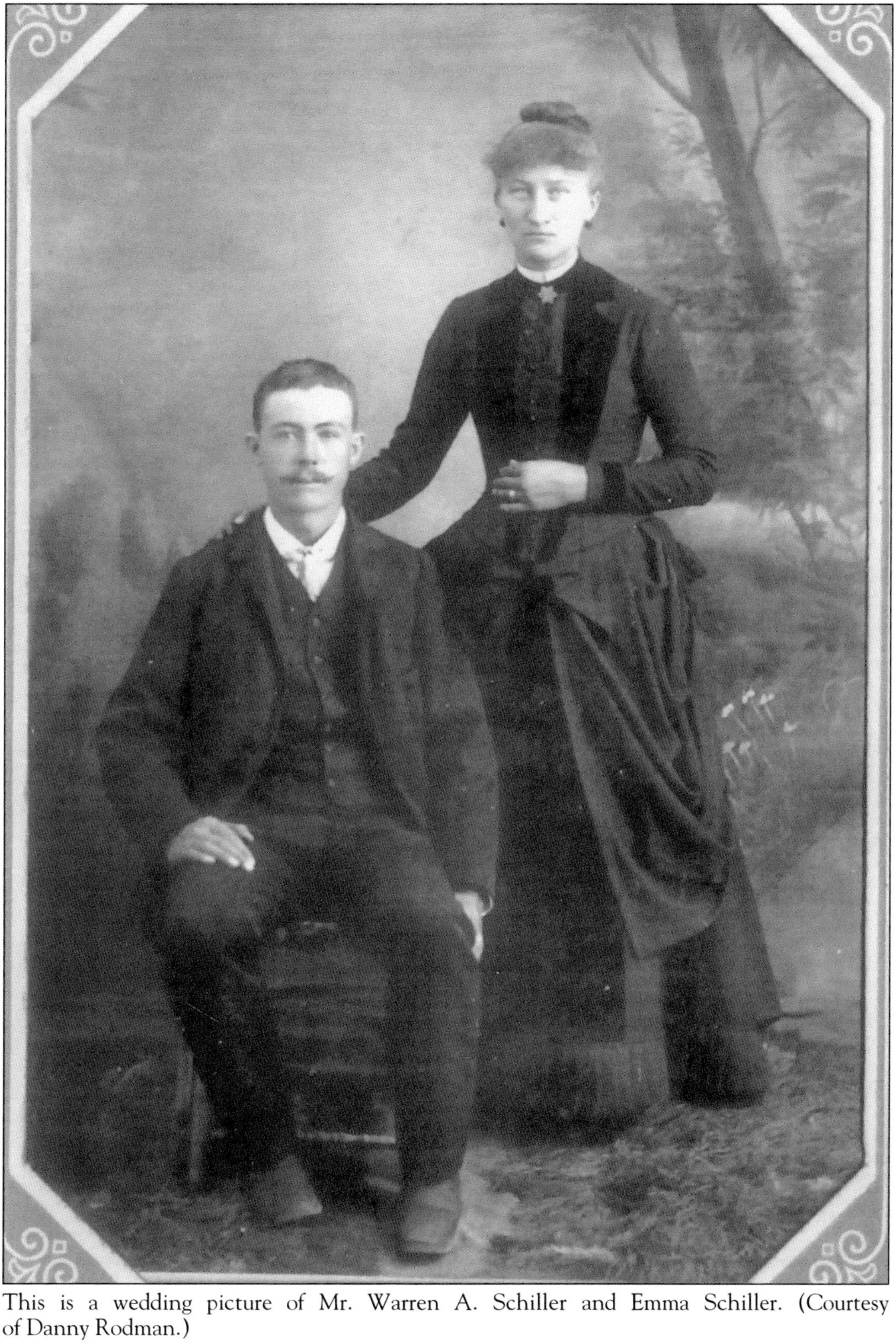

This is a wedding picture of Mr. Warren A. Schiller and Emma Schiller. (Courtesy of Danny Rodman.)

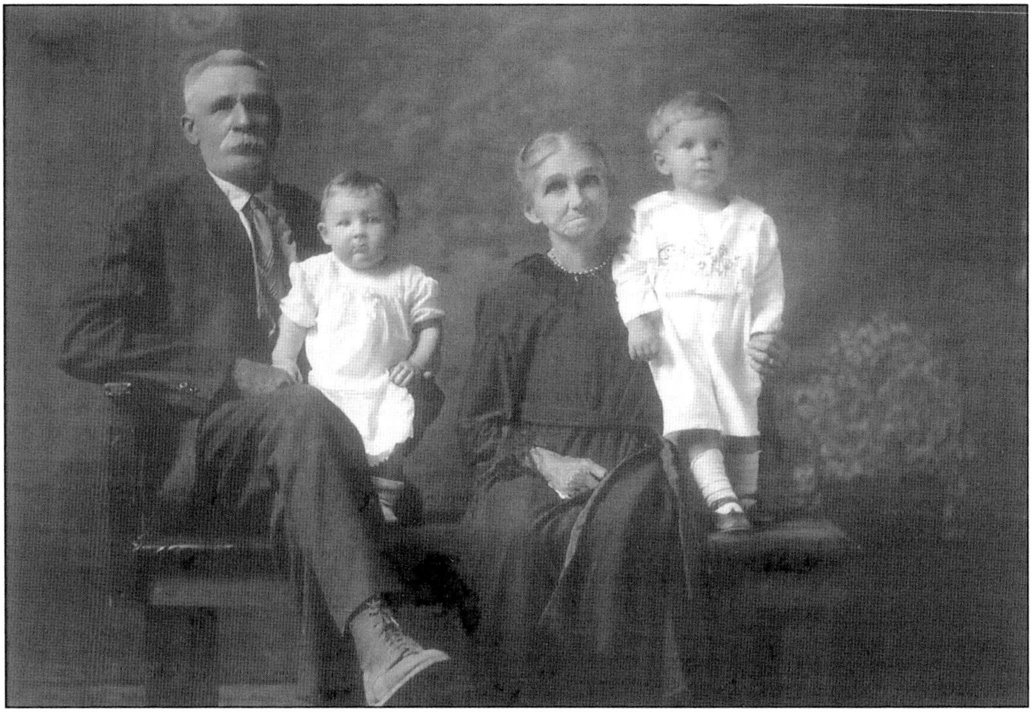

Pictured here are James McKinney, his wife, and his grandchildren. They are, from left to right, James, Edith, Susan, and Dean. (Courtesy of Kenny Montgomery.)

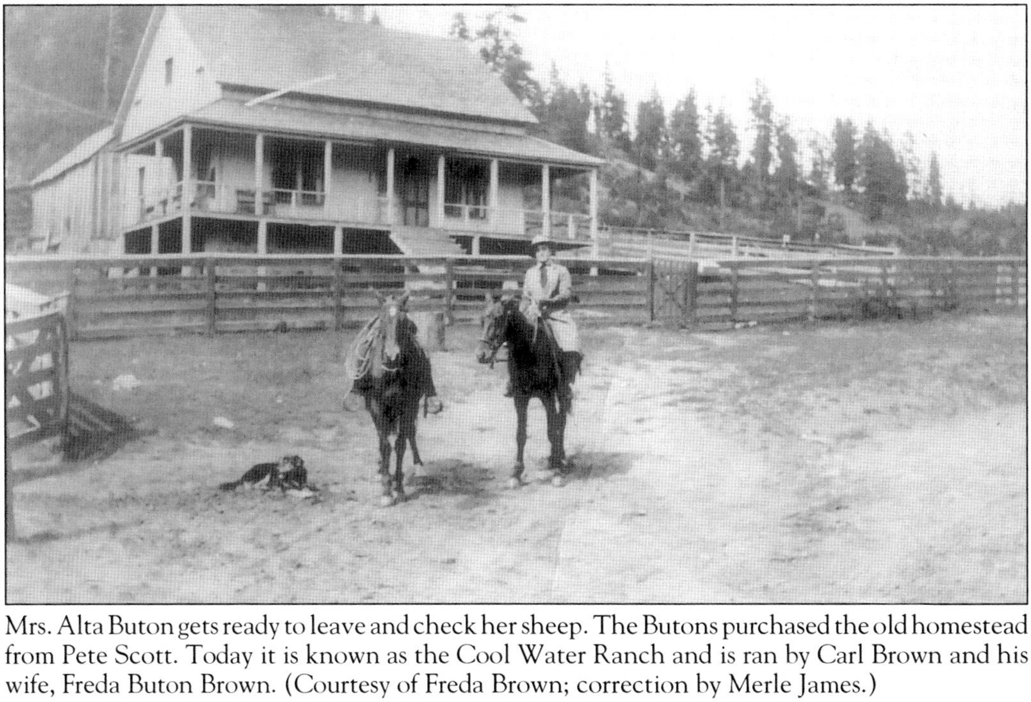

Mrs. Alta Buton gets ready to leave and check her sheep. The Butons purchased the old homestead from Pete Scott. Today it is known as the Cool Water Ranch and is ran by Carl Brown and his wife, Freda Buton Brown. (Courtesy of Freda Brown; correction by Merle James.)

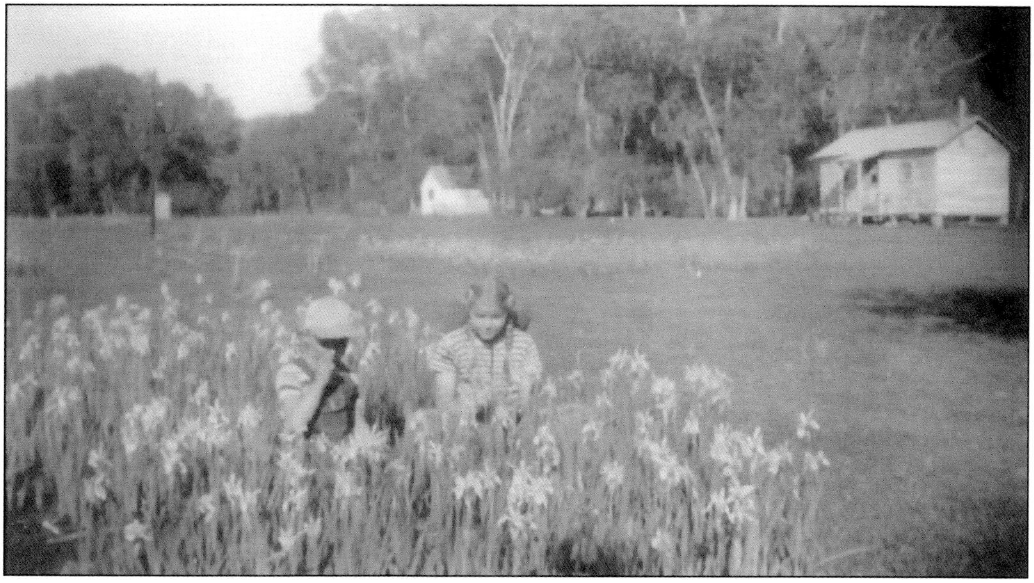

Two children sit among the wild iris that grow along the banks of the Pine River. The cabins in the background belong to the Cool Water Ranch. There were cabins up on the road also, but they are now all down along the river. (Courtesy of Freda Brown.)

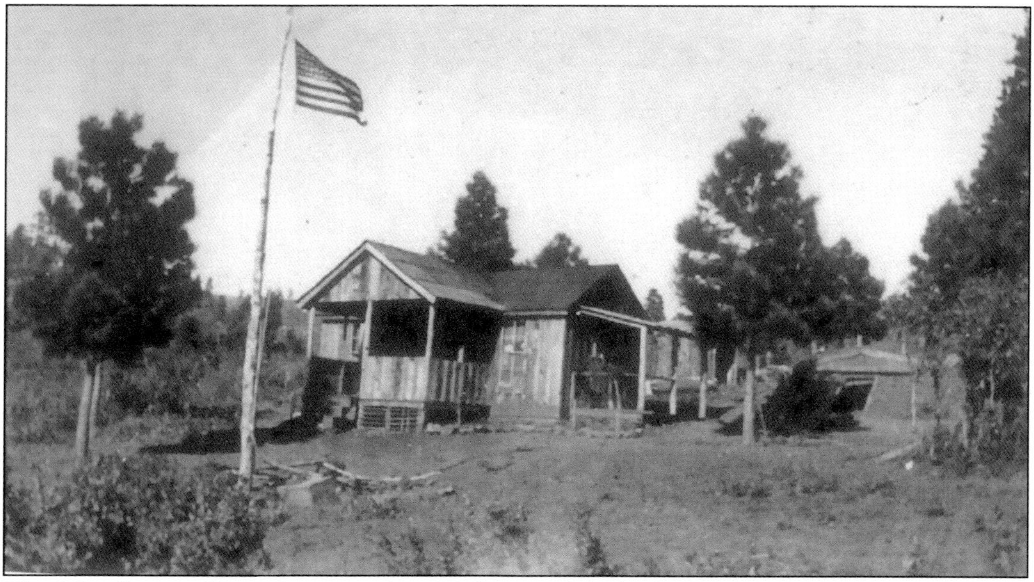

The John Burtrand Barr homestead in Wallace Gulch displays the American flag in its front yard. (Courtesy of Roberta Barr.)

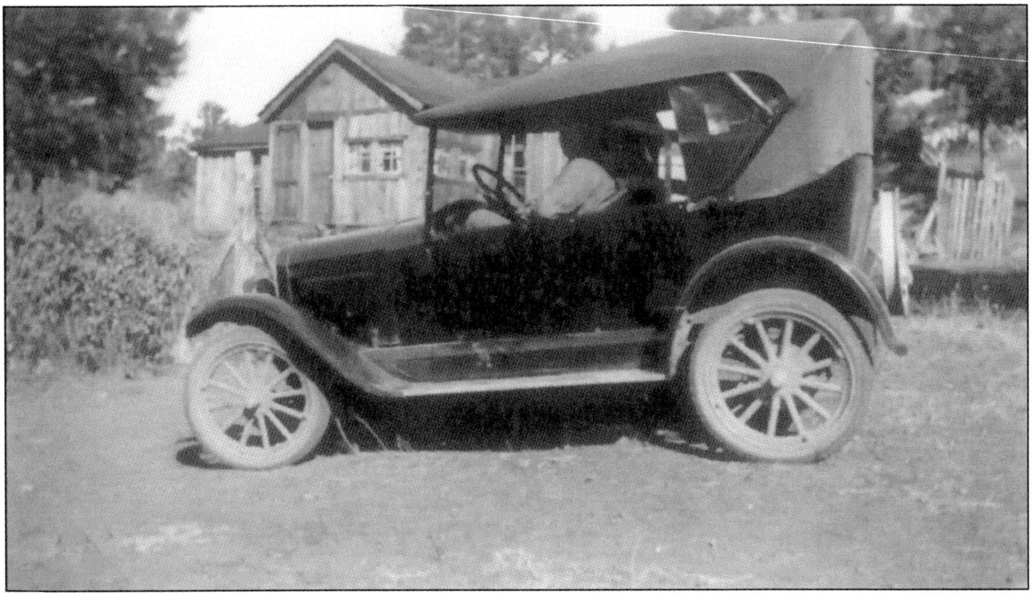

Robert Barr sits in his new car in front of the Lyons homestead in Wallace Gulch. The Lyons and the Barrs were neighbors. (Courtesy of Roberta Barr.)

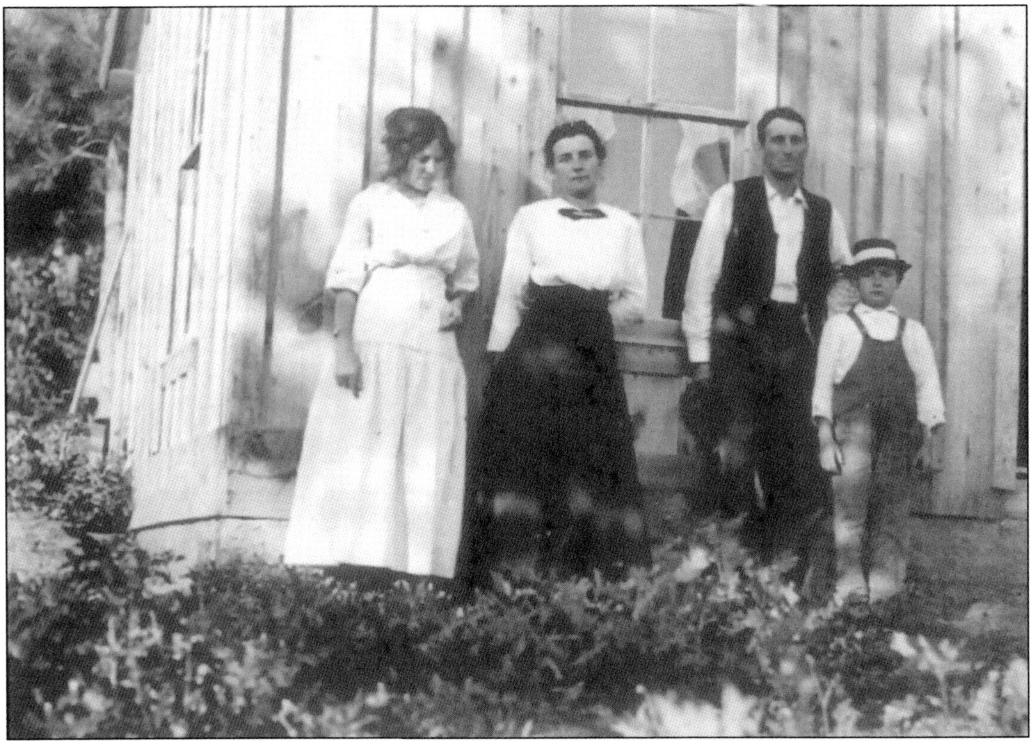

Robert Barr stands with his mother, father, and a neighbor in front of the Barr home in Wallace Gulch. Pictured, left to right, are unidentified, Alice Barr, John Burtrand Barr, and Robert Barr. (Courtesy of Roberta Barr.)

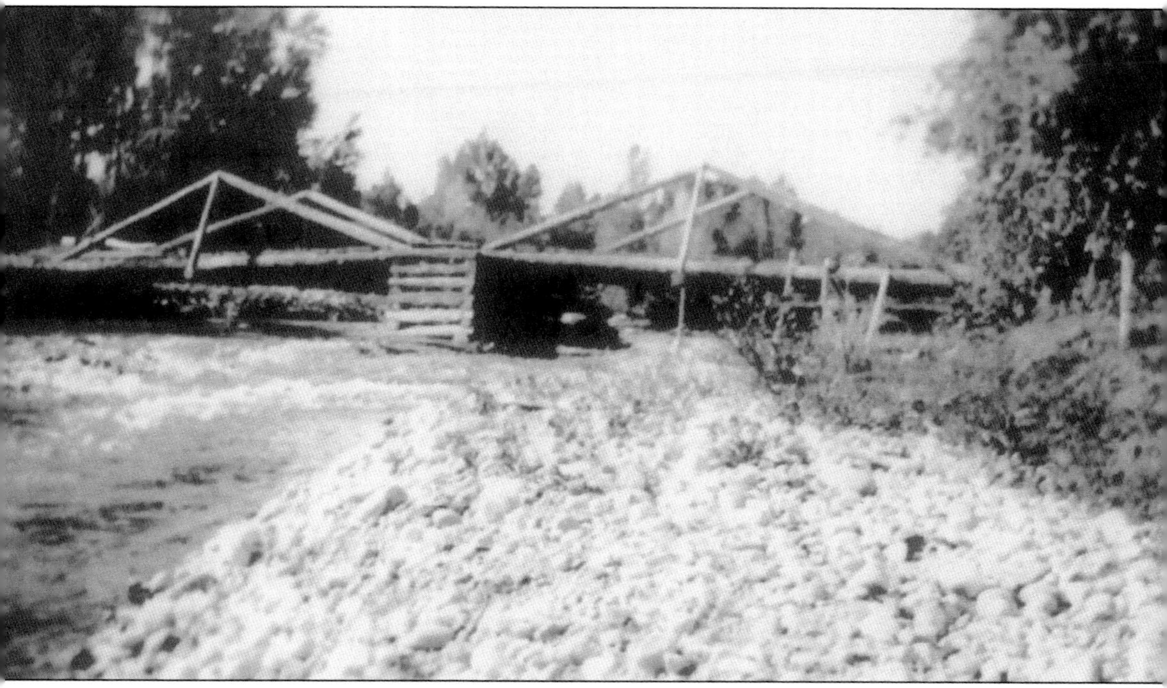

The Middle Bridge crossed the Pine River at the settlement of Los Pinos, which was one of the first settlements in the Pine River Valley. The road came out from Animas City and went through Los Pinos on its way to Pagosa Springs, Colorado. Los Pinos had a stage station, hotel, and post office and was located on the east side of the Pine River. The city suffered an unfortunate fire, and was rebuilt on the west side of the river. In 1879, the road was a toll road but it did not last long. Los Pinos was located about 4 miles up the valley from present day Bayfield. (Courtesy of Roberta Barr.)

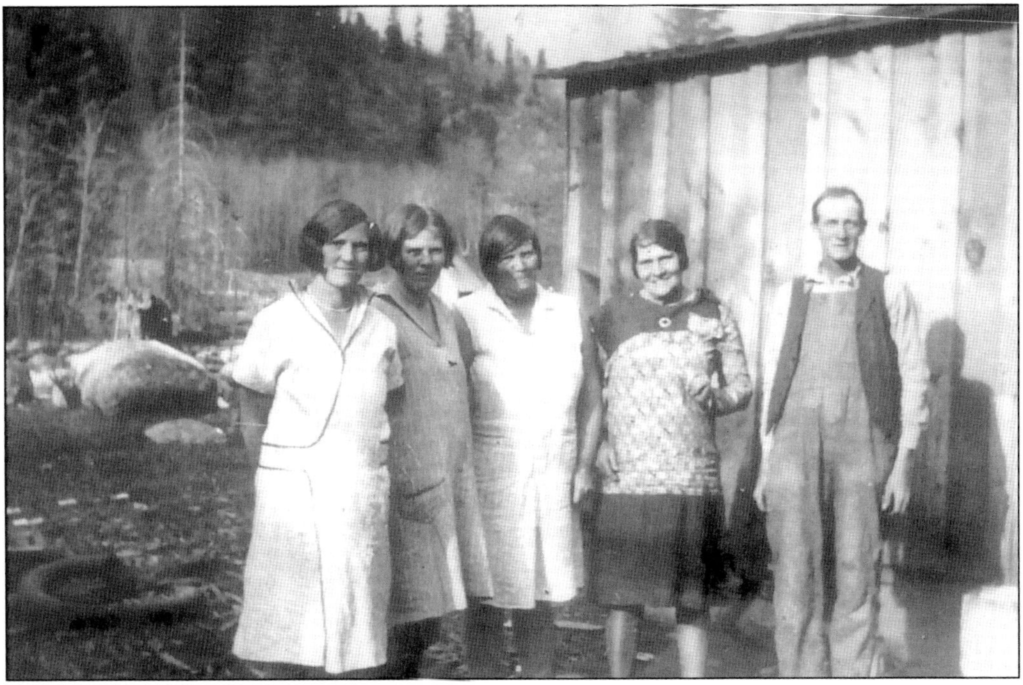

Pictured, from left to right, are Lena Davis, Edna Davis, Cora Montgomery, Clara Bates, and George Wiser. (Courtesy of Poncho McNew Collection; identification by Georgia Micheli.)

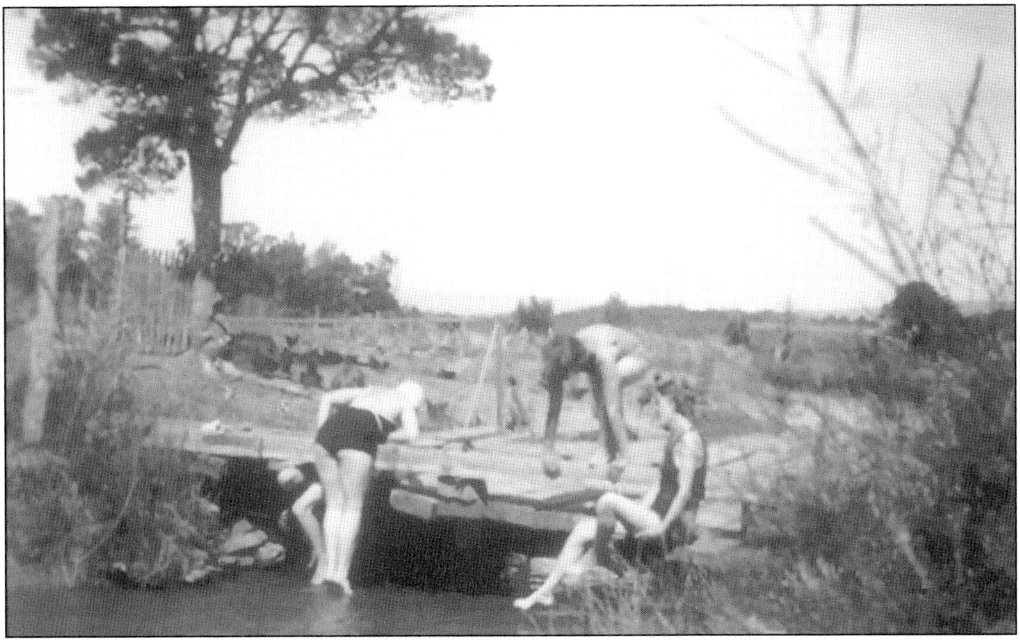

These girls had fun in King Ditch that ran by the McCoy home. The King Ditch is one of the early ditches in the Valley. (Courtesy of Melba McCoy.)

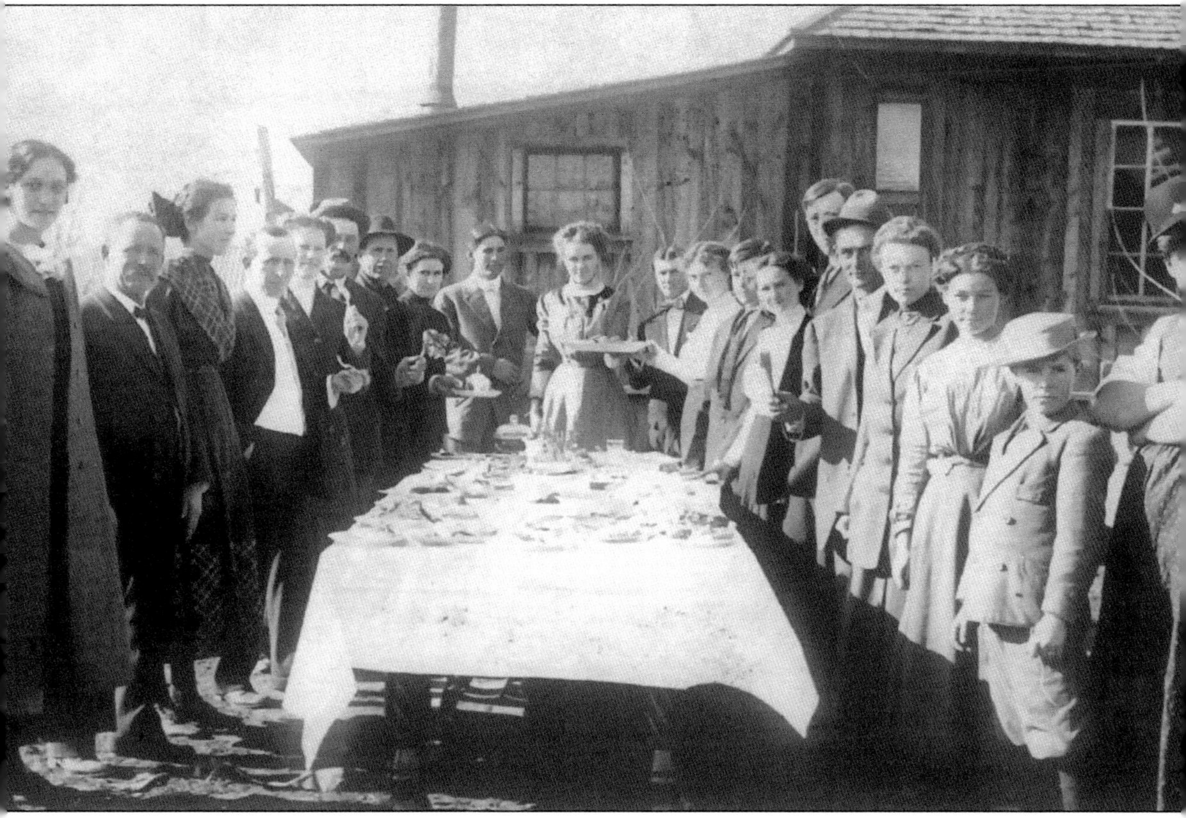

The Frahm friends pose for this photo before participating in a picnic. Pictured, beginning from the left front, are Edna Townsend, J. M. Springer, Albee Taylor, Mel Slayer, Ron Sullivan, J. R. Gibbs, Mrs. (?) Jenkins, Clyde (?), Cecil (?), Fred Stouffer, Estey Maloy, Millie Bay, Leone H. (?), Charles McClair, Frank Gibbs, Edna Mador Gibbs, Jessie Green, Merna Schaffer, and Ray (?). (Courtesy of Fred Fraham.)

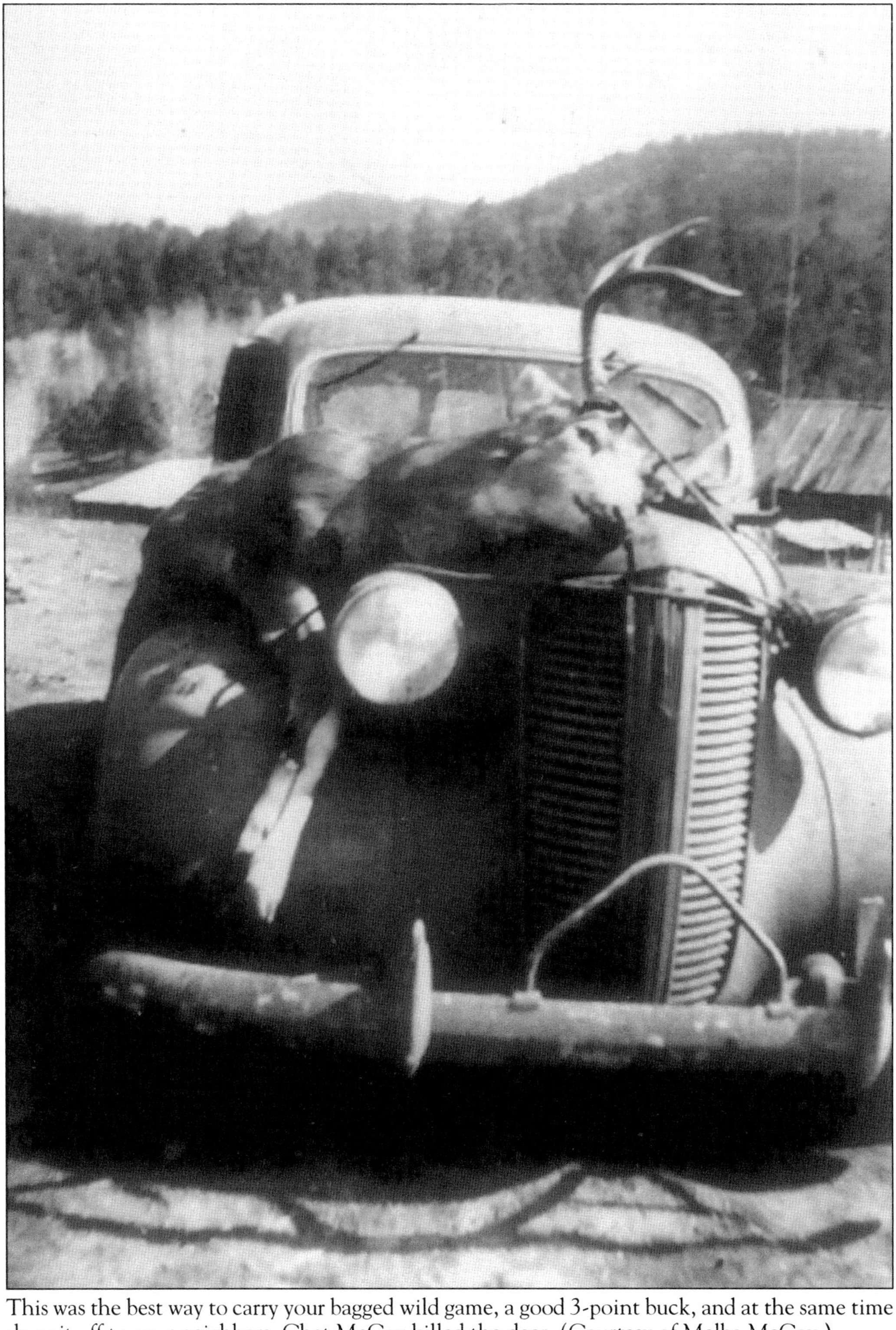

This was the best way to carry your bagged wild game, a good 3-point buck, and at the same time show it off to your neighbors. Chet McCoy killed the deer. (Courtesy of Melba McCoy.)

Three

SCHOOLS

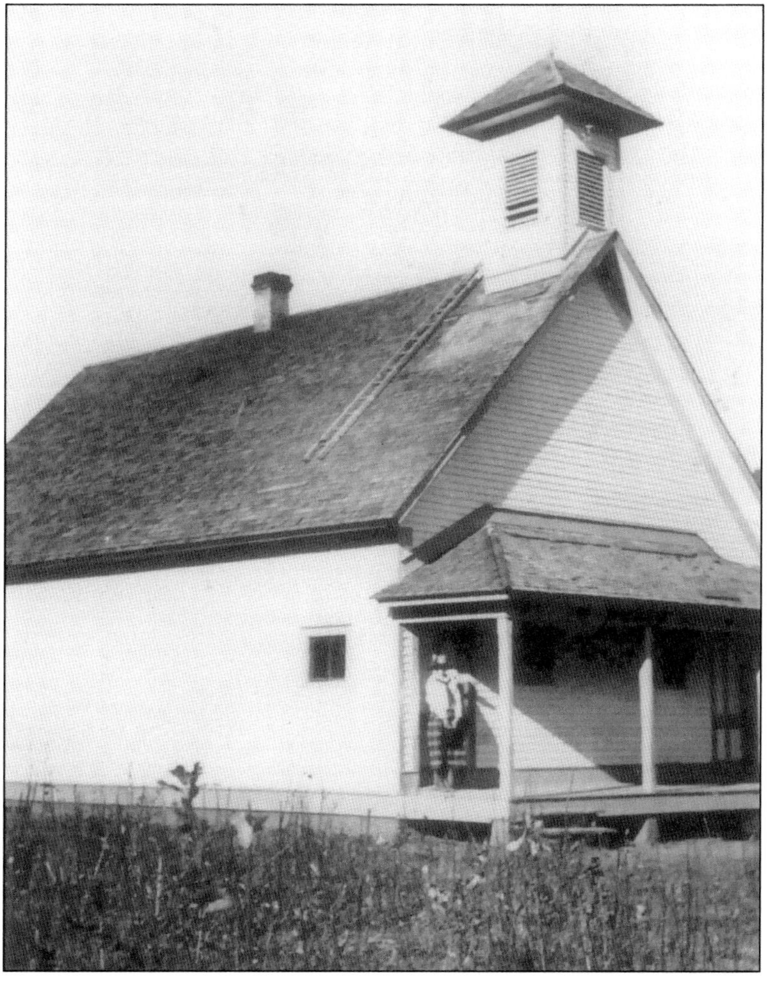

The Columbus School was one of the first schoolhouses built in the upper Pine River Valley. This building is now a home and is occupied by Mr. Gregg and Debra Janus, both teachers. They also own the teacherage that was next door; it is also a home. (Courtesy of Debra Janus.)

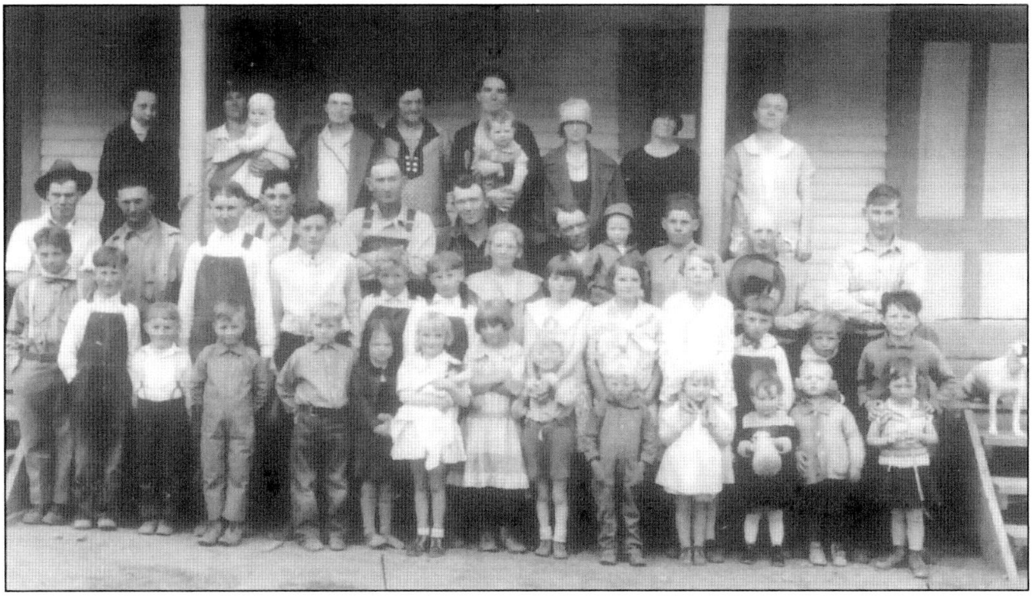

Pictured is the Class of 1929, at Columbus School. Pictured, from left to right, are (first row) Rosemary Richards, Ernie Parks, Audry McCoy, Francis Wilbourn, Harlan Blackmore, Charles Dunsworth, Rosie Blackmore, Edith Dunsworth, Ruth Richards, Clyde Wilbourn, Archie Blackmore, and Dale McCoy; (second row) Earl Blackmore, Orville McCoy, Elsie Blackmore, Laura Dunsworth, Ester Percell, Melva Wilbourn, Harold McCoy, Henry Parks, John Richards, Rex McCoy, and Clem Knight; (third row) Ivan Parks, Harry Norris, Chester McCoy, Dan Percell, Dayton Percell, Fred McCoy, Chester Green, Luther Wilbourn, Laurence Wilbourne, Richard Percell, Bill Richards, and Merle McCoy; (fourth row) Edith Waggoner, Ted McCoy, Amy McCoy, Lydia Parks, Mamie Percell, Laura Jane Richards, Esther Richards, Cora Wilbourn, Jessie Bird, and Grace Morse. (Courtesy of Debra Janus.)

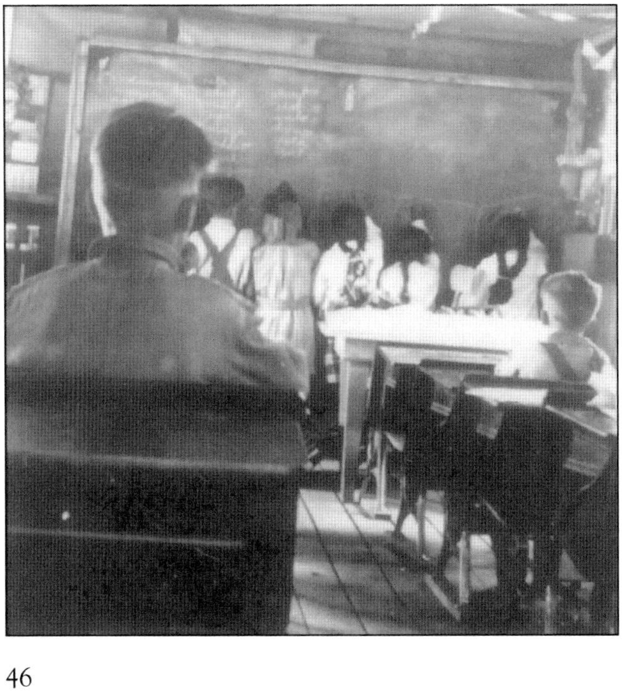

A group of students work on the blackboard as their classmates watch in the Benn Springs one-room schoolhouse. (Courtesy of Roberta Barr.)

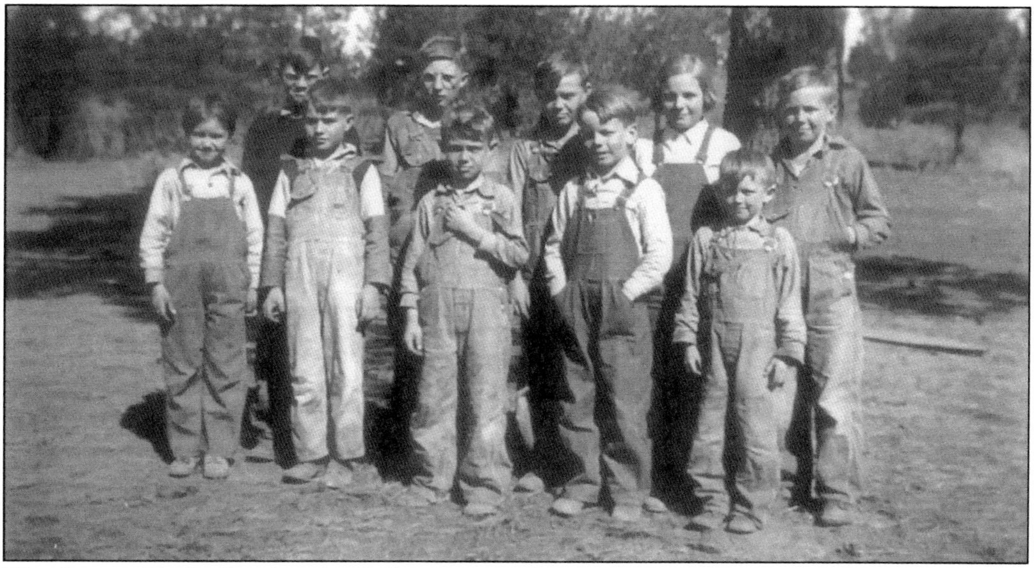

This day was Tacky Day for Mrs. Roberta Barr's class at Benn Springs School. Notice that there is only one girl in the class. Mrs. Barr said that most of her students were male, and that some classes would have no girls at all. (Courtesy of Roberta Barr.)

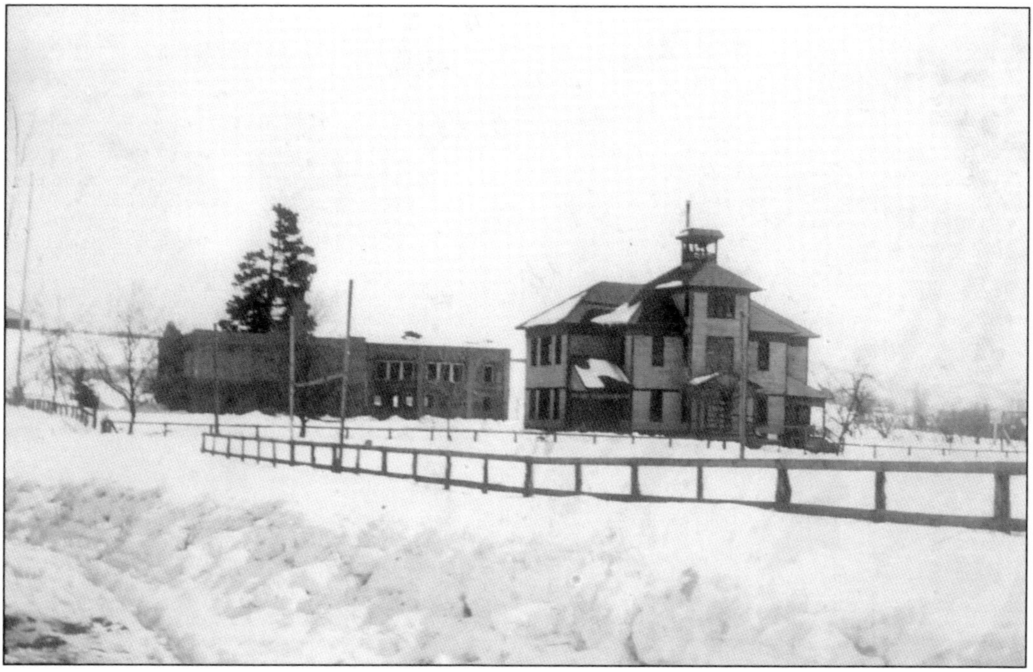

Pictured is a wintry view of the Old Yellow School and the New High School. Notice the large ponderosa pine tree behind the high school. (Courtesy of Glade Stowell.)

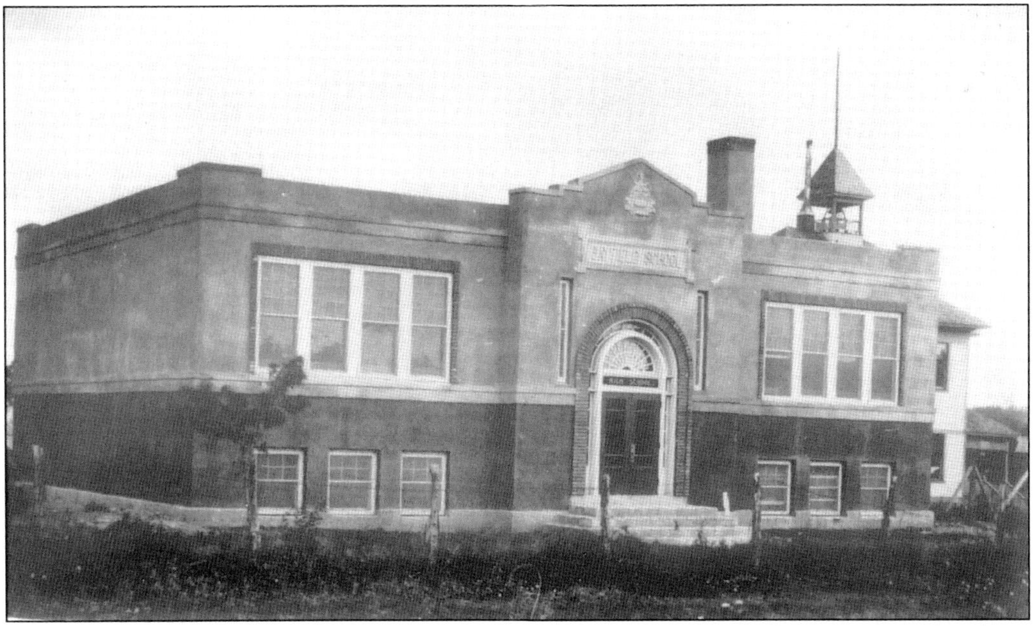

As the student body grew, the Old Yellow School became too small, and a new high school was necessary. Construction on the Bayfield High School began in 1923 and was completed in 1925. However, part of the new high school was used in 1924. The Yellow School bell tower can be seen over the right corner of the high school. Courtesy of Jo Griffin.)

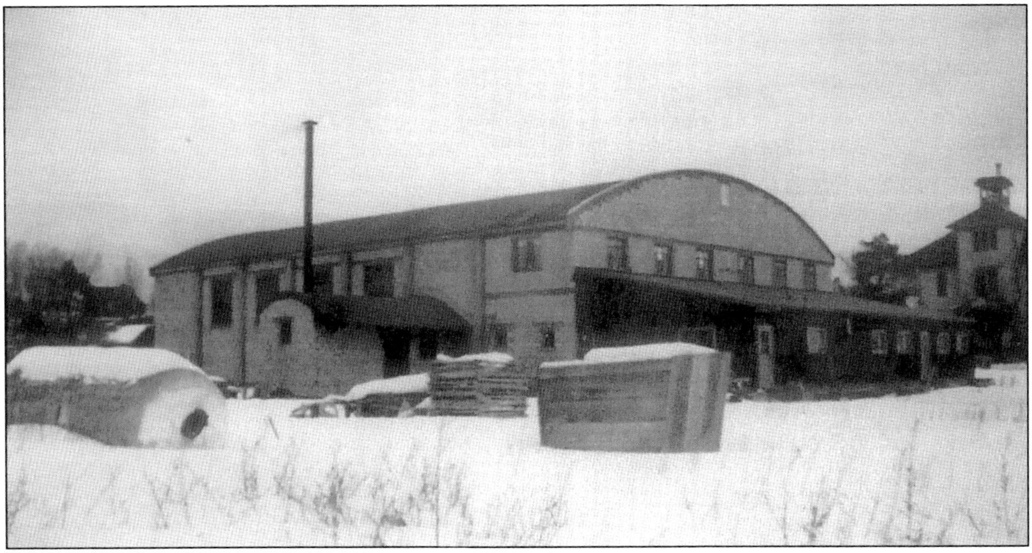

The community built the gymnasium through donations, fund raising, and donated labor; upon completion it was given to the school district. In 1946, a group of men decided that the youth of Bayfield needed a gym. The school athletes played basketball in Akers Hall, which was over Stocks Garage. It had only a 12-foot ceiling and no bleachers, leaving the spectators to just stand around the court. A committee was formed and started campaigning in the community. Even the young people saved their pennies so they could buy a cinder block. They had dances, roller-skating, and donkey basketball games, or just anything to help pay for it before turning it over to the school district. (Courtesy of Meryl James.)

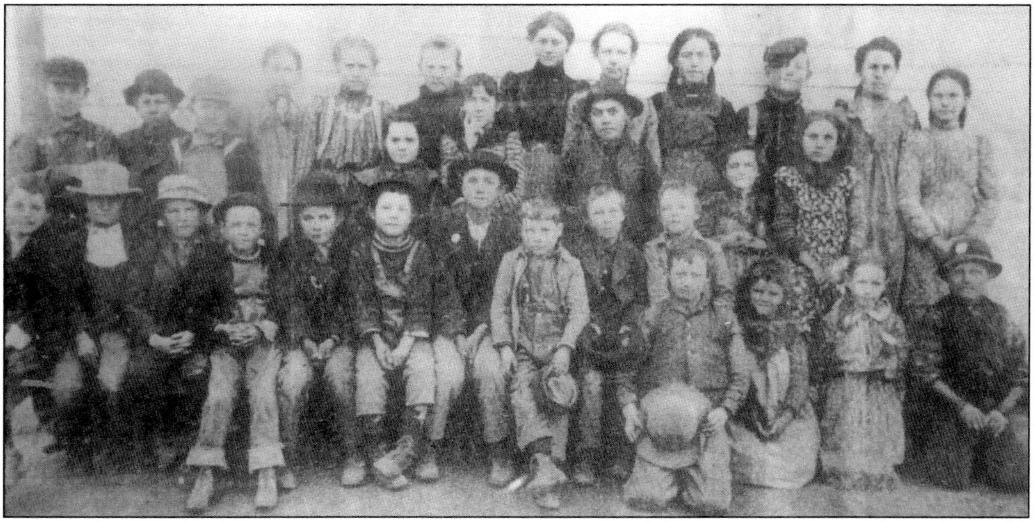

Here is the 1901–1902 class near Los Pinos, La Plata County. The school was located near where U.S. Highway 160 now goes northeast of the present town of Bayfield. They are all unidentified except the fifth boy from left, front row (Walter Ostwald) and the boy sixth from the left (Herbert Ostwald). (Courtesy of L.T. Ostwald Collection.)

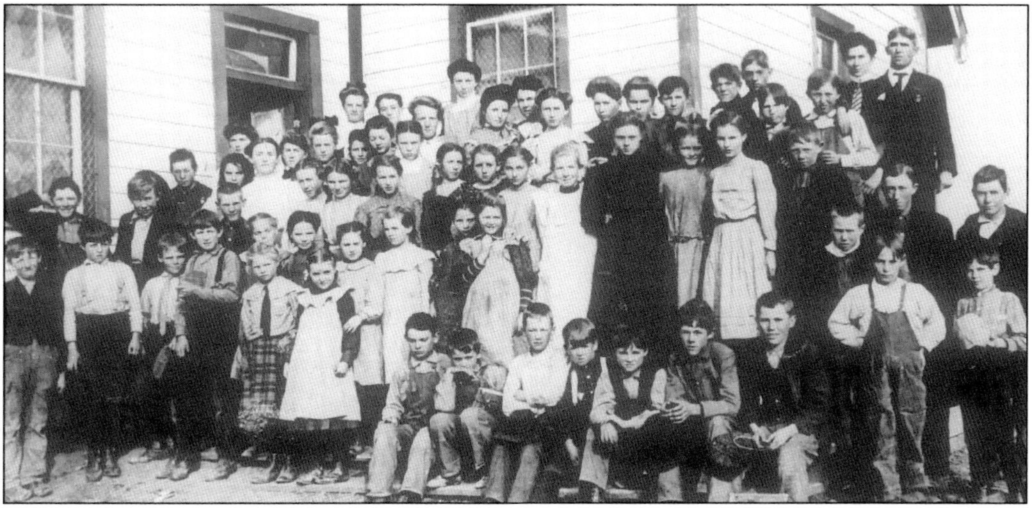

The Los Pinos school was located outside town on a hill that was leveled for the construction of U.S. Highway 160. This 1903–1904 class attended that school. Pictured, from left to right, are (first row) two unidentified students, Vernon Drury, unidentified, Ruby Bates, Levie Parson, Adrian Lock, unidentified, Joe Wilmer, Duke Martin, Wes Schiller, Joe Carmack, and three unidentified students; (second row) Carl Bay, unidentified, Carl Rollman, Loretta Sutton, Lenie Parson, three unidentified students, Dotie Org, unidentified, Charlie Martin, and Lee Ray Wheeler; (third row) Joe Myers, Sylvester Schroeder, unidentified, Lulu Taylor, Edna Martin, unidentified, and Vera E. Ostwald; (fourth row) Chris Schiller, Mary Olsen, Emma Vossmer, Bessie Springer, unidentified, Abie Taylor, Myrtle Salyer, two unidentified students, Anna Olson, Estey Malloy, Pauline Newman, Earl Morrison, and unidentified; (fifth row) Amelia Lessels Green, Lucy Morrison, unidentified, Elsie Martin, unidentified, Many Olsen, unidentified, Agnes Underhill, Cecil Springer, unidentified, Archie Org, Cecil Malloy, Frances Carr, and Authur Carr. (Courtesy of L.T. Ostwald Collection.)

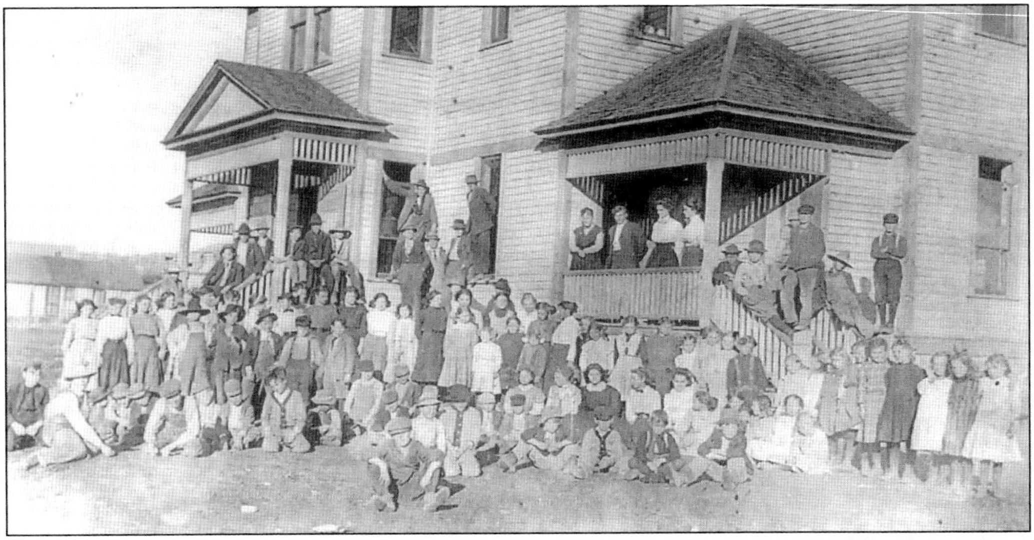

It looks like the whole school turned out for this photo taken in front of the Old Yellow School built in 1906. It appears that the teachers are on the porch on the right of the photo. (Courtesy of Kenny Montgomery Collection.)

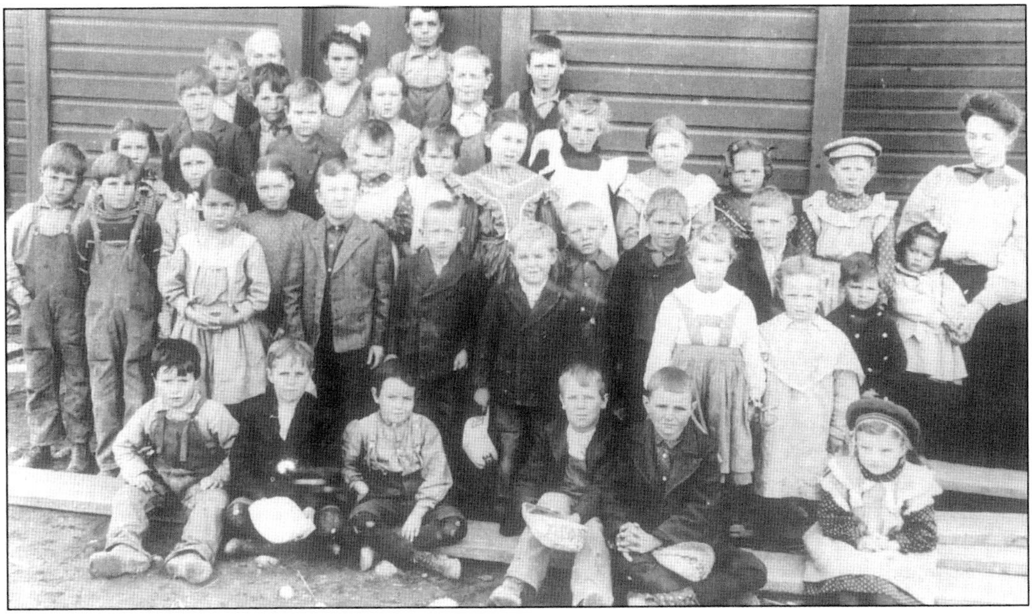

The first, second, and third grades were held at the Union Church on Mill Street. Pictured, from left to right, are (first row) Vernon Tinnin, Oscar Meyers, Monroe Everett, Monroe Everett, Oscar Meyers, and Ona Disatell; (second row) Harry Scott, Fred Palmer, Lucile Locke, Joe Morley, Clive Peterson, Marion Everett, Floyd Peterson, Ducan Meyers, Josie Schiller, Nellie Montgomery, Walter Newland, and Hazel Disatell; (third row) unidentified, unidentified, Shirley Hartley, Nila Davenport, Zano Davenport, Lilly Underhill, Meta Montgomery, unidentified, Mona Bates, unidentified, Luella Bates, and Miss Jewett Palmer; (fourth row) Jennings Ong, Guy Morrison, Vial Davenport, Emma Schiller, William Worrel, and Jewett Palmer (fifth row) Neil Morrison, Addie Morrison, unidentified, and Adrian Locke. (Courtesy of L.T. Ostwald Collection.)

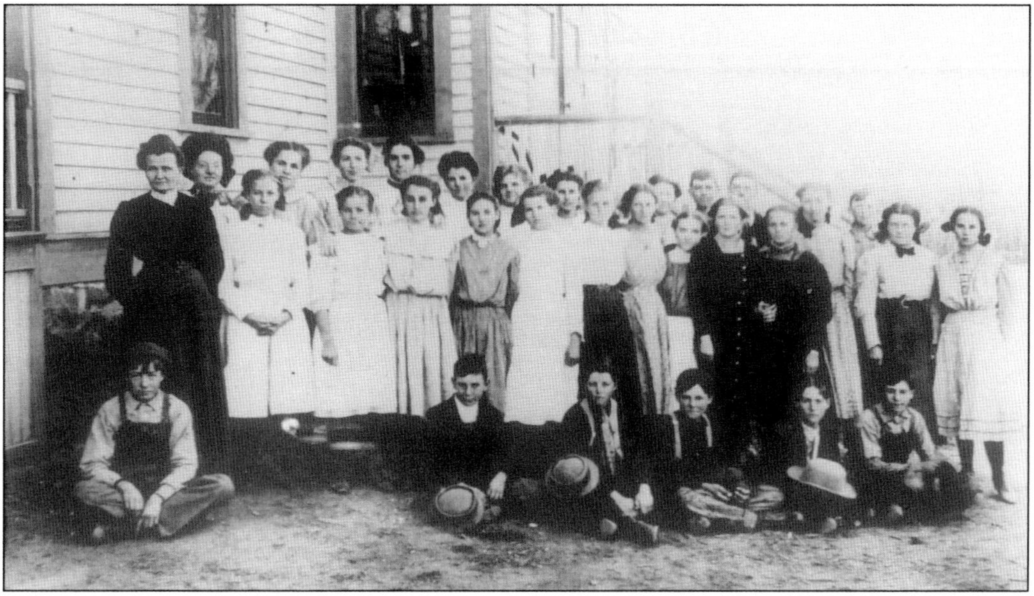

Pictured is a 1909–1910 class of older students at the Old Yellow School. Notice the two students standing in the window. (Courtesy of L.T. Ostwald Collection.)

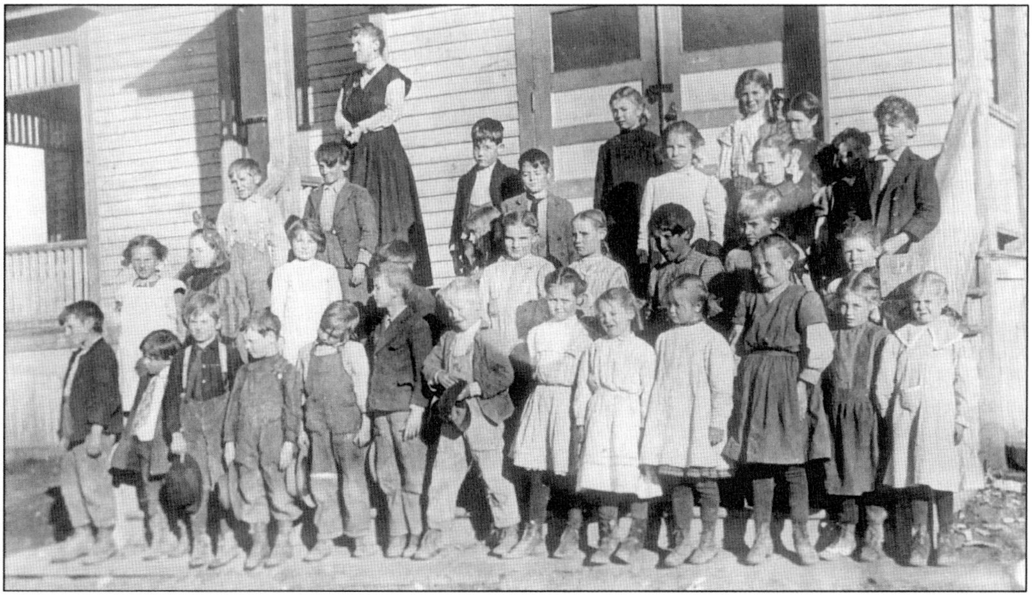

Bayfield School class of 1911 stands with their teacher Mrs. O'Conner who is standing at the top of the stairs. Frank Carmack is in the front row, fifth boy, with his head cocked to left, and the girl at the end of the first row is Lena Carmack. The rest are unidentified. (Courtesy of L.T. Ostwald Collection.)

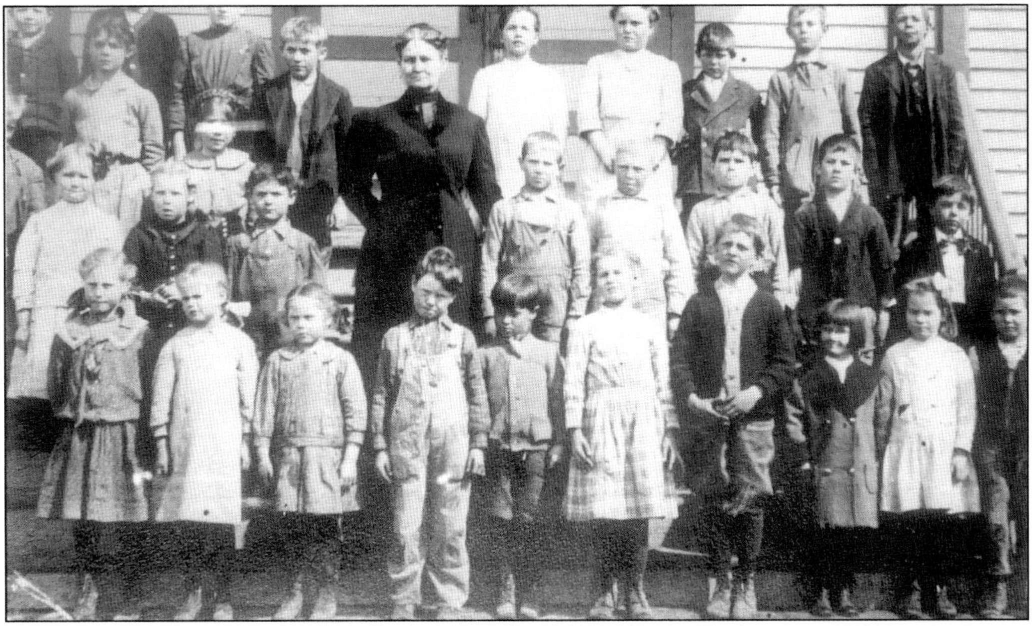

This is the 1911–1912 Bayfield School class at the Old Yellow School. Pictured, left to right, are (front row) Montie Montgomery, Lena Carmack, Florence Hayes, Bradley Currie, Carson Tinnin, Nora Von Dusen, Charles Coulson, Louise Singleton, Verlene Davenport, and Clifford Palmer; (middle row) Frank Carmack, Frieda Schiller, Velma Everett, Josephine Cudnay, Bruce Alfred, Ted Montgomery, Sam Everett, Frank Beebee, Roy Palmer, and Raymond Egger; (back row) Jean Campbell, Florence Alfred, Walter Taylor, Edna Lane, Carl Ostwald, Mrs. Prewitt, Vadna Davenport, Ruth Graves, Walter Newland, Jim Townsend, and Ralph Dockstadler. (Courtesy of L.T. Ostwald Collection.)

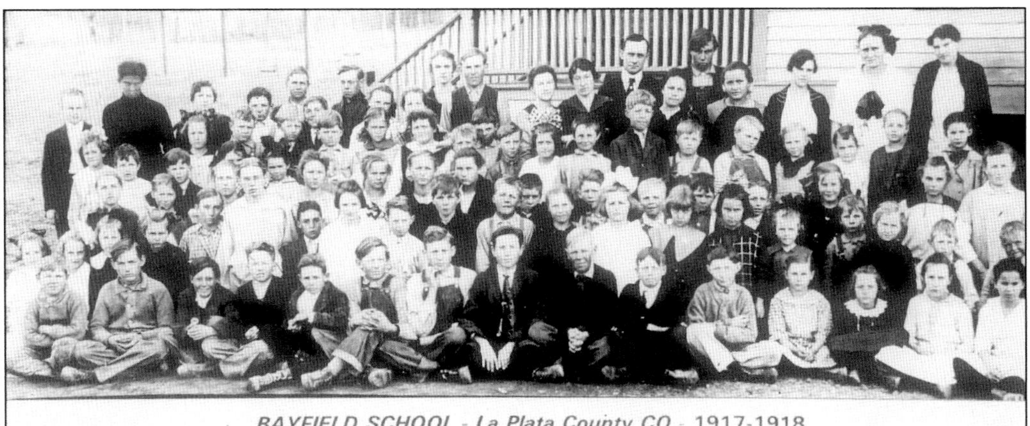

The Bayfield School class of 1917–1918 is pictured here at the Old Yellow School. Student identification is in the following photograph. (Courtesy of L.T. Ostwald Collection.)

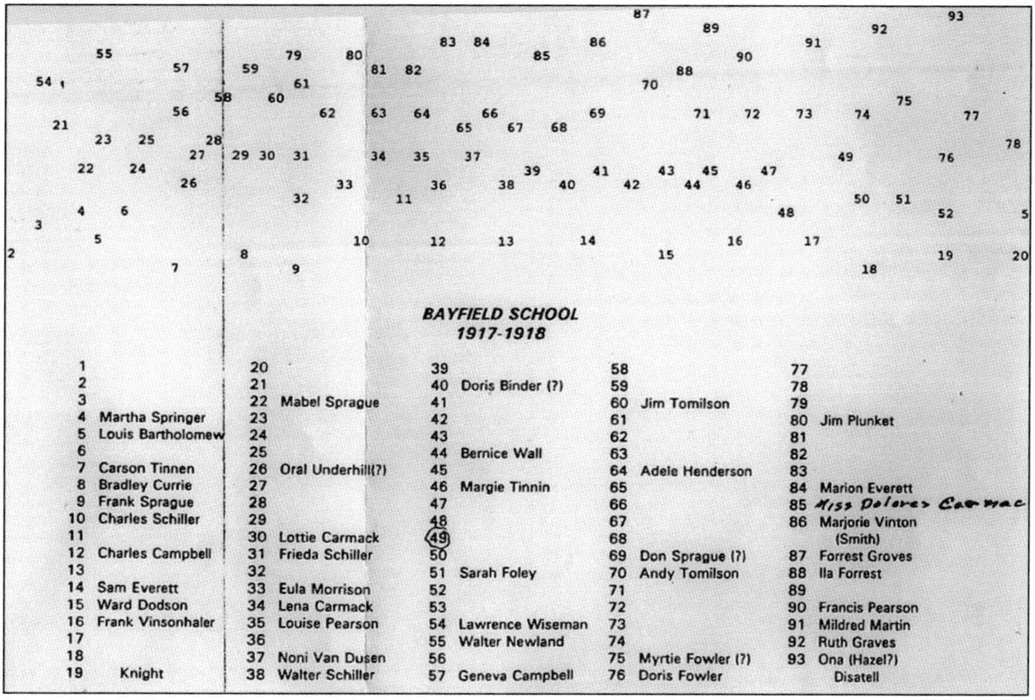

BAYFIELD SCHOOL
1917-1918

1
2
3
4 Martha Springer
5 Louis Bartholomew
6
7 Carson Tinnen
8 Bradley Currie
9 Frank Sprague
10 Charles Schiller
11
12 Charles Campbell
13
14 Sam Everett
15 Ward Dodson
16 Frank Vinsonhaler
17
18
19 Knight
20
21
22 Mabel Sprague
23
24
25
26 Oral Underhill(?)
27
28
29
30 Lottie Carmack
31 Frieda Schiller
32
33 Eula Morrison
34 Lena Carmack
35 Louise Pearson
36
37 Noni Van Dusen
38 Walter Schiller
39
40 Doris Binder (?)
41
42
43
44 Bernice Wall
45
46 Margie Tinnin
47
48
49
50
51 Sarah Foley
52
53
54 Lawrence Wiseman
55 Walter Newland
56
57 Geneva Campbell
58
59
60 Jim Tomilson
61
62
63
64 Adele Henderson
65
66
67
68
69 Don Sprague (?)
70 Andy Tomilson
71
72
73
74
75 Myrtie Fowler (?)
76 Doris Fowler
77
78
79
80 Jim Plunket
81
82
83
84 Marion Everett
85 Miss Dolores Carmac
86 Marjorie Vinton (Smith)
87 Forrest Groves
88 Ila Forrest
89
90 Francis Pearson
91 Mildred Martin
92 Ruth Graves
93 Ona (Hazel?) Disatell

This is the student identification of previous photograph. Blank spaces are unidentified. (Courtesy of L.T. Ostwald Collection.)

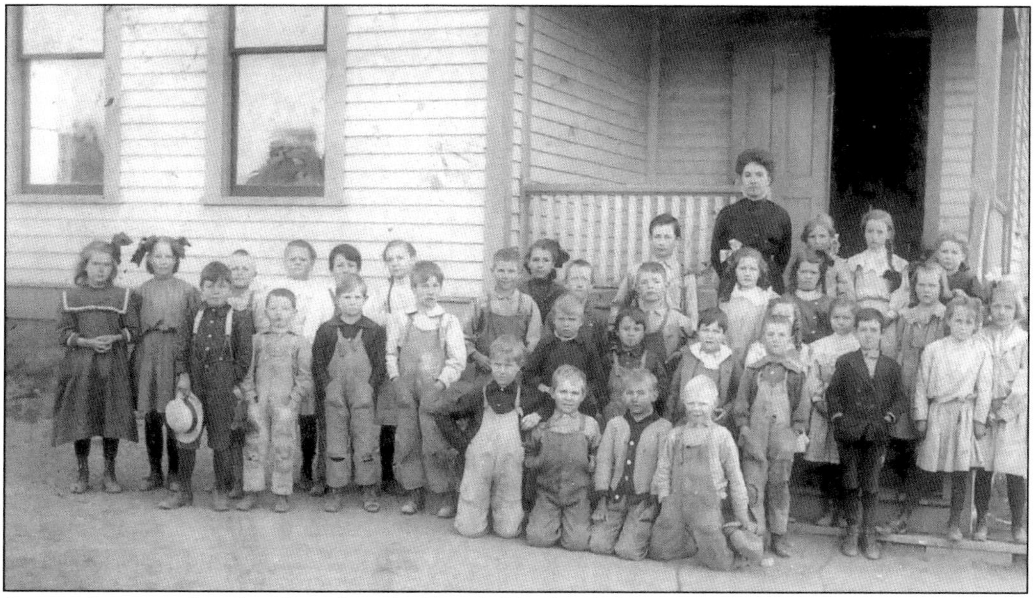

Pictured is an undated and unidentified Bayfield school class in front of the Old Yellow School. (Courtesy of Poncho McNew Collection.)

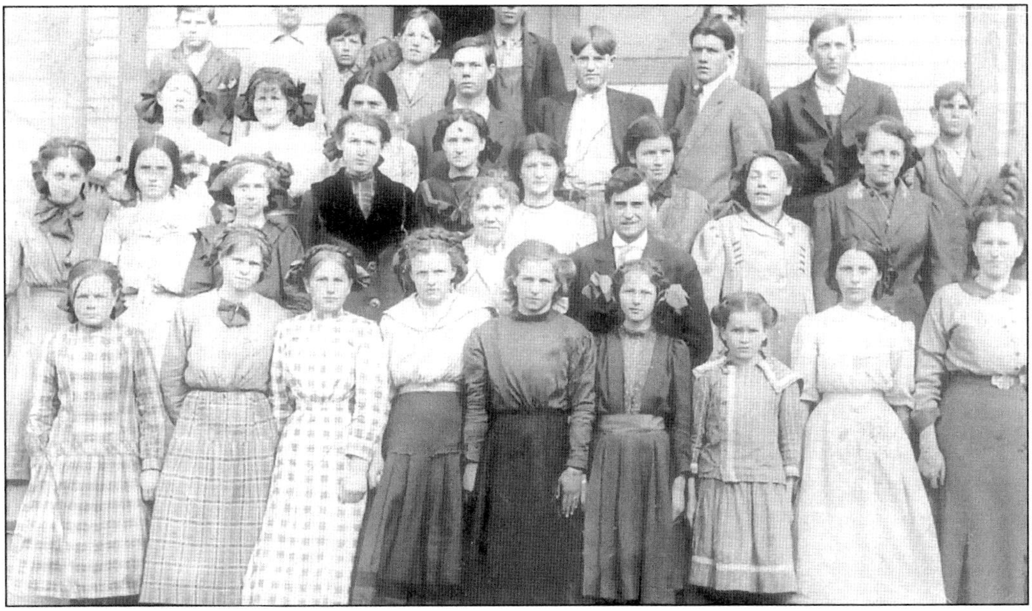

This is another undated and unidentified older school class at the Old Yellow School. (Courtesy of Poncho McNew Collection.)

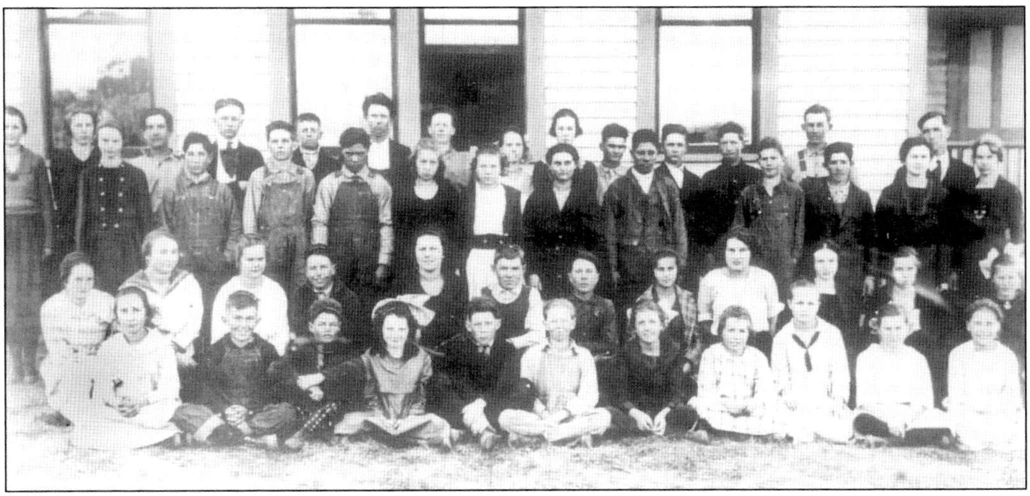

Pictured is the 1918–1919 Bayfield School class at the Old Yellow School. Identification is as follows, left to right: (first row) Zoro Wagner, Harold Springer, Frank Humiston, Louise Fergesson, Paul Duvic, Sam Warlick, Ila Mallory, Helen Pierce, unidentified, Mildred Farrow, and Mae Binder; (second row) Eula Morrison, Ora Underhill, Lena Carmack, Frank Humiston, Ila Forrest, John Tickson, Lydiala Forrest, Lottie Carmack, Nona Van Dusen, unidentified, Happy Weiser, and Alice Fraham; (third row) Louise Pearson, Zelpha Farrow, Frank Foltz, Lynn Bartholomew, unidentified, Bradley Currie, unidentified, Berthan Payson, John Martinez, unidentified, Lloyd Pierce, and two unidentified students; (fourth row) Edna Weiser, Farrell Lacy, unidentified, Ward Dodson, Lewis Wells (?), unidentified, Mildred Carmack, Evelyn Duvic, Ellery Parson, Carl Rollman, Marion Well, Dan Sprague, and unidentified. (Courtesy of O. T. Ostwald Collection.)

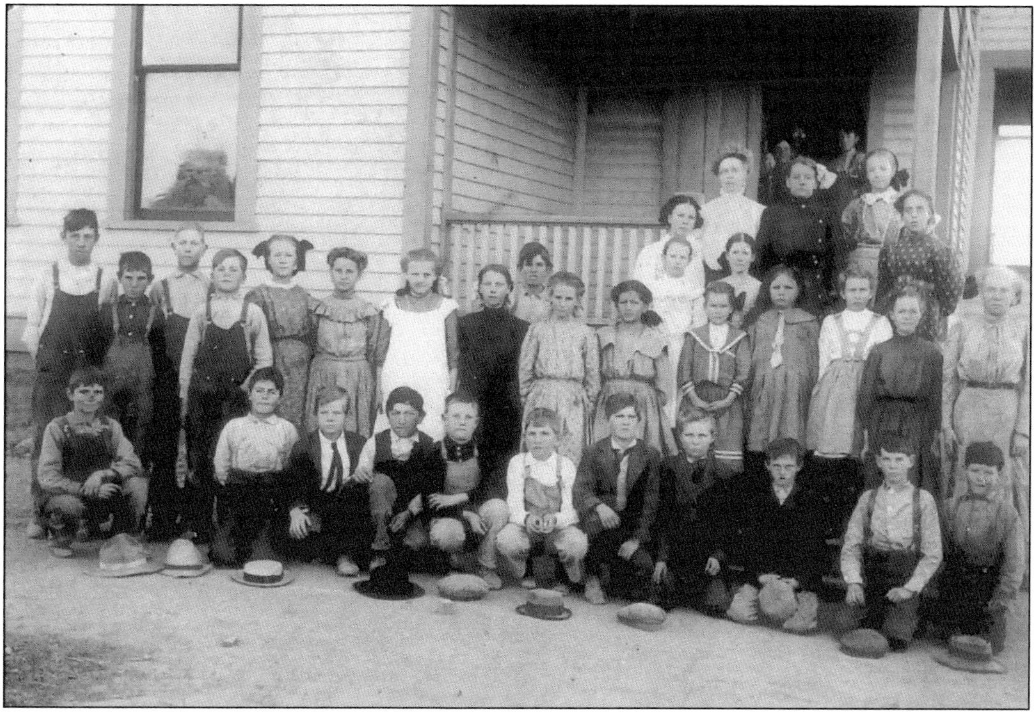

Pictured here is another unidentified and undated Bayfield School class by the Old Yellow School. Notice how all the boys, except one, front row, have laid their hats on the ground. (Courtesy of Poncho McNew Collection.)

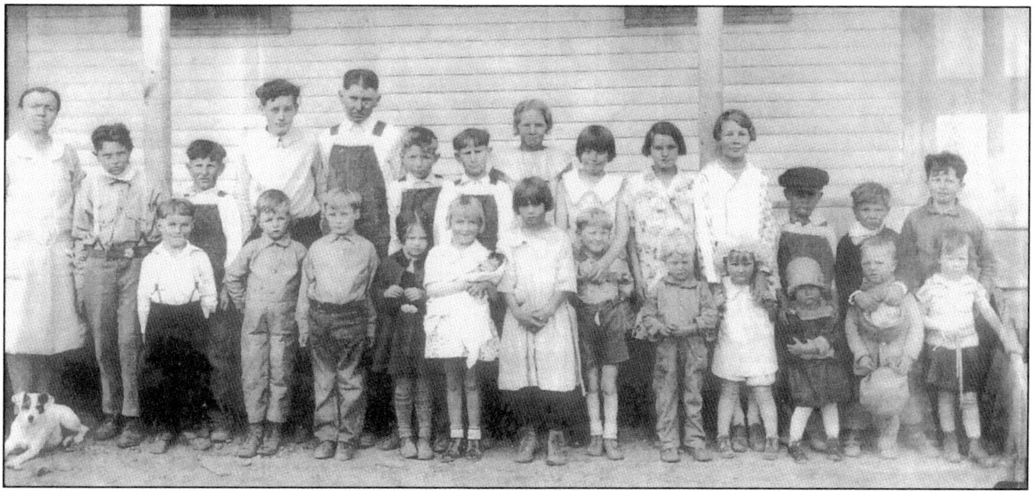

Mrs. Grace Morse stands with her 1929 class in front of the Columbus School, which is now the home of Gregg and Debra Janus. Pictured, left to right, are (front row) Dale McCoy, Archie Blackmore, Clyde Wilbourn, Ruth Richards, Edith Dunsworth, Rosie Blackmore, Charles Dunsworth, Harlan Blackmore, Frances Wilbourn, Audry McCoy, Ernie Parks, and Rosemary Richards; (back row) Mrs. Grace Morse, Clem Knight, Res McCoy, Dayton Percell, Chester McCoy, Earl Blackmore, Orville McCoy, Elsie Blackmore, Laura Dunsworth, Esther Percell, Melvia Wilbourn, Harold McCoy, Henry Parks, and Jonnie Richards. (Courtesy of Henry Parks.)

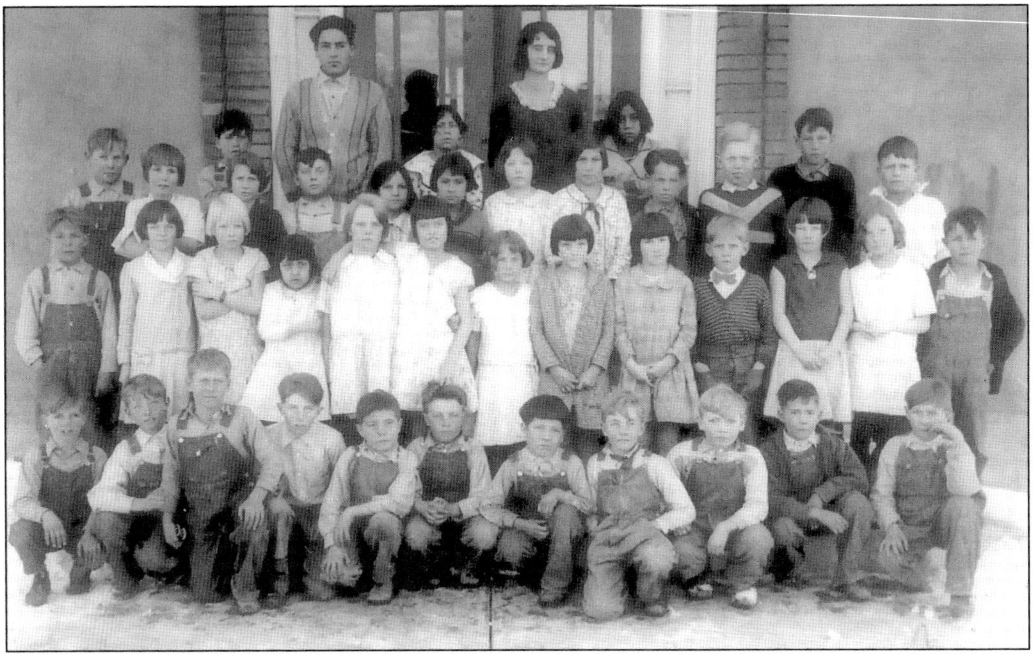

The two people at the top of this photo are possibly teachers. (Courtesy of Kenny Montgomery Collection.)

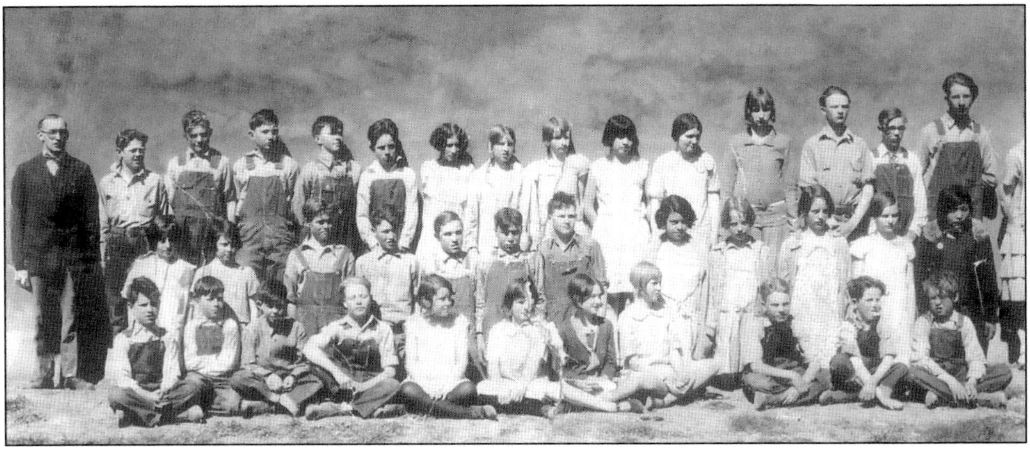

A Bayfield School class of unidentified members poses on the east side of the high school. The teacher in back row, left, is also unidentified. (Courtesy of Poncho McNew Collection.)

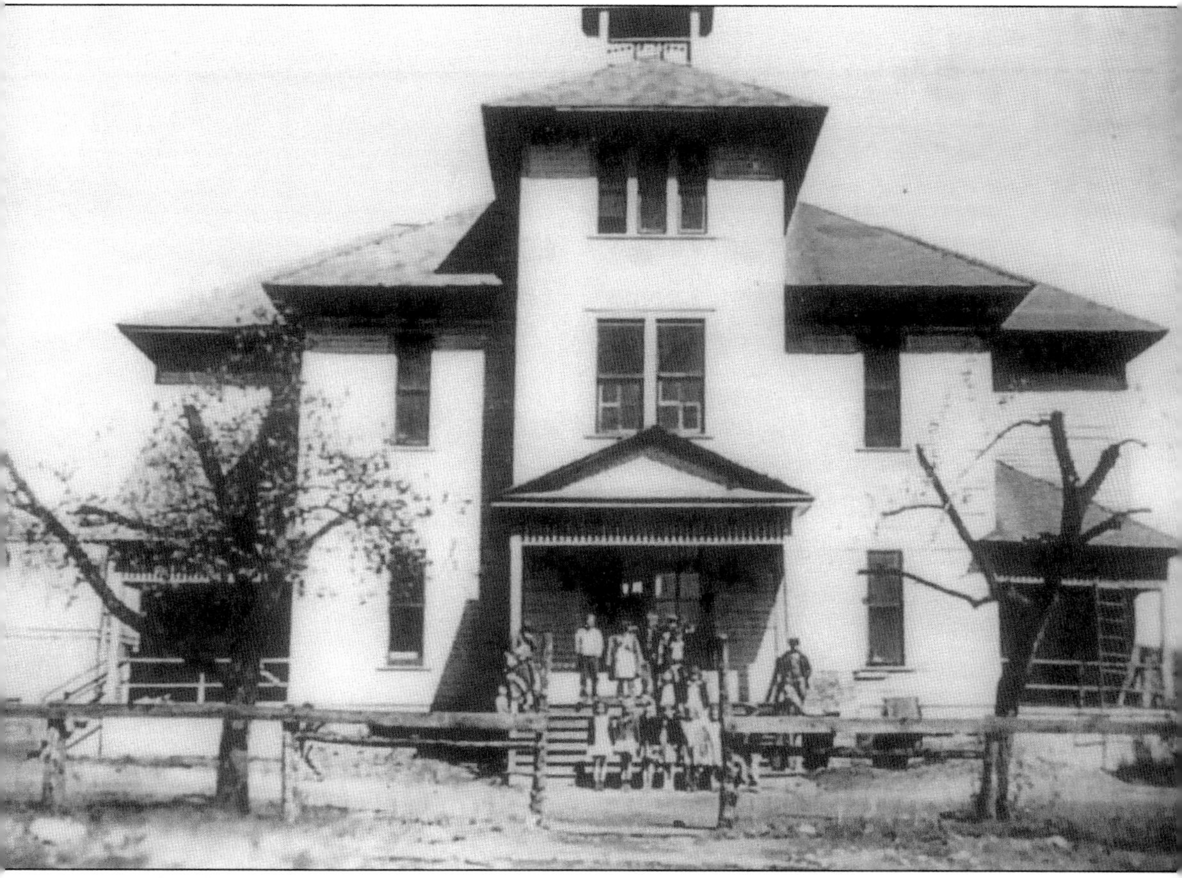

A group of students stands on the front steps of the Old Yellow School. The undated photo has to be after 1925, because the chimney of the new high school can be seen on the right side. The two trees are still there today. The school burned in the late 1950s and had to be torn down. (Courtesy of Tim Walters.)

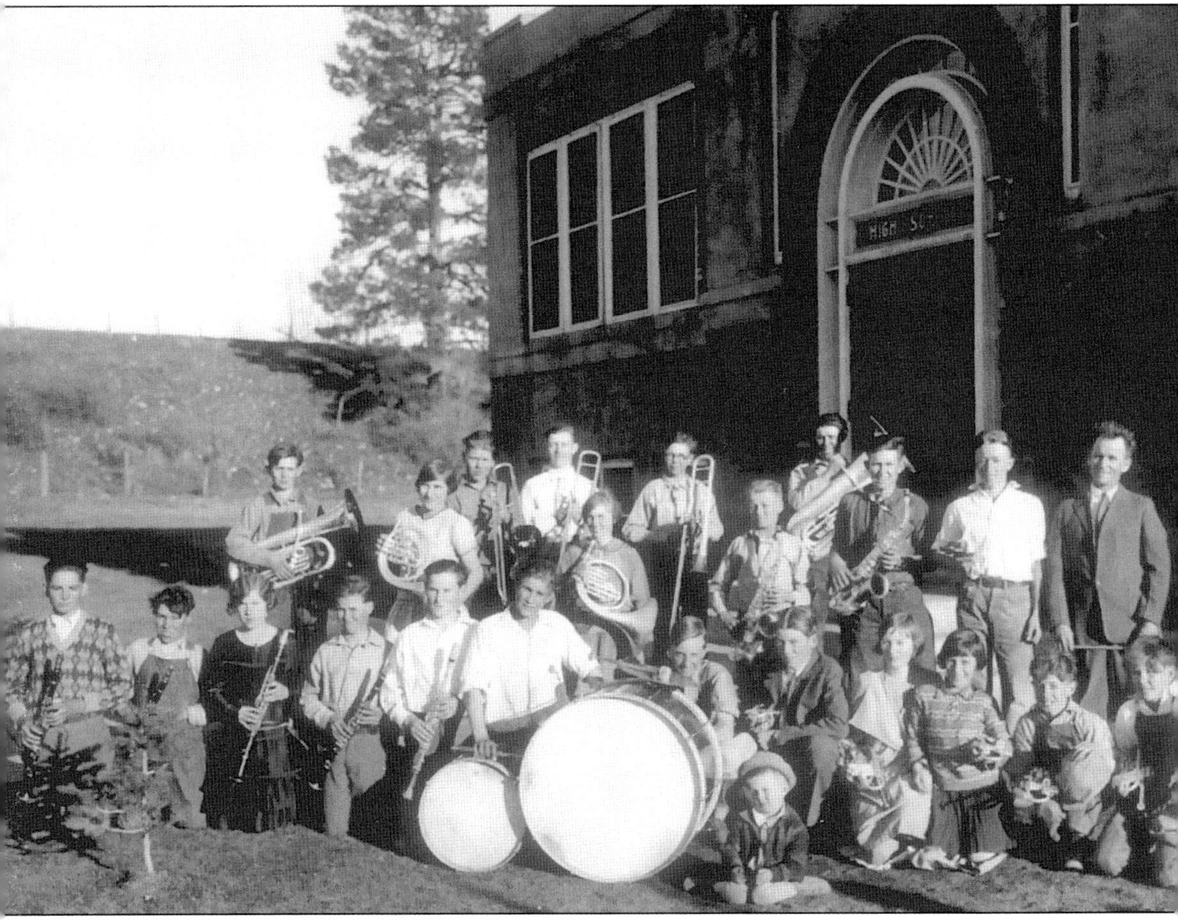

The 1930–31 Bayfield High School band poses in front of the high school. Note the size of the spruce trees. Spruce trees were planted all over town in the early 1930s, and today they are about the same size. Pictured, from left to right, are (front row) Conrad Burks (Ignacio), Logan Shelhamer, Genelle Salazar, Edwin Green, Leonard Jenkins, Chester Rodman, Edgar Branson, Cecil Sower, Dorothy Gearhart, Geneva Salabar, Richard Frahan, Delmar Jenkins, Jack Emery (son of the director, is the small boy by the base drum); (back row) Melvin Holt, Doris Binder, Dan Townsend, Ernestine Gearhart, Kenneth Gearhart, Bryan Whitney, Elmer Shelhamer, Ray Copeland (Ignacio), Loren Bell (Ignacio), unidentified, and director W.J. Emery. (Courtesy of Tim Walters.)

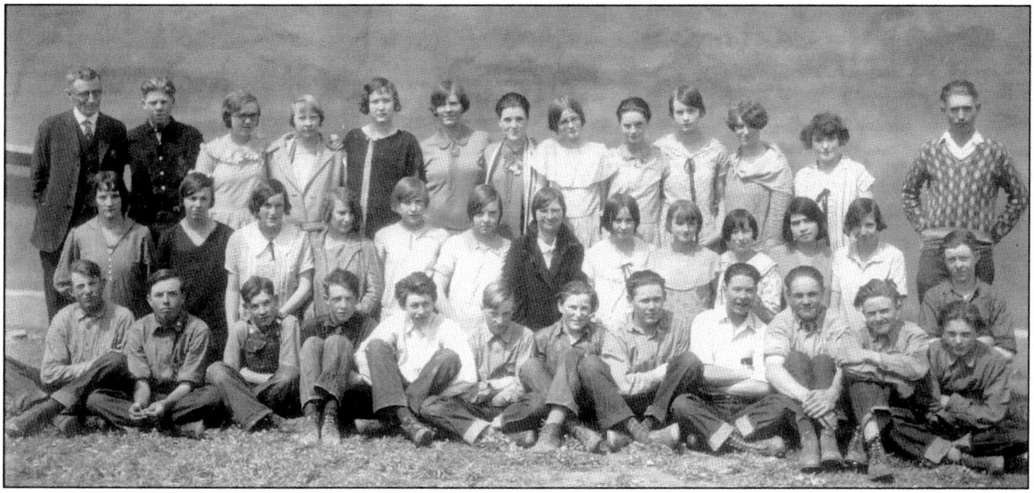

This is an early 1930s Bayfield High School class. (Courtesy of Colorado Historical Society.)

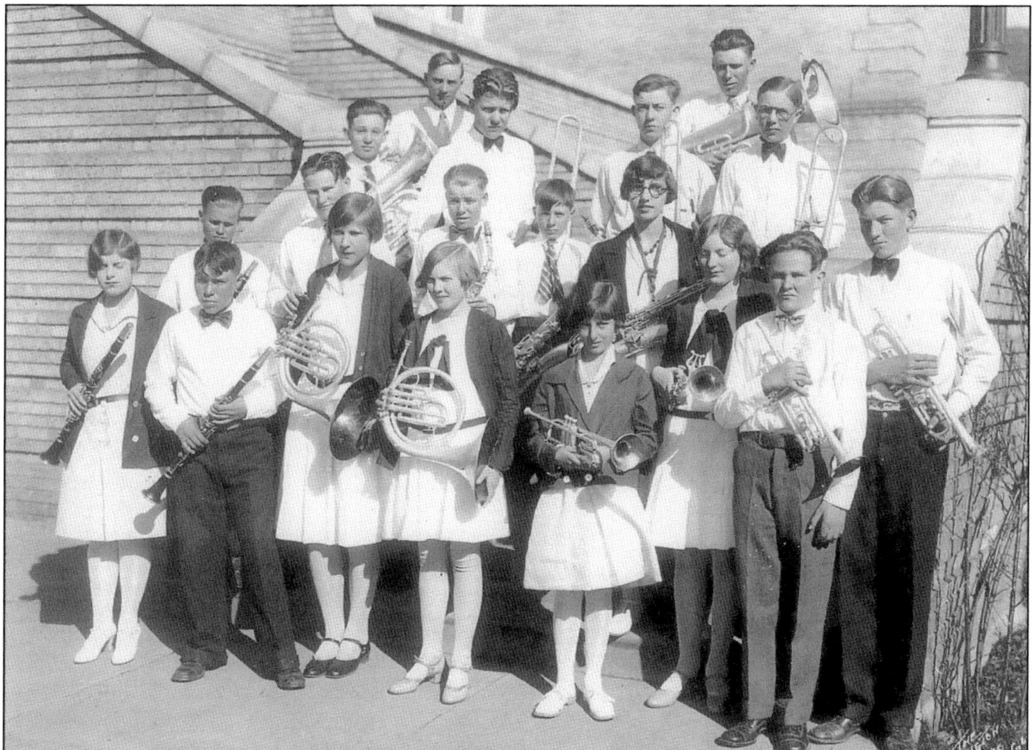

The 1930–31 Bayfield High School band members pose at the bottom of the stairs at Durango High School, Durango, Colorado, where they participated in a regional band competition, taking first place. Pictured from left to right are, (first row) Genelle Salabar, Logan Shelhamer, Doris Binder, Ernestine Gerhart, Geneva Salabar, Dorothy Gerhart, Delmar Jenkins, and Cecil Sower; (second row) Bryan Greenley, Leonard Jenkins, Bryon Whitney, Alfred Shelhammer, Norma (?), (third row) unidentified, (?) Holt, Guy Binder, Kenneth Gearhart; (fourth row) Bud (?), (?) Branson, Alfred Shelhamer, and Edgar (?). (Courtesy of Cecil Sower.)

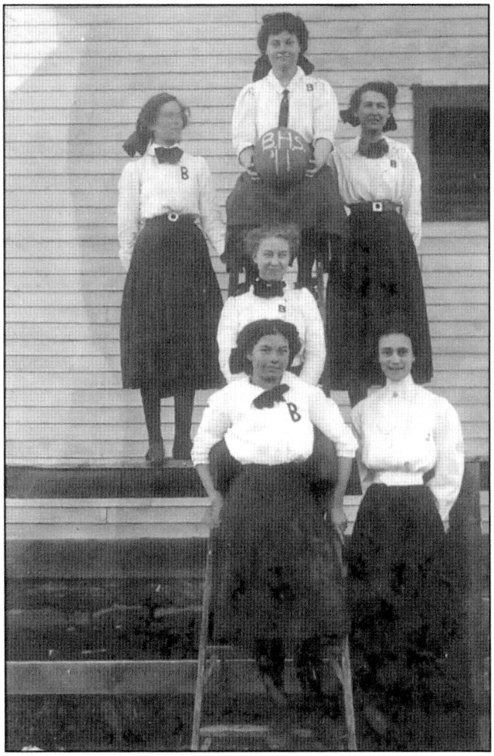

Here is the 1911 Bayfield High School girl's basketball team. Pictured, from left to right, are (first row) Georgie Turner, and Coach Mable Vallient Gibbs; (second row) Lou Alta Melton; (third row) Abbie Taylor, and Elsie Eads; (fourth row) Elsie Maloy. (Courtesy of Melba McCoy.)

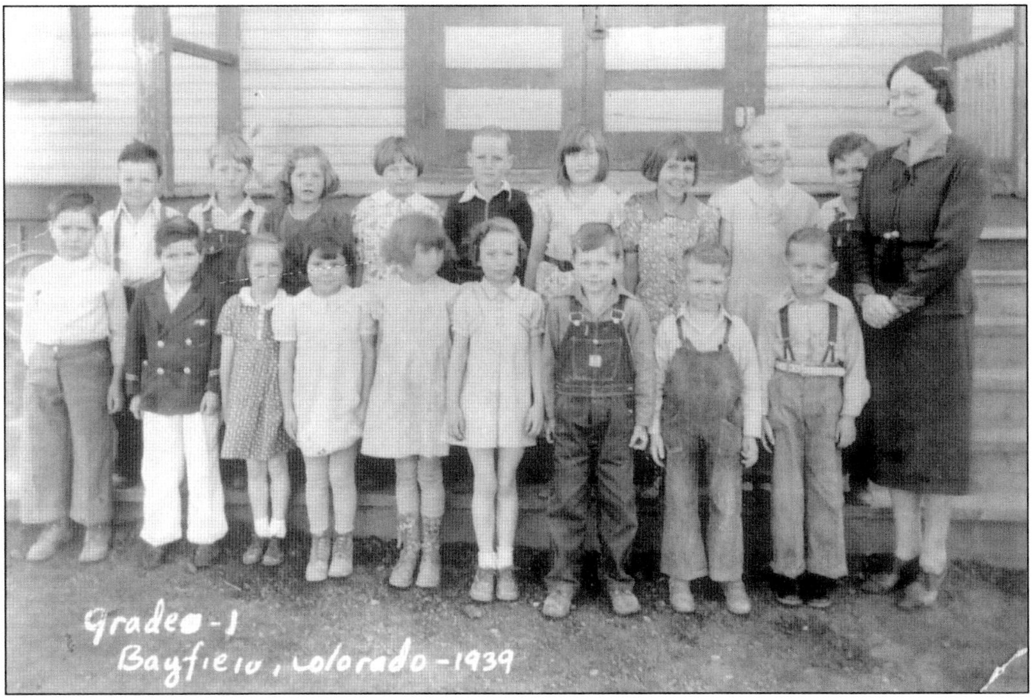

This first grade class of Bayfield Elementary School poses with their teacher, Miss Helen McDonald, in front of the Old Yellow School in this 1939 photo. (Courtesy of Poncho McNew Collection.)

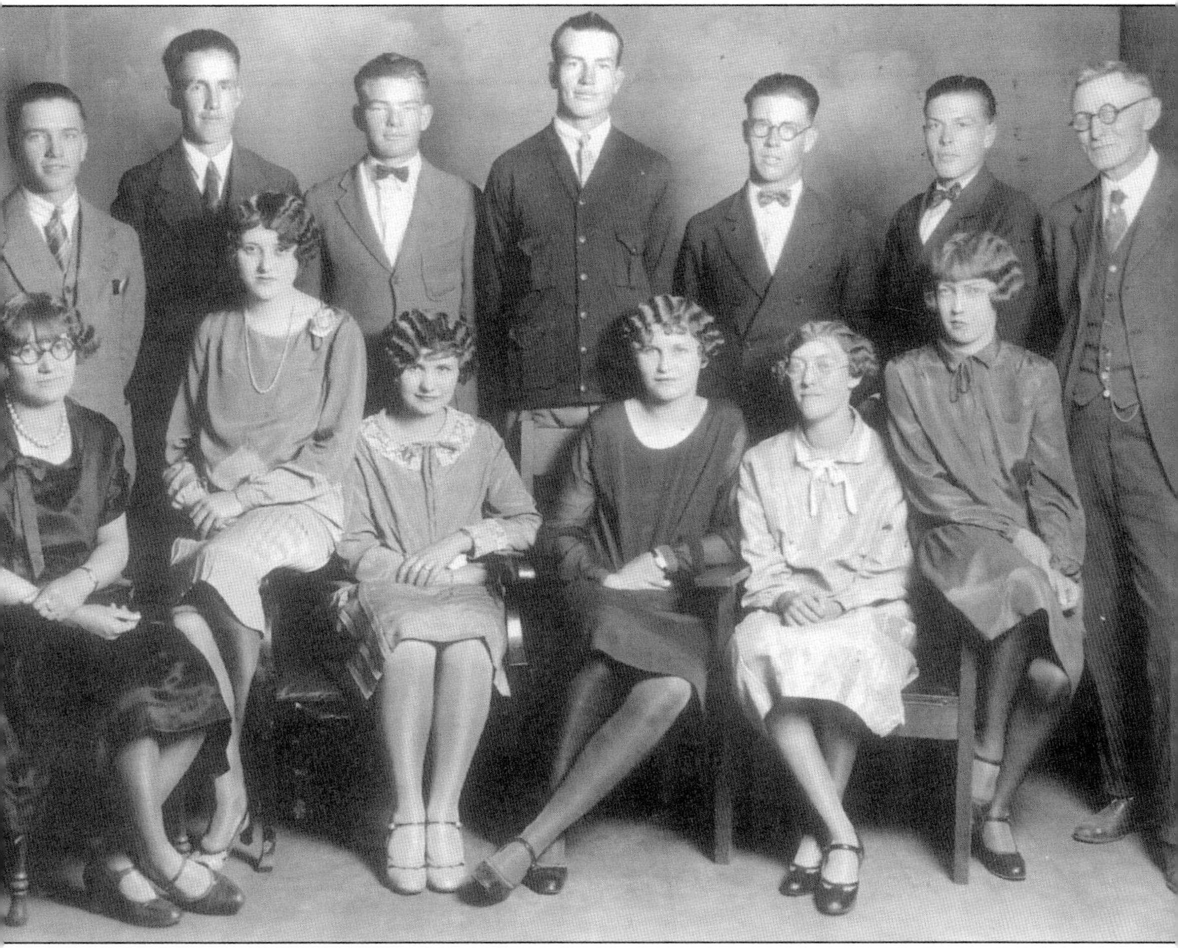

The 1927 Bayfield High School Senior Class poses for a class portrait. Note the similar hairstyles amongst the girls. Pictured, from left to right, are (front row) Annie Long, Lylene Darnell, Marceille Leming, Frances Pierson, Iva Sapp, and Virginia Wall; (back row) Lloyd Barnes, Rowland Carmack, Darl Davenport, Deb Davenport, Keith Paisley, Hugh Fredeen, and Principal Lorenz. (Courtesy of Colorado Historical Society.)

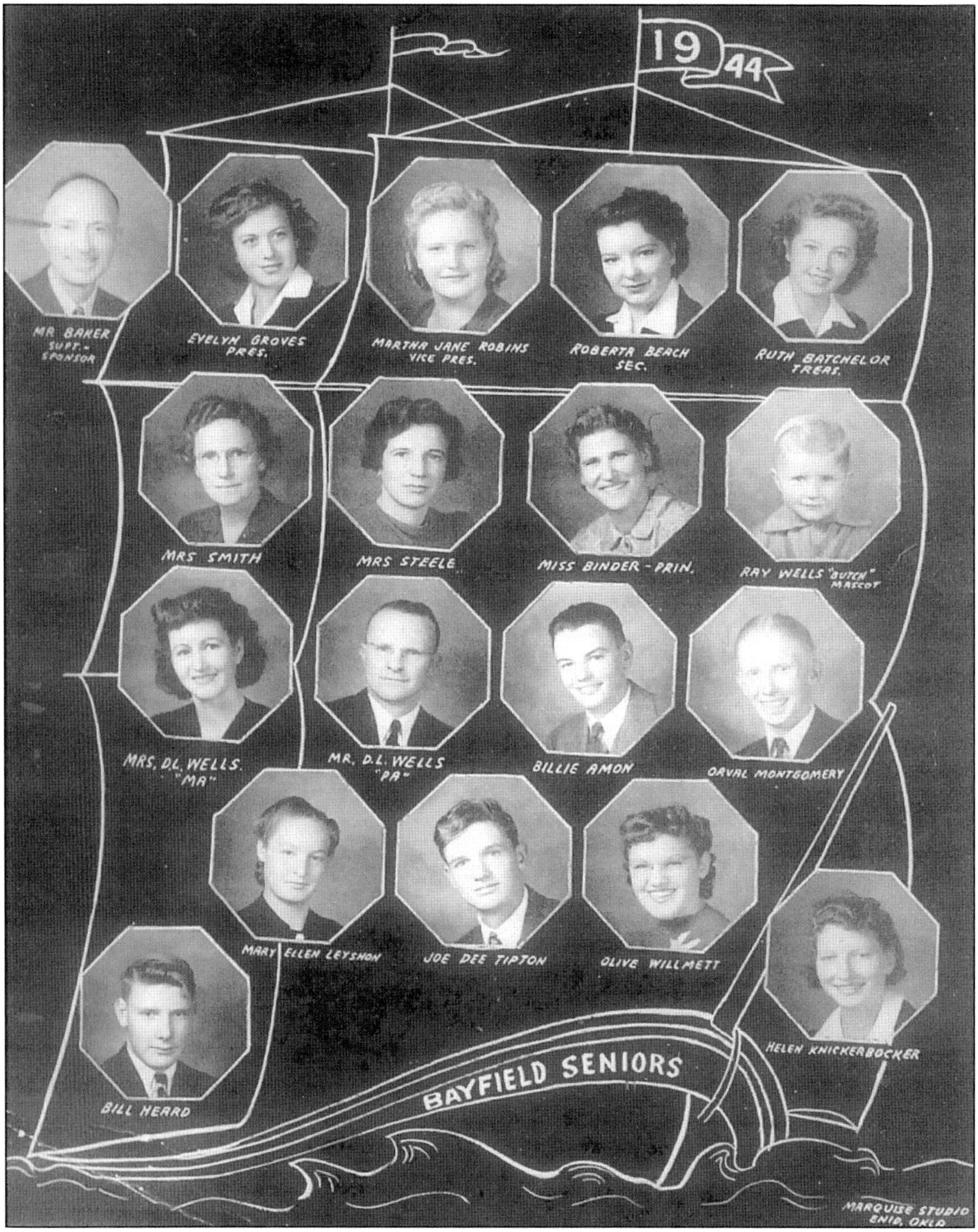

This 1944 Bayfield Senior Class photo appeared in the 1944 Bayfield Wolverine School annual. Pictured, from left to right, are (first row) Bill Herrd and Helen Knickerbocker; (second row) Mary Ellen Leyshon, Joe Dee Tipton, and Olive Willmett; (third row) Mrs. D.L. "Ma" Wells, Mr. D.L. "Pa" Wells, Billie Amon, and Orval Montgomery; (fourth row) Mrs. Smith, Mrs. Steele, Principal Binder, mascot Ray "Butch" Wells; (fifth row) Superintendent Baker, president Evelyn Groves, vice president Martha Jane Robins, secretary Roberta Beach, and treasurer Ruth Batchelor. (Courtesy of Hugh Percell.)

Four

HISTORIC BAYFIELD

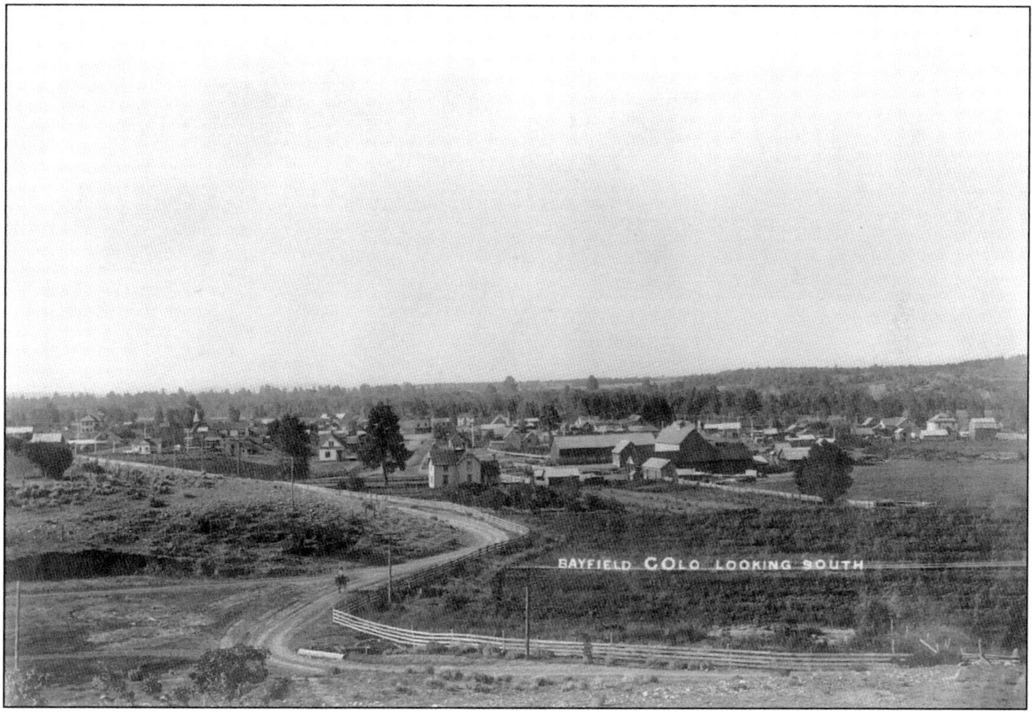

As the picture states, "Bayfield, Colorado Looking South," this view shows the road that is now called the Buck Highway. The large two-story house belonged to William Bay. His ranch was named the "Lone Pine Ranch" because of the lone ponderosa pine that stands to the left of the house. The barn and outbuilding are to the right of the house. They are no longer there today. The steeple of the Calvary Presbyterian Church can be seen in the distance on the left side of photo. (Courtesy of Colorado Historical Society.)

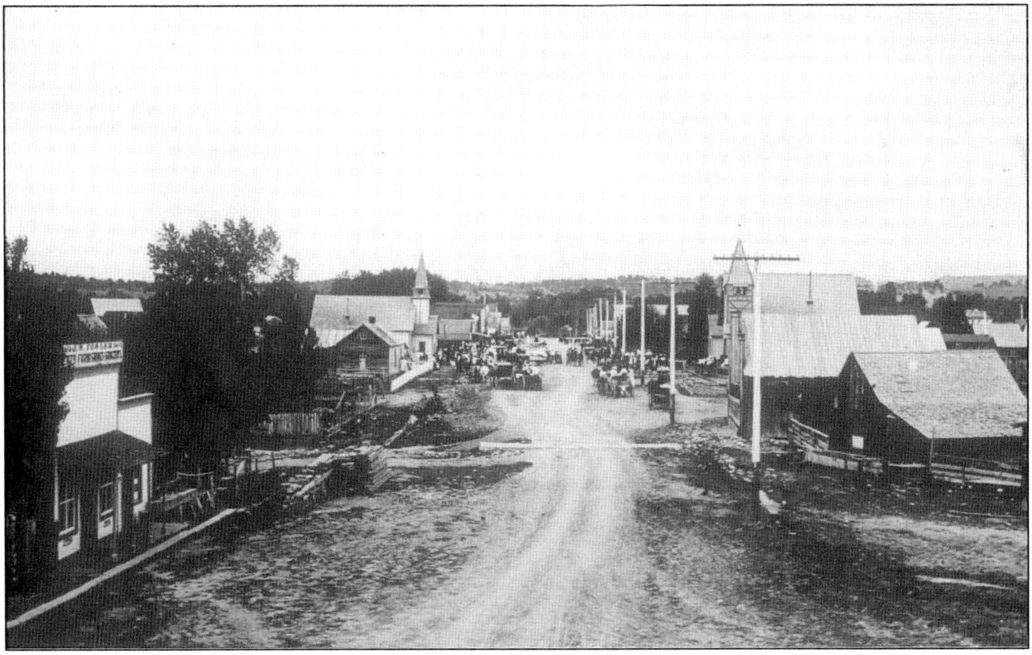

This view is of Bayfield's Mill Street (main), looking west. With the amount of people and wagons gathered by the churches, this could be a Sunday and church is just letting out. The Union Church is on the left and the Calvary Presbyterian Church on the right. While this photo is undated, there are some available clues in determining its date : if those are telephone lines, not telegraph lines, then the photo is after 1904, because that is when the telephone lines came through town. (Courtesy of Tom Moga Collection, Shoreline Inn, Vallecito Lake.)

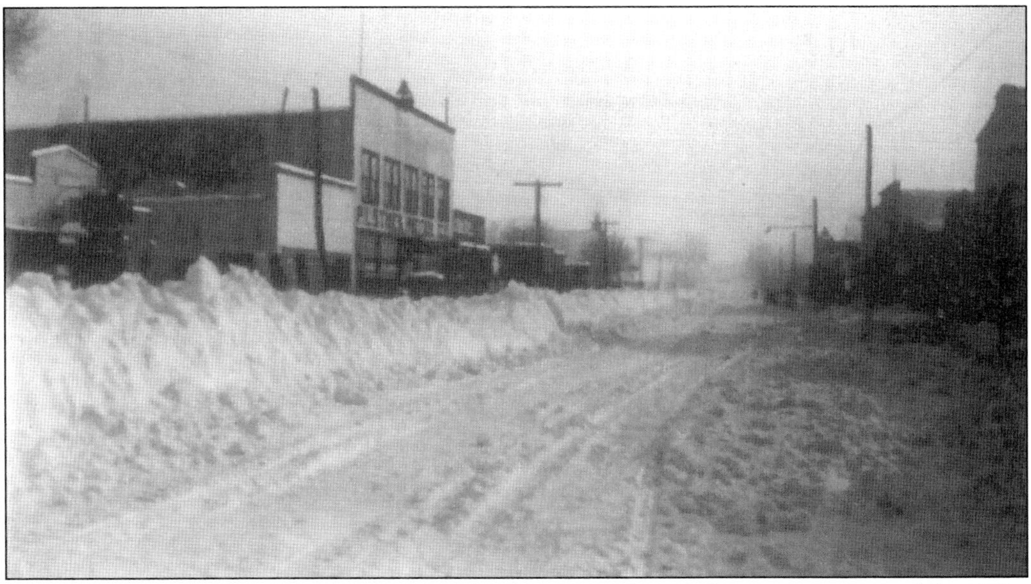

This is a very wintry Mill Street in Bayfield. They have plowed the snow to the middle of the street, and still do it today. The large building on the left is Stocks Garage with the Bayfield Hall, formally Akers Hall, above, where the basketball team played its games. The two church steeples can vaguely be seen on each side of the street. (Courtesy of Nobel Wells.)

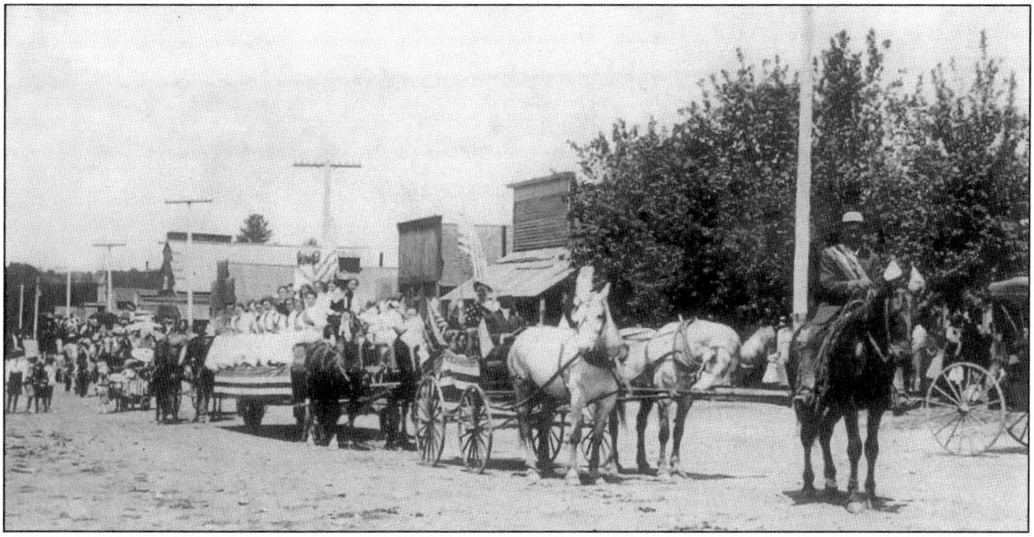

This 1906 Fourth of July parade is shown coming up Mill Street in Bayfield. The Parade Marshall, on the lead horse, is Charles Swick, and the lady in the following buggy, with the white team, is Lulu Taylor. Notice the stars of the flag draped over her left shoulder. (Courtesy of La Plata County Historical Society Animas Museum Photo Archives.)

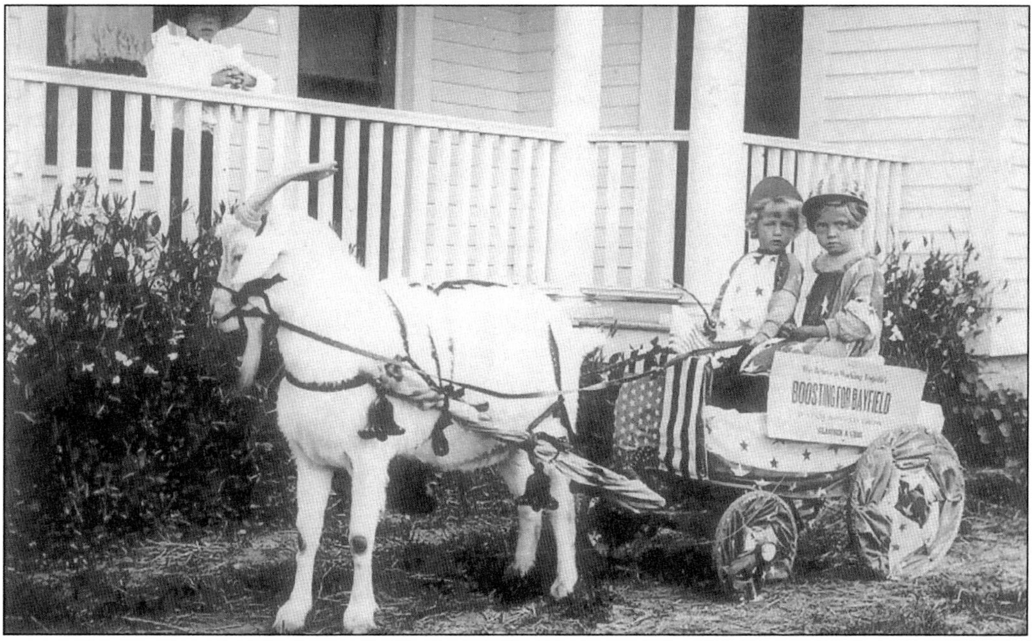

The Glasser's son Harold and his sister are ready for their big day in the Bayfield 1909 Fourth of July Parade, as they sit in a small wagon being pulled by a white goat. It made a hit with the spectators. The banner on the side of the cart reads: "We Believe in Working Together; Boosting for Bayfield; Watch Bayfield Grow; Glasser & Gibbs." In 1911, Harold Glasser again entered the parade with his goat cart. However, this time he had two other boys: Harold Springer and Claude Stuffer. They represented the Bayfield Juniors and carried their bats, gloves, and other implements for the national game. They won first prize. (Courtesy of Poncho McNew Collection.)

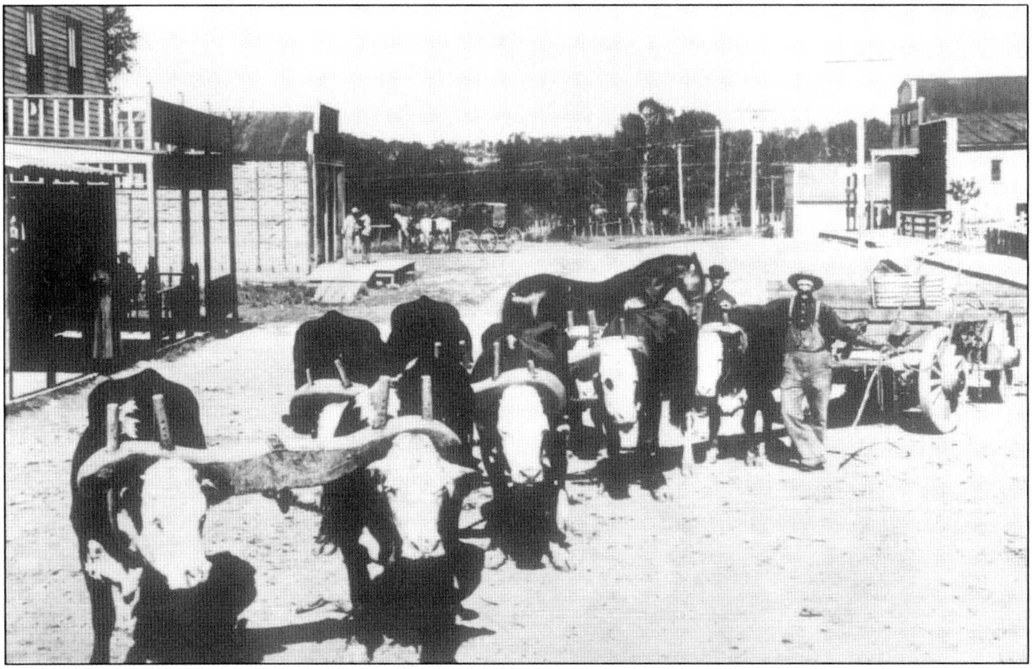

In this 1907 photo, a four-yoke oxen team is pictured pausing on Mill Street with its load of lumber. The man in front of the horse is Will Simpson and the one by the oxen is Nate Johnston. Oxen were used in many logging camps, especially at the logging camps in Sauls Creek, which is a small area east of Bayfield that runs into Beaver Creek. Later, the town of Bayfield put its dump out on Sauls Creek. (Courtesy of Glade Stowell.)

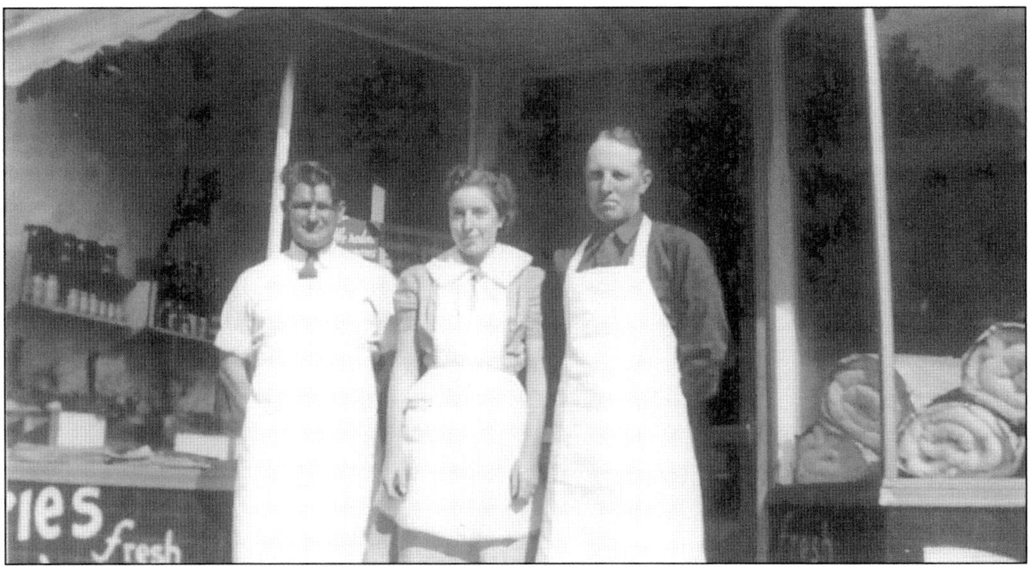

Pictured, from left to right, are Cecil Lewis, Pauline Cobb, and Dick Berry, standing in front of Lewis Mercantile, located on Mill Street. When Cecil Lewis bought the business from the Coulson Brothers he changed the name to Lewis Mercantile. (Courtesy of Elaine Baird.)

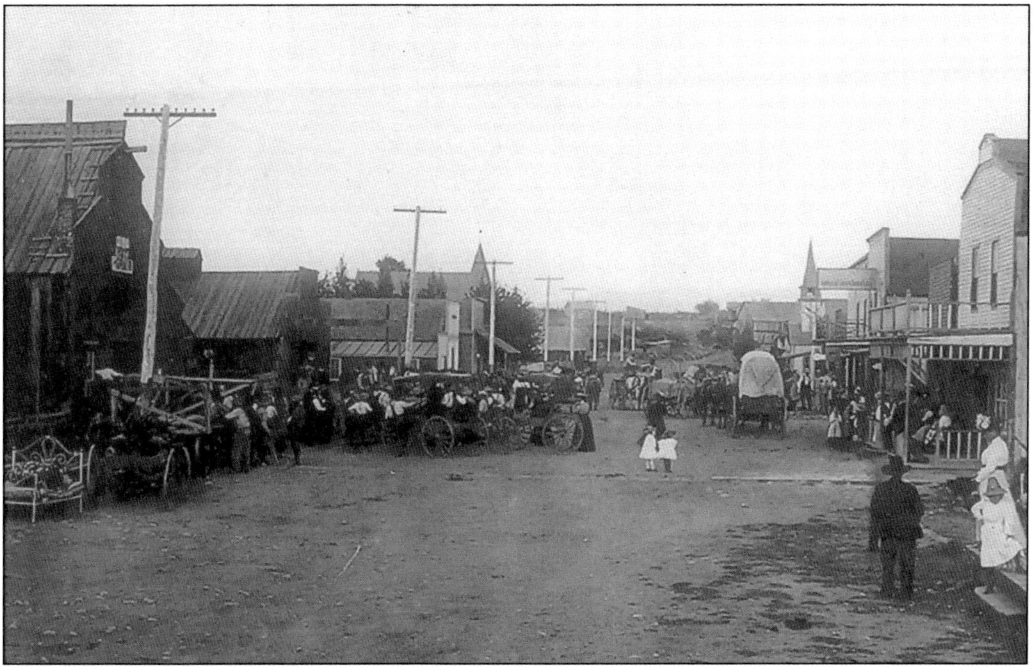

Looking down Mill Street, there seems to be quite a lot of activity. Again, it could be some sort of celebration or special event as most of the men are in white shirts and the ladies are dressed up. Notice the beds on both sides of the street in the foreground. Apparently, they needed extra beds for all the people coming into town for the event and put some on the street. (Courtesy of Barb Fjerstad.)

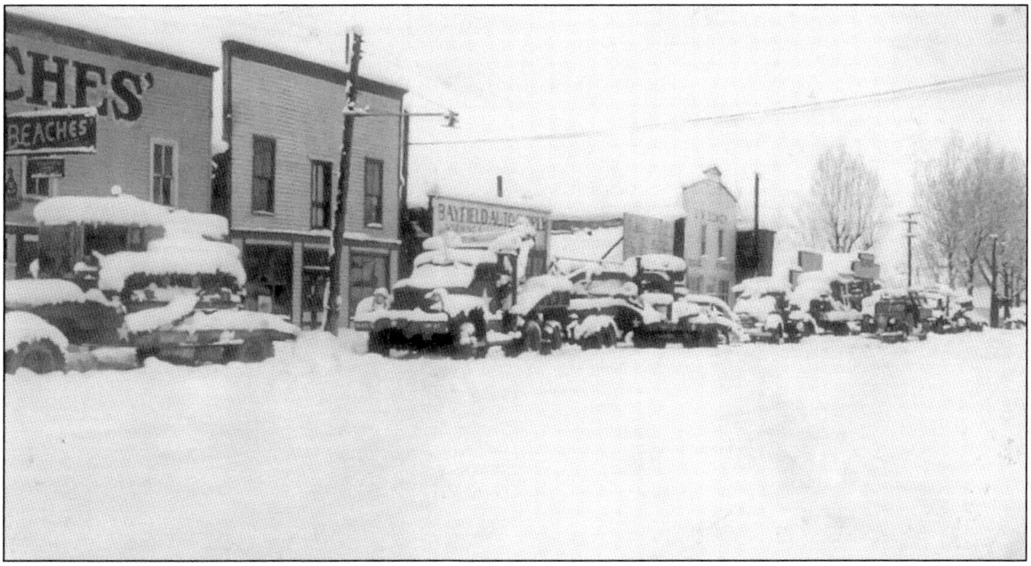

Mill Street lies under a heavy 30-inch snowfall, January 24, 1943. The south side of the street is lined with army vehicles that were passing through and stopped because of the inclement snowfall. The buildings are identified as, from left to right, Beaches Hardware, Pool Hall, with rooms above, Bayfield Auto Shop, Hotel, the "wall," Beaches Grocery Store, and a liquor store. (Courtesy of Jack Carmack.)

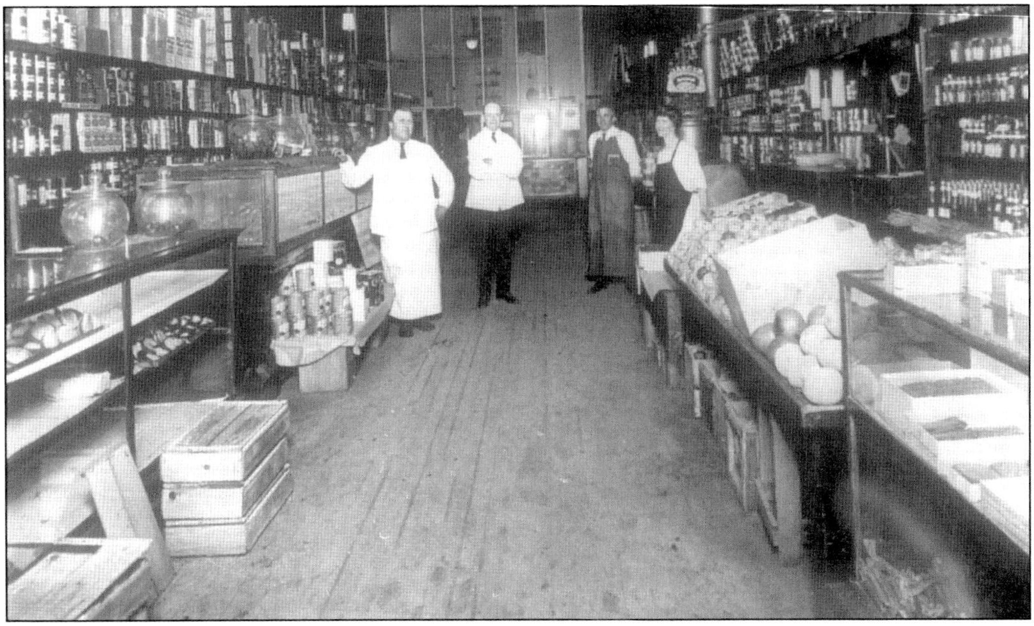

Inside view of Bayfield's first drug store built by Dr. E.W. Newland. He built it right after moving to Bayfield in 1900, and sold it in 1910 to Olwald Keene (left) and L.E. Jenkins (right). Also pictured are two unidentified clerks. (Courtesy of Tom Moga Collection, Shoreline Inn, Vallecito Lake.)

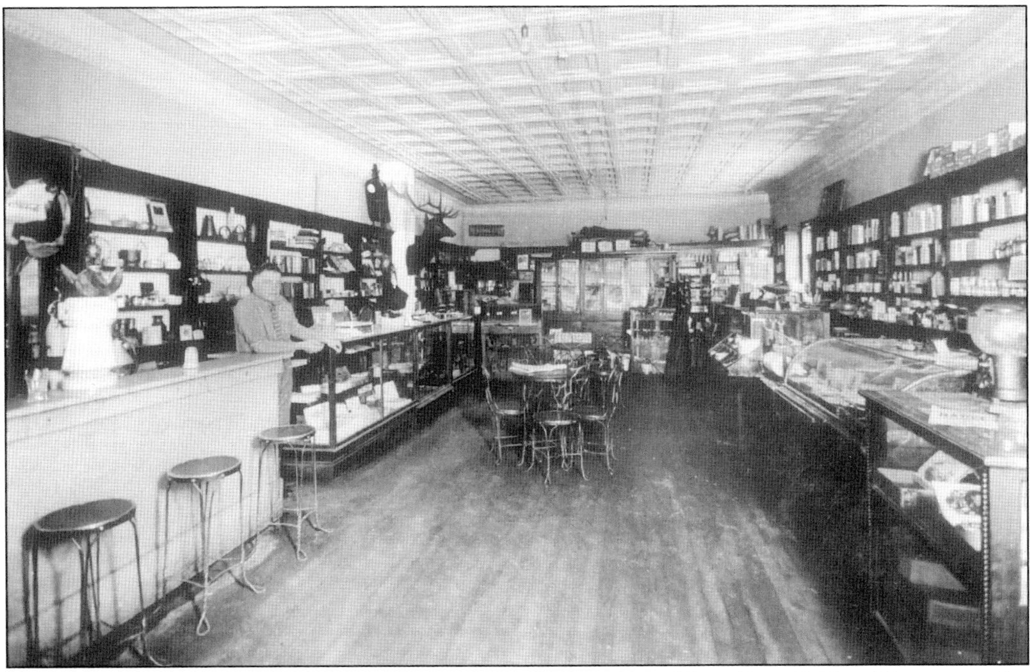

This is the interior of the Jenkins Drug store after it was sold to Roy Gibbs. He put in the soda fountain. Note the "wire legged" stools by the counter, and the tables and chairs, the same as the stools, in the center of the store. (Courtesy of Tom Moga Collection, Shoreline Inn, Vallecito Lake.)

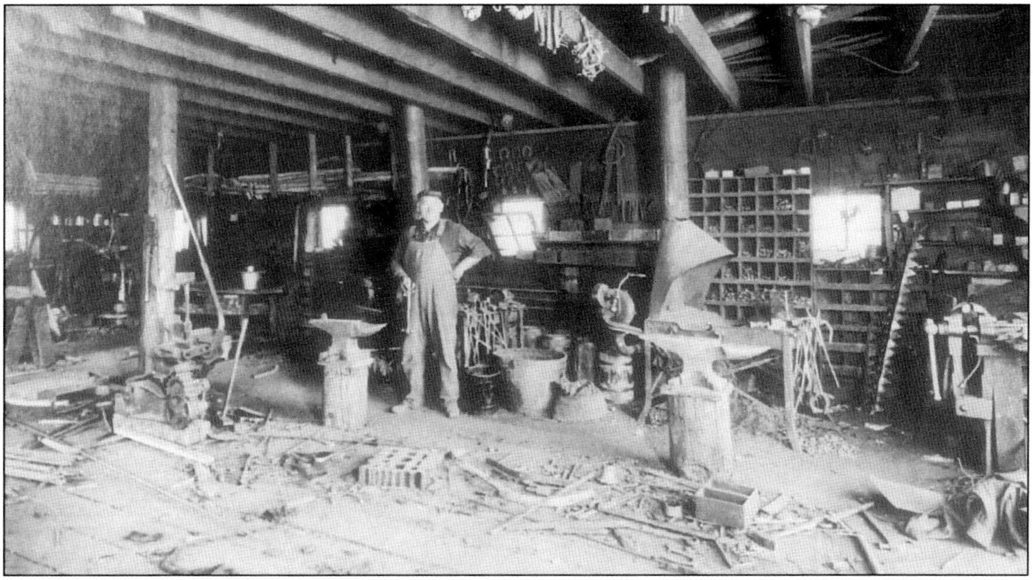

Frank Binder stands in the interior of the blacksmith shop built by his father in 1910. Frank remembers helping his father shoe the horses that were brought in to be shod. "We would heat the shoes up and bend them to fit the horse, just as good as possible, then cool them in a bucket of water, before nailing them on." (Courtesy of Tom Moga Collection, Shoreline Inn, Vallecito Lake. Quote from *People of the Pine*, a short account of Bayfield and the Valley, written by a high school class in the late 1970s.)

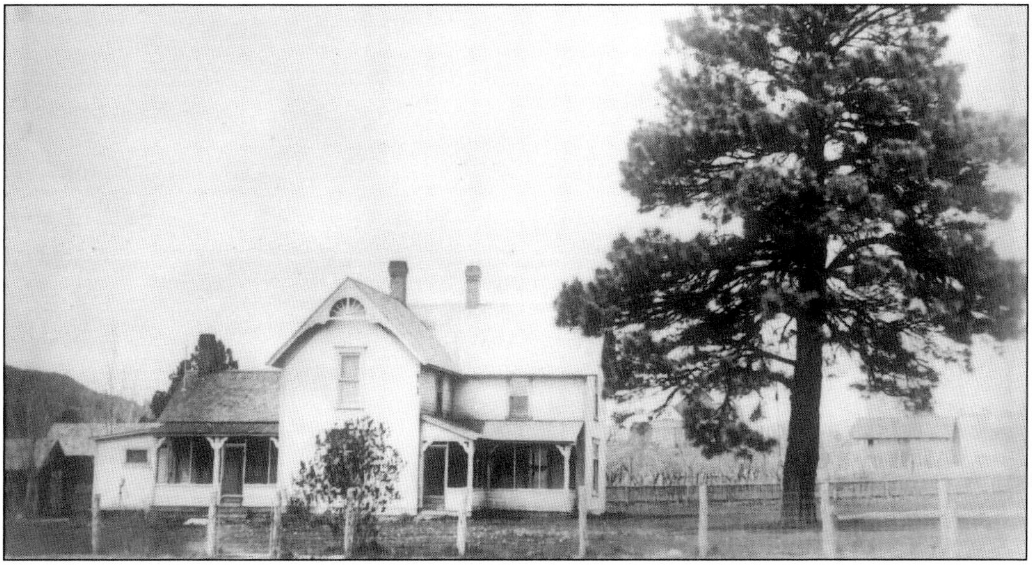

Pictured is the William Bay home with the lone ponderosa pine tree in the front yard. Mr. Bay named his ranch "The Lone Pine Ranch" because of this pine tree. In 1978, a Bayfield junior high school class did a project under the direction of their science teacher, Gregg Janus, to find the oldest tree in Bayfield, Colorado. This ponderosa pine was the oldest, being 260 years old! The tree is still doing well today; you do the math. Today, the house is also surrounded by large spruce trees that were planted in the early 1930s. (Courtesy of Grace Schirard. Tree information by Gregg Janus.)

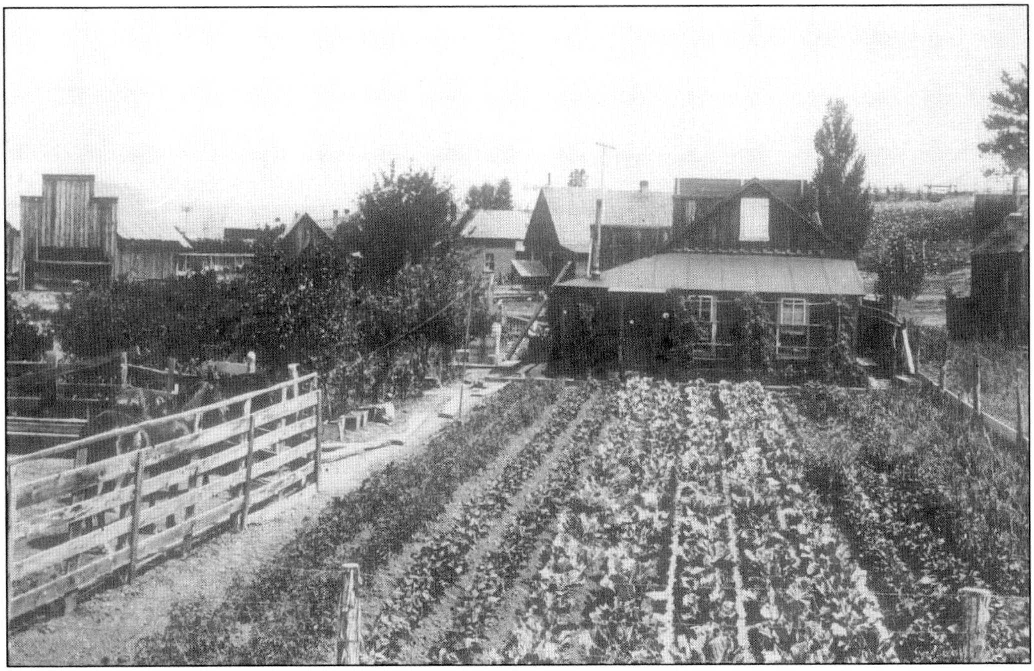

This is Mrs. Schiller's garden behind their business and home. The Schillers also had corrals for the settlers when they came to town; part of this can be seen on the left. The well and watering trough were just west of this. (Courtesy of Danny Rodman.)

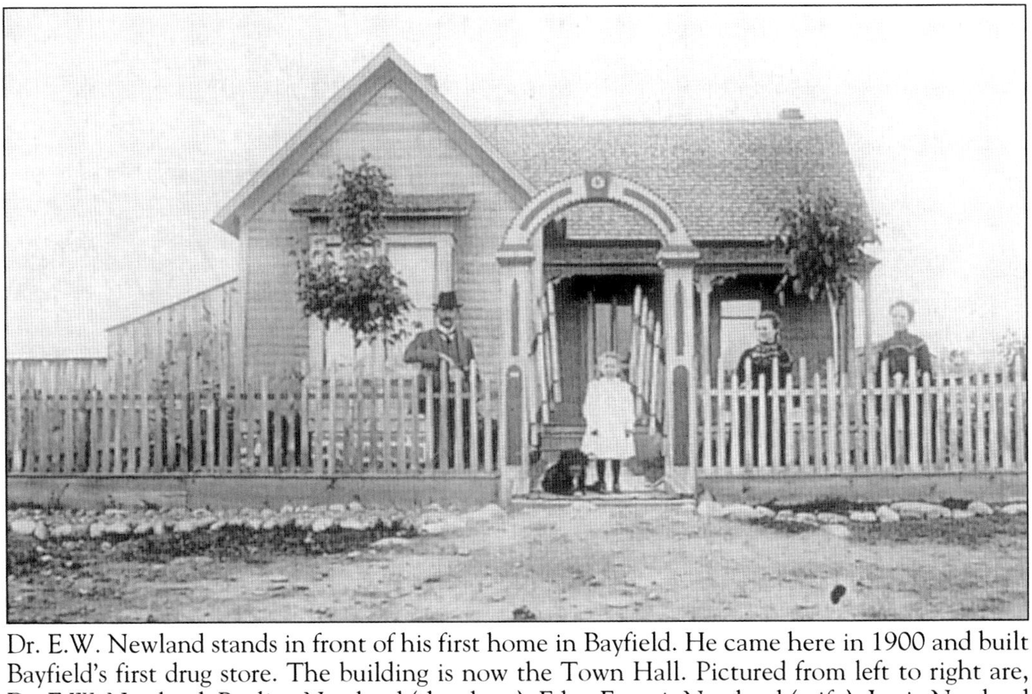

Dr. E.W. Newland stands in front of his first home in Bayfield. He came here in 1900 and built Bayfield's first drug store. The building is now the Town Hall. Pictured from left to right are, Dr. E.W. Newland, Pauline Newland (daughter), Edna Francis Newland (wife), Junie Newland (sister). (Courtesy of Jess Newland.)

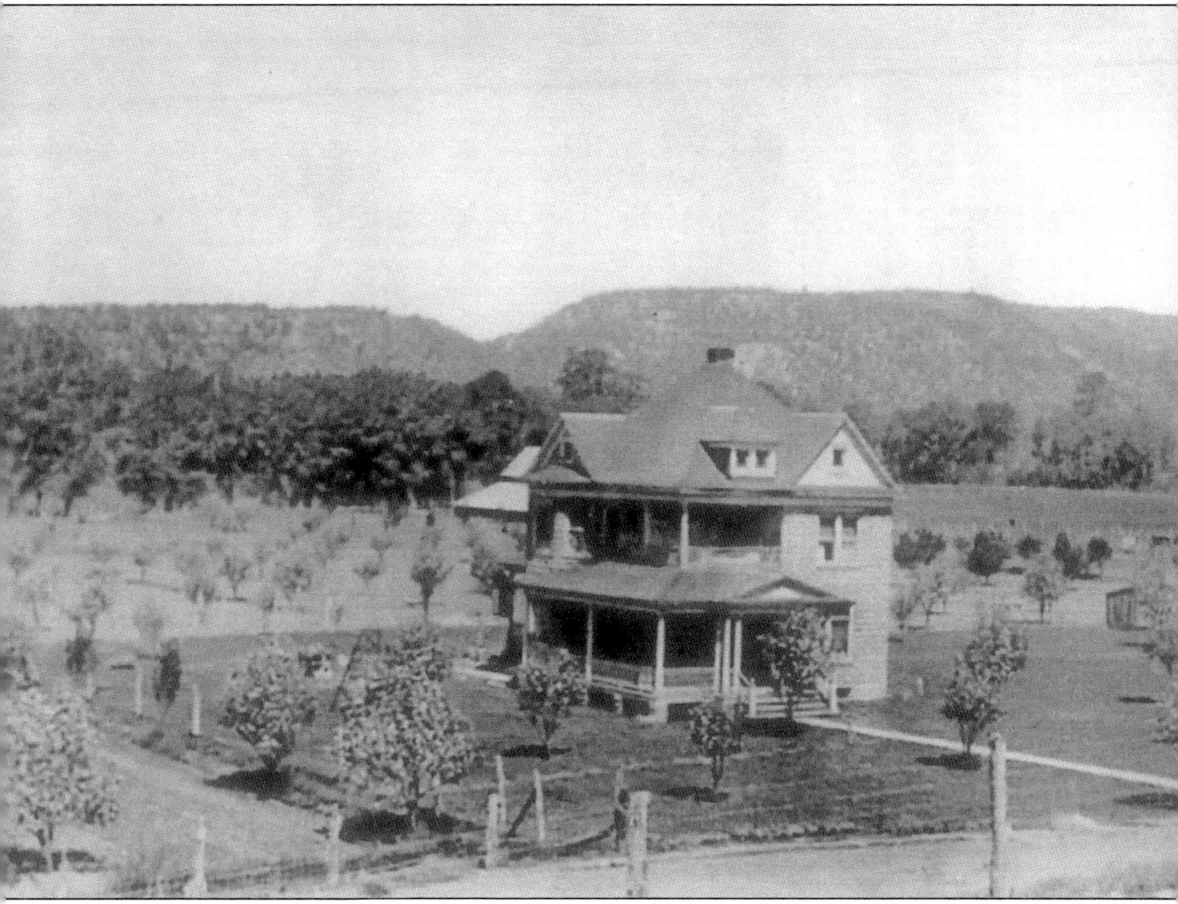

Dr. Newland's second home was built in 1911. It is a pre-fab house, ordered from the Sears & Roebuck Catalogue. All the material, including plans, were shipped by rail to Ignacio, Colorado, the railhead located 15 miles south of Bayfield, and brought by freight wagons to Bayfield. The cement blocks were made on site. There are three other such home in the area, but two of them are only two story. Part of the fruit trees shown are still productive today. However, today the house is surrounded by tall spruce trees like those that were planted all around town in the early 1930's, and they are taller than the house. (Courtesy of Jess Newland.)

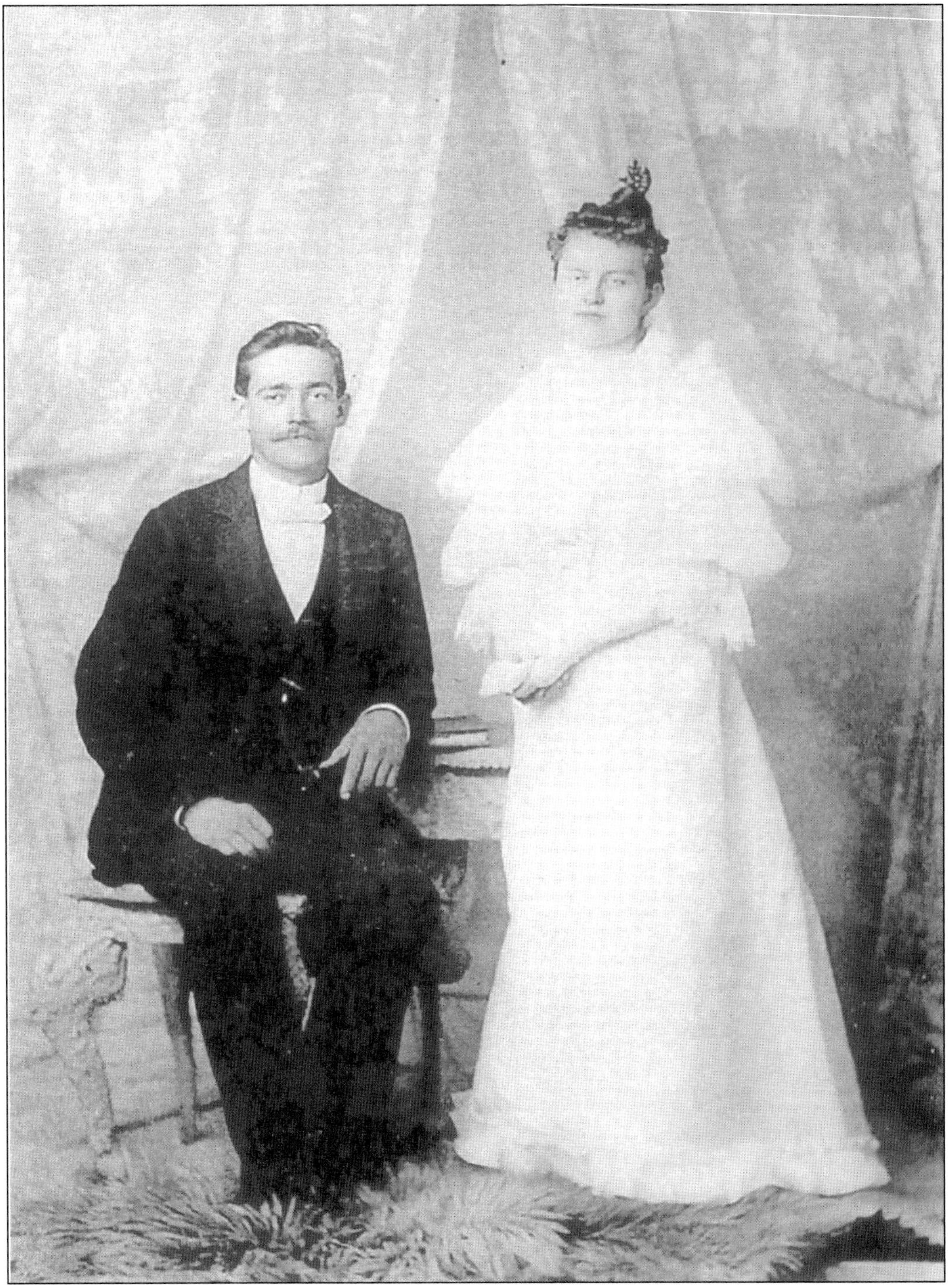

This is Dr. E.W. Newland and Edna Francis Bell Newland's wedding photo. They were married five years before moving to Bayfield in 1900. (Courtesy of Jess Newland.)

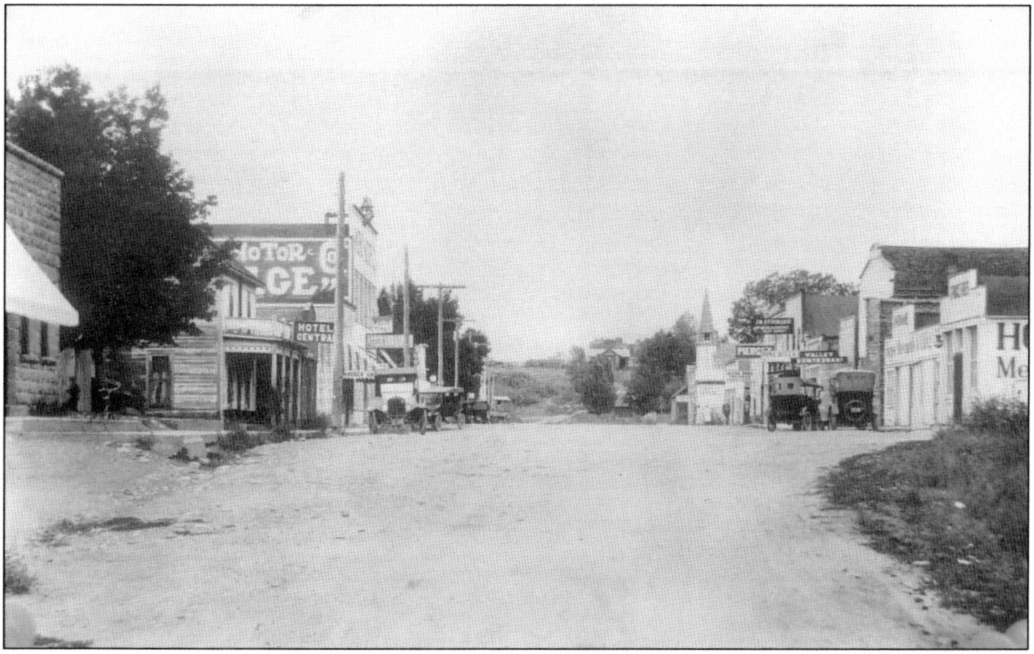

This is a view of Mill Street, 1922. Some of the buildings on the right side of photo, south side of street, later burned down. Notice the fire wall after the first two false front buildings, on the right side. The wall separates the next building as well as the rest on up the street. The fire wall was built after part of the town burned, with the intention of protecting the whole side of the street from another fire. (Courtesy of Colorado Historical Society.)

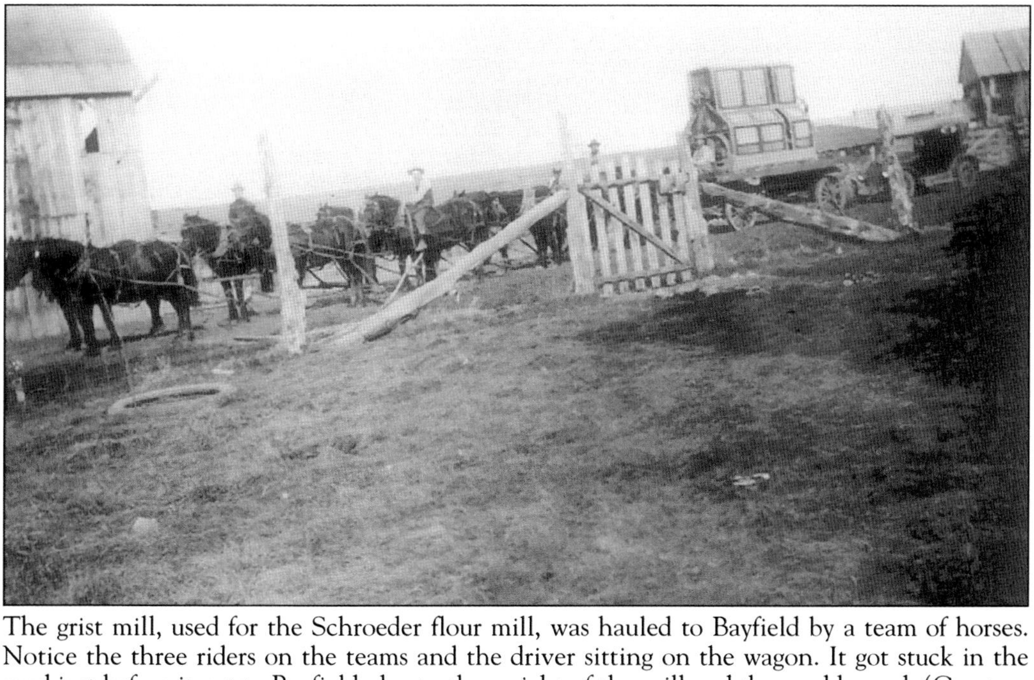

The grist mill, used for the Schroeder flour mill, was hauled to Bayfield by a team of horses. Notice the three riders on the teams and the driver sitting on the wagon. It got stuck in the mud just before it got to Bayfield, due to the weight of the mill and the muddy road. (Courtesy of Jewell LePlatt.)

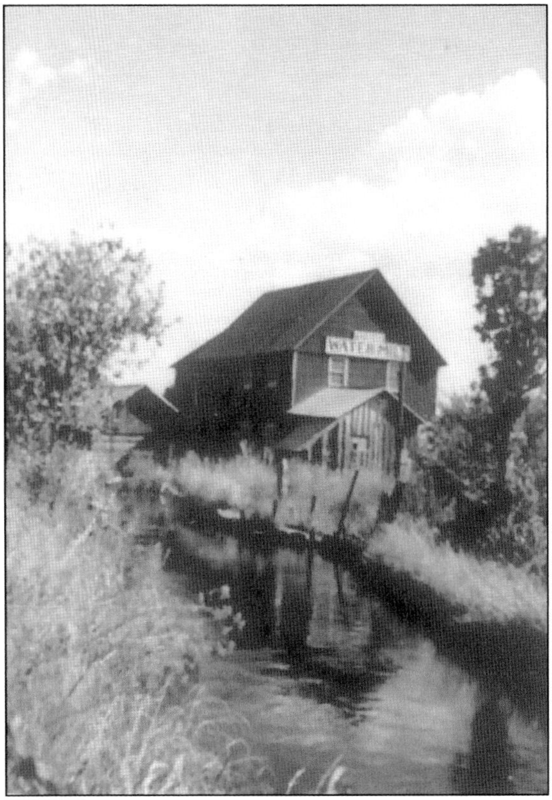

Mr. H. G. Schroeder built the first water-powered flour mill on the Mill Ditch just south of Mill Street. It burned in 1943, causing some damage to the town. Another flour mill, built by Halworth Tanner, was powered by a diesel engine. They bought their grain locally, as did the other mill, and produced White Rose flour. When the mill burned, and the Pine River farmers switched from raising grain to hay, they moved to Cortez, Colorado, to be closer to where the grain was being raised. (Courtesy of Betty Fahrion.)

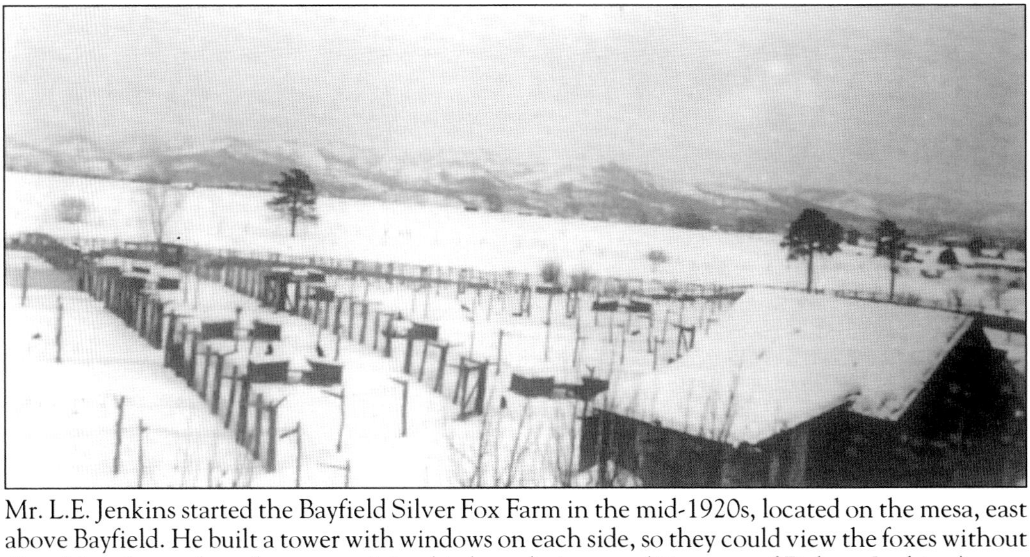

Mr. L.E. Jenkins started the Bayfield Silver Fox Farm in the mid-1920s, located on the mesa, east above Bayfield. He built a tower with windows on each side, so they could view the foxes without disturbing them when they were giving birth to their pups. (Courtesy of Delmar Jenkins.)

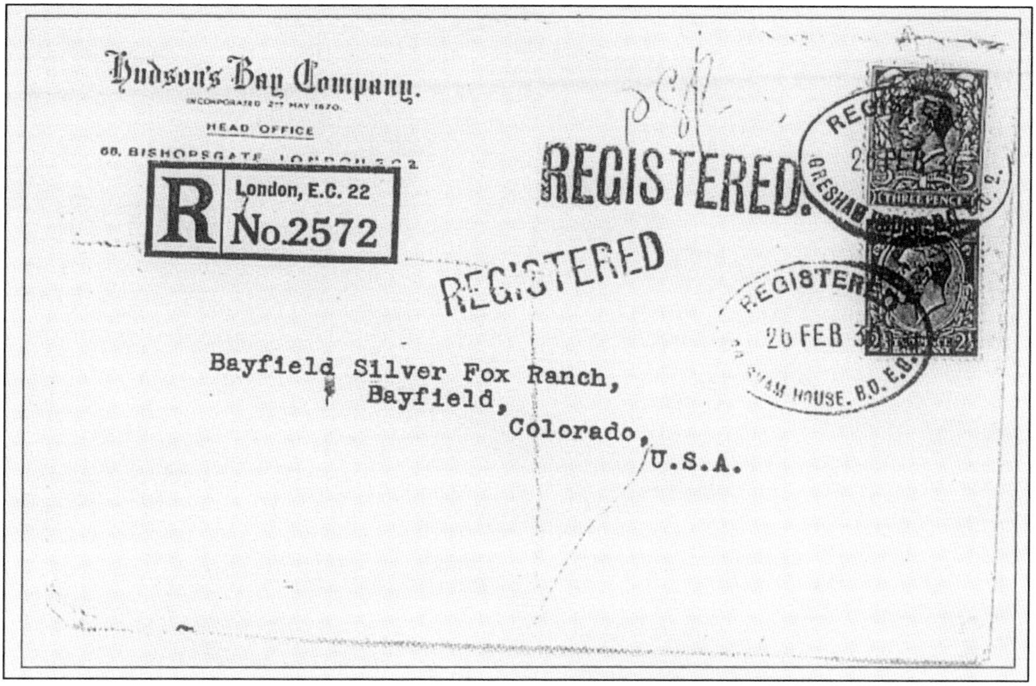

This is a copy of the front of an envelope that contained the first payment the Jenkins received, dated February 26, 1930, from the Hudson Bay Company, London, England. The payment was for the silver fox pelts they had sent from their fox farm in Bayfield. The check was in English pounds, the currency of England. (Courtesy of Delmar Jenkins.)

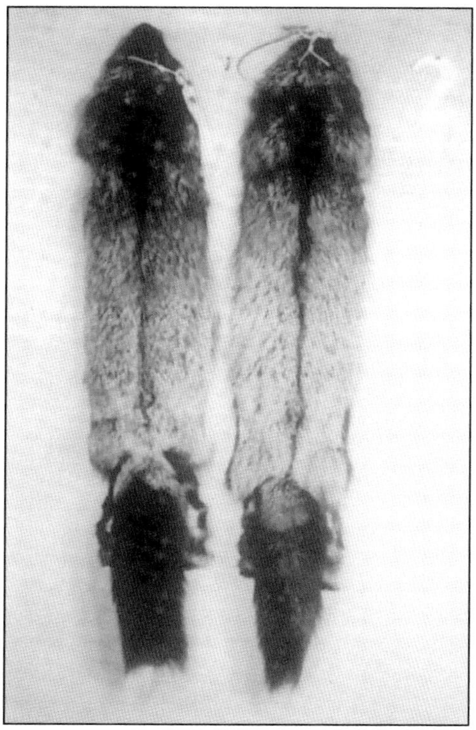

These are two silver fox pelts like the ones sent to the Boston Fur Company in New York, who then sent them on to the head office in London, England. (Courtesy of Delmar Jenkins.)

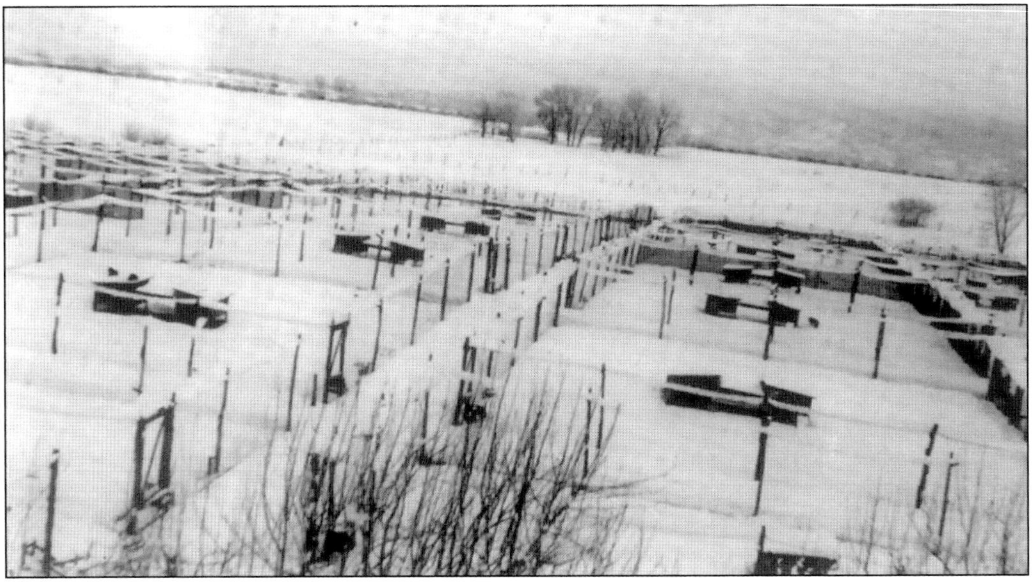

Here is a different view of the fox pens of the Bayfield Silver Fox Farm. After the death of her husband, the farm continued to be operated by Mrs. Emma Jenkins. The field where the pens were located is now just a pasture. (Courtesy of Delmar Jenkins.)

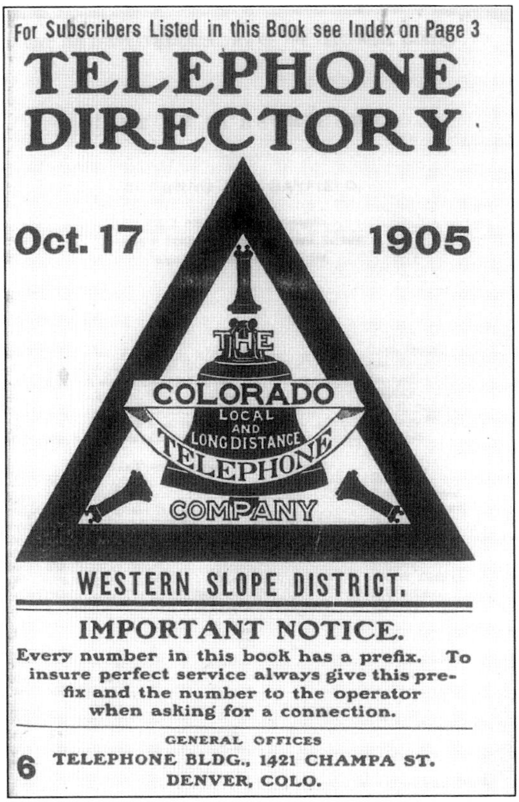

This is the cover of the first telephone book in 1905 from the Colorado Telephone Company, to include Bayfield. Rights-of-way were acquired from landowners by the Colorado Telephone Company in 1904. Some sold the rights-of-way through their land for just $1, while others sold theirs for $20. The book listed the names as either "white" or "blue" lines. Example: Blue 102 Akers, H.W. & Co. Saw Mill–Bayfield; White 32 Taylor, Geo. J.–Residence–Bayfield. Mr. Chas P. Foreman was the exchange manager in Bayfield, and Laura Ostwald was the first "hello girl." (Courtesy of Telecommunications History Group, Inc., Denver.)

This is an ad from the 1909 *Bayfield Blade*, Bayfield's local newspaper. There were quite a few independent, private telephone companies set up for farmers, and the one closest to the main line would hook up, and the rest hook to him. The bills were paid to the main company. (Courtesy of Southwest Studies Film Archives, *Bayfield Blade*, Catherine Conrad.)

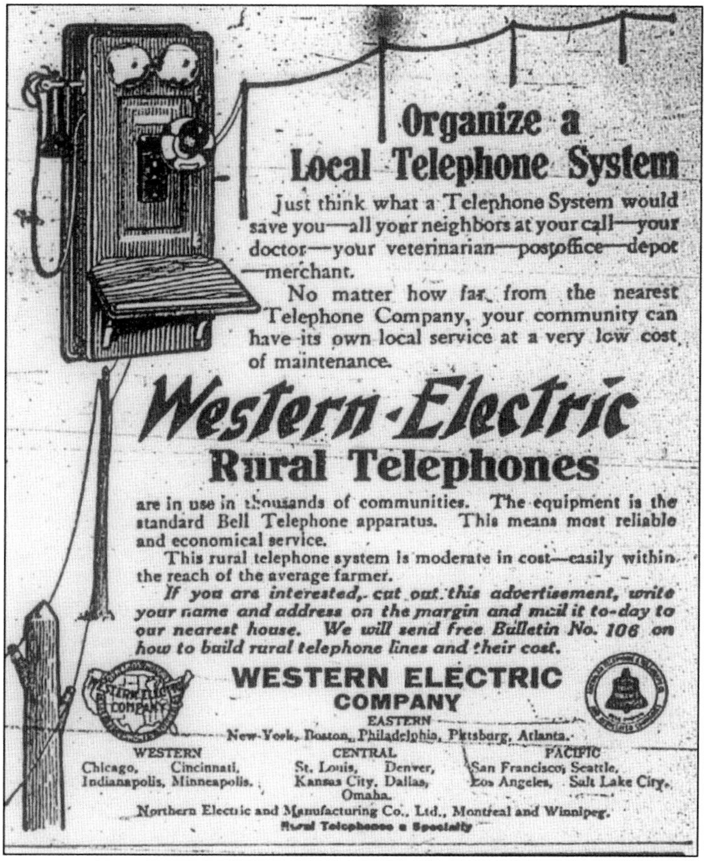

This image is of the history in pictures of the "Bell" in the Bell System from 1889 to the present time. (Courtesy of Mountain Bell A US West Company website, www.mountainbell,com.)

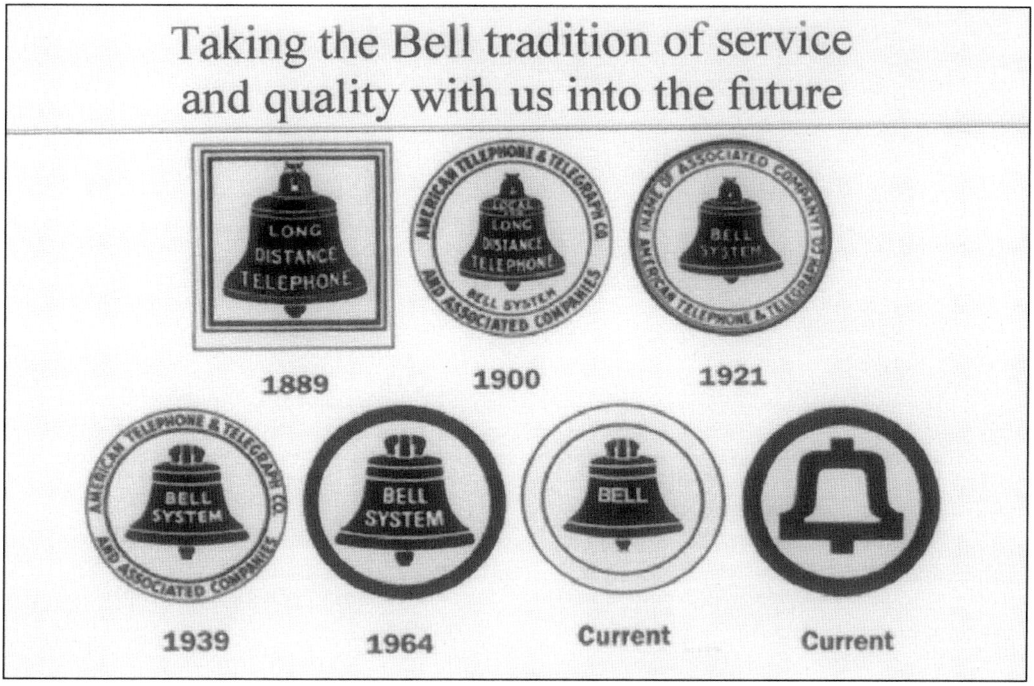

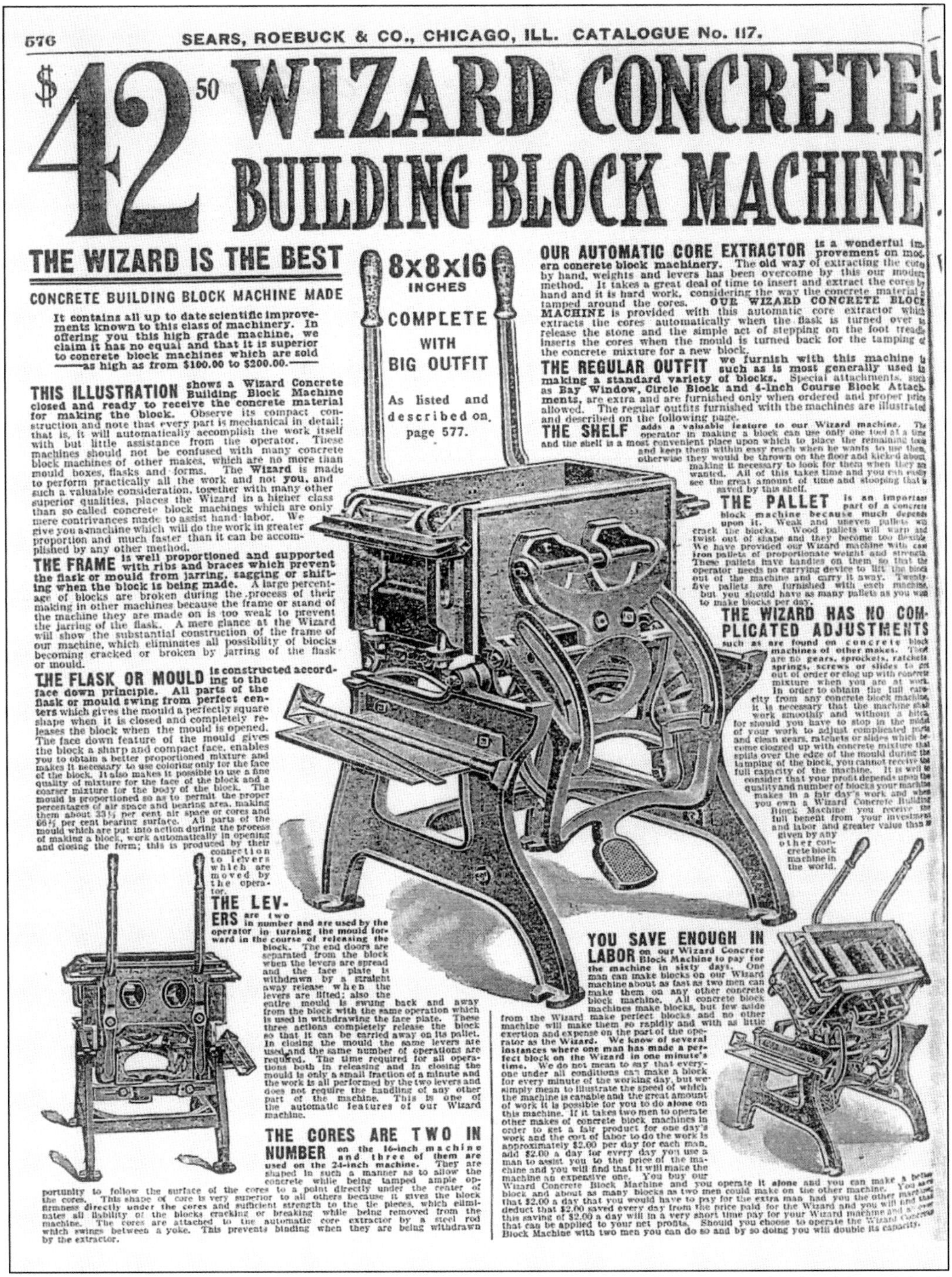

576 SEARS, ROEBUCK & CO., CHICAGO, ILL. CATALOGUE No. 117.

$42[50] WIZARD CONCRETE BUILDING BLOCK MACHINE

THE WIZARD IS THE BEST CONCRETE BUILDING BLOCK MACHINE MADE

It contains all up to date scientific improvements known to this class of machinery. In offering you this high grade machine, we claim it has no equal and that it is superior to concrete block machines which are sold as high as from $100.00 to $200.00.

8x8x16 INCHES COMPLETE WITH BIG OUTFIT As listed and described on page 577.

THIS ILLUSTRATION shows a Wizard Concrete Building Block Machine closed and ready to receive the concrete material for making the block. Observe its compact construction and note that every part is mechanical in detail; that is, it will automatically accomplish the work itself with but little assistance from the operator. These machines should not be confused with many concrete block machines of other makes, which are no more than mould boxes, flasks and forms. The **Wizard** is made to perform practically all the work and not **you**, and such a valuable consideration, together with many other superior qualities, places the Wizard in a higher class than so called concrete block machines which are only mere contrivances made to assist hand labor. We give you a machine which will do the work in greater proportion and much faster than it can be accomplished by any other method.

THE FRAME is well proportioned and supported with ribs and braces which prevent the flask or mould from jarring, sagging or shifting when the block is being made. A large percentage of blocks are broken during the process of their making in other machines because the frame or stand of the machine they are made on is too weak to prevent the jarring of the flask. A mere glance at the Wizard will show the substantial construction of the frame of our machine, which eliminates all possibility of blocks becoming cracked or broken by jarring of the flask or mould.

THE FLASK OR MOULD is constructed according to the face down principle. All parts of the flask or mould swing from perfect centers which gives the mould a perfectly square shape when it is closed and completely releases the block when the mould is opened. The face down feature of the mould gives the block a sharp and compact face, enables you to obtain a better proportioned mixture and makes it necessary to use coloring only for the face of the block. It also makes it possible to use a fine quality of mixture for the face of the block and a coarser mixture for the body of the block. The mould is proportioned so as to permit the proper percentages of air space and bearing area, making them about 33⅓ per cent air space or cores and 66⅔ per cent bearing surface. All parts of the mould which are put into action during the process of making a block, work automatically in opening and closing the form; this is produced by their connection to levers which are moved by the operator.

THE LEVERS are two in number and are used by the operator in turning the mould forward in the course of releasing the block. The end doors are separated from the block when the levers are spread and the face plate is withdrawn by a straight away release when the levers are lifted; also the entire mould is swung back and away from the block with the same operation which is used in withdrawing the face plate. These three actions completely release the block so that it can be carried away on its pallet. In closing the mould the same levers are used and the same number of operations are required. The time required for all operations both in releasing and in closing the mould is only a small fraction of a minute and the work is all performed by the two levers and does not require the handling of any other part of the machine. This is one of the automatic features of our Wizard machine.

THE CORES ARE TWO IN NUMBER on the 16-inch machine and three of them are used on the 24-inch machine. They are shaped in such a manner as to allow the concrete while being tamped ample opportunity to follow the surface of the cores to a point directly under the center of the cores. This shape of core is very superior to all others because it gives the block firmness directly under the cores and sufficient strength to the tie pieces, which eliminates all liability of the blocks cracking or breaking while being removed from the machine. The cores are attached to the automatic core extractor by a steel rod which swings between a yoke. This prevents binding when they are being withdrawn by the extractor.

OUR AUTOMATIC CORE EXTRACTOR is a wonderful improvement on modern concrete block machinery. The **old way** of extracting the cores by hand, weights and levers has been overcome by this our modern method. It takes a great deal of time to insert and extract the cores by hand and it is hard work, considering the way the concrete material is tamped around the cores. **OUR WIZARD CONCRETE BLOCK MACHINE** is provided with this automatic core extractor which extracts the cores automatically when the flask is turned over to release the stone and the simple act of stepping on the foot treadle inserts the cores when the mould is turned back for the tamping of the concrete mixture for a new block.

THE REGULAR OUTFIT we furnish with this machine is such as is most generally used in making a standard variety of blocks. Special attachments, such **as Bay Window, Circle Block and 4-inch Course Block Attachments,** are extra and are furnished only when ordered and proper price allowed. The regular outfits furnished with the machines are illustrated and described on the following page.

THE SHELF adds a valuable feature to our Wizard machine. The operator in making a block can use only one tool at a time and the shelf is a most convenient place upon which to place the remaining tools and keep them within easy reach when he wants to use them, otherwise they would be thrown on the floor and kicked about, making it necessary to look for them when they are wanted. All of this takes time and you can easily see the great amount of time and stooping that is saved by this shelf.

THE PALLET is an important part of a concrete block machine because much depends upon it. Weak and uneven pallets will crack the blocks. Wood pallets will warp and twist out of shape and they become too flexible. We have provided our Wizard machine with cast iron pallets of proportionate weight and strength. These pallets have handles on them so that the operator needs no carrying device to lift the block out of the machine and carry it away. Twenty-five pallets are furnished with each machine, but you should have as many pallets as you want to make blocks per day.

THE WIZARD HAS NO COMPLICATED ADJUSTMENTS such as are found on concrete block machines of other makes. There are no gears, sprockets, ratchets, springs, screws or slides to get out of order or clog up with concrete mixture when you are at work. In order to obtain the full capacity from any concrete block machine, it is necessary that the machine shall work smoothly and without a hitch, for should you have to stop in the midst of your work to adjust complicated parts and clean gears, ratchets or slides which become clogged up with concrete mixture that spills over the edge of the mould during the tamping of the block, you cannot receive the full capacity of the machine. It is well to consider that your profit depends upon the quality and number of blocks your machine makes in a fair day's work and when you own a Wizard Concrete Building Block Machine you receive the full benefit from your investment and labor and greater value than is given by any other concrete block machine in the world.

YOU SAVE ENOUGH IN LABOR on our Wizard Concrete Block Machine to pay for the machine in sixty days. One man can make blocks on our Wizard machine about as fast as two men can make them on any other concrete block machine. All concrete block machines make blocks, but few aside from the Wizard make perfect blocks and no other machine will make them so rapidly and with as little exertion and expense on the part of the operator as the Wizard. **We know of several instances where one man has made a perfect block on the Wizard in one minute's time.** We do not mean to say that everyone under all conditions can make a block for every minute of the working day, but we simply mean to illustrate the speed of which the machine is capable and the great amount of work it is possible for you to do **alone** on this machine. If it takes two men to operate other makes of concrete block machines in order to get a fair product for one day's work and the cost of labor to do the work is approximately $2.00 per day for each man, add $2.00 a day for every day you use a man to assist you to the price of the machine and you will find that it will make the machine an expensive one. You buy our Wizard Concrete Block Machine and you operate it **alone** and you can make a better block and about as many blocks as two men could make on the other machine. You save that $2.00 a day that you would have to pay for the extra man had you the other machine; deduct that $2.00 saved every day from the price paid for the Wizard and you will find that this saving of $2.00 a day will in a very short time pay for your Wizard machine and after that can be applied to your net profits. Should you choose to operate the Wizard Concrete Block Machine with two men you can do so and by so doing you will double its capacity.

Here is an ad from the 1898 Sears & Roebuck Catalogue advertising the building block machine. A machine like this was used to build houses, the L.E. Jenkins Drug Store, and the Farmers and Merchants Bank. (Courtesy of La Plata County Historical Society Animas Museum Book Archives.)

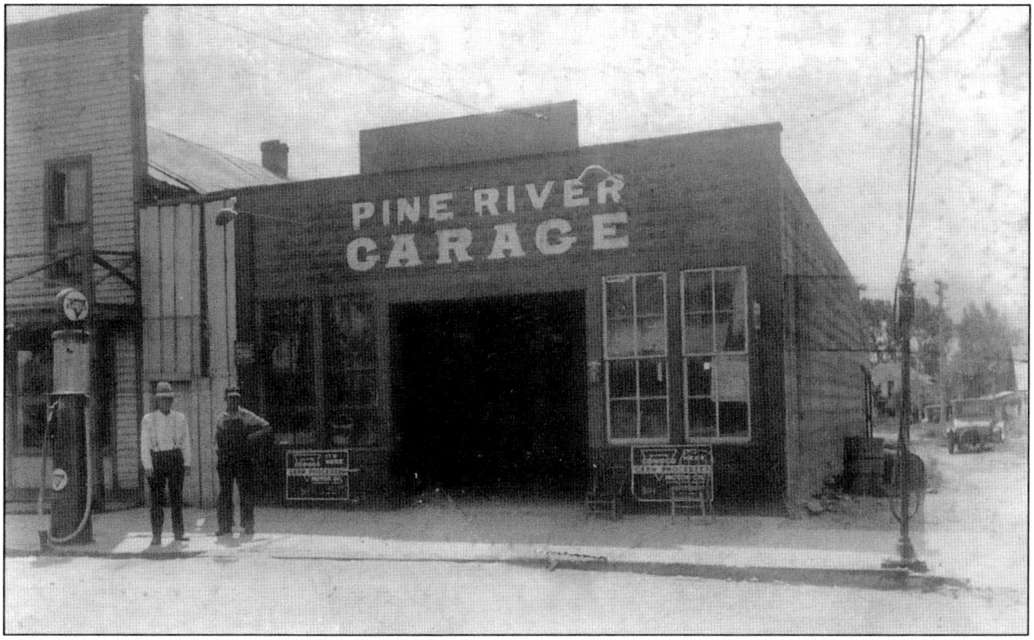

The Pine River Garage, owned by Warren A. Schiller, was located on the south side of Mill Street in Bayfield. It sold Conoco gas in the hand gas pump located on the left side of the photo. An unidentified man (left) stands with Mr. Schiller. (Courtesy of Danny Rodman.)

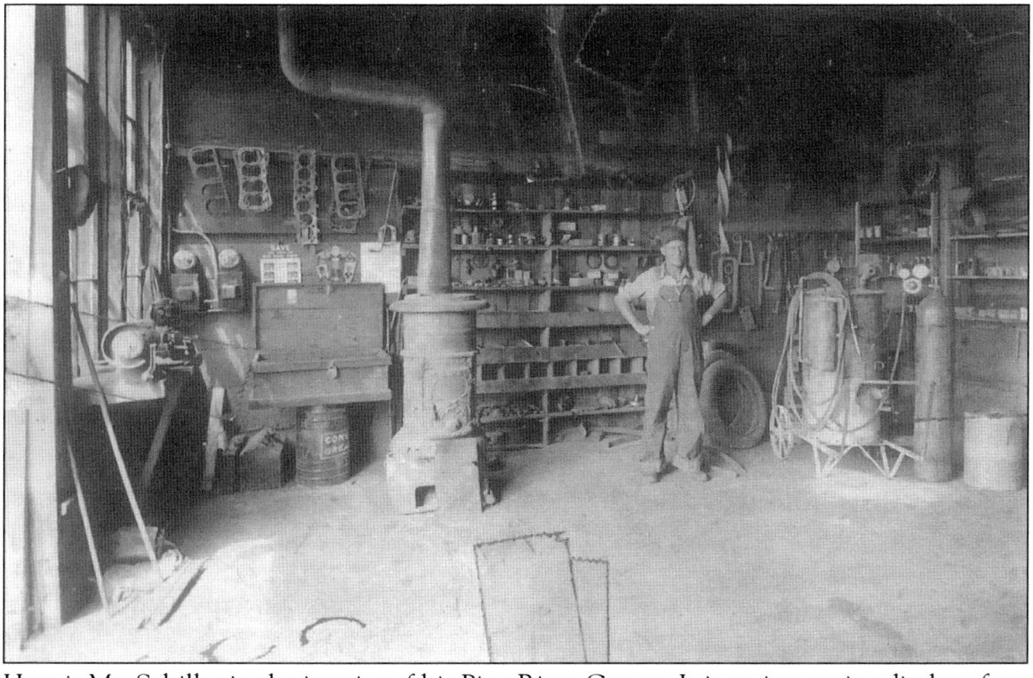

Here is Mr. Schiller in the interior of his Pine River Garage. It is an interesting display of car parts, including the tool box sitting on a small Conoco oil drum and the acetylene welding set up (right). (Courtesy of Danny Rodman.)

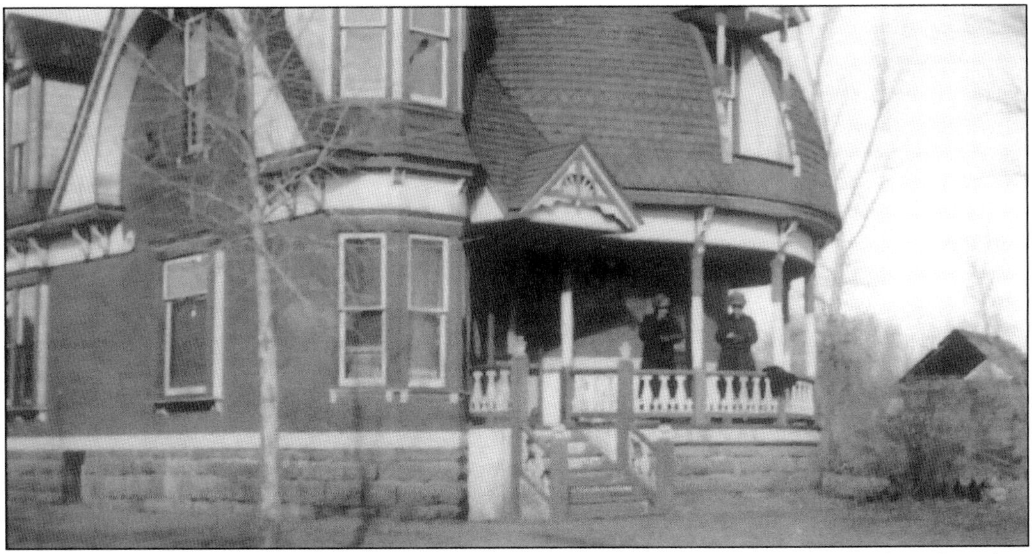

The Riverside Home, also called the Hartman Hotel, was down on what people referred to as the "island." This was because the Little Pine River and the Mill Ditch separated it from the rest of the town. The Riverside Home was an elegant place for social affairs in its heyday. An ad in the 1911 *Bayfield Blade* read: "When in Bayfield stop at the Riverside Home. Good Accommodation. Reasonable Rates." The Home was owned by Mr. and Mrs. F.M. Salyer. (Courtesy of Fred Frahm.)

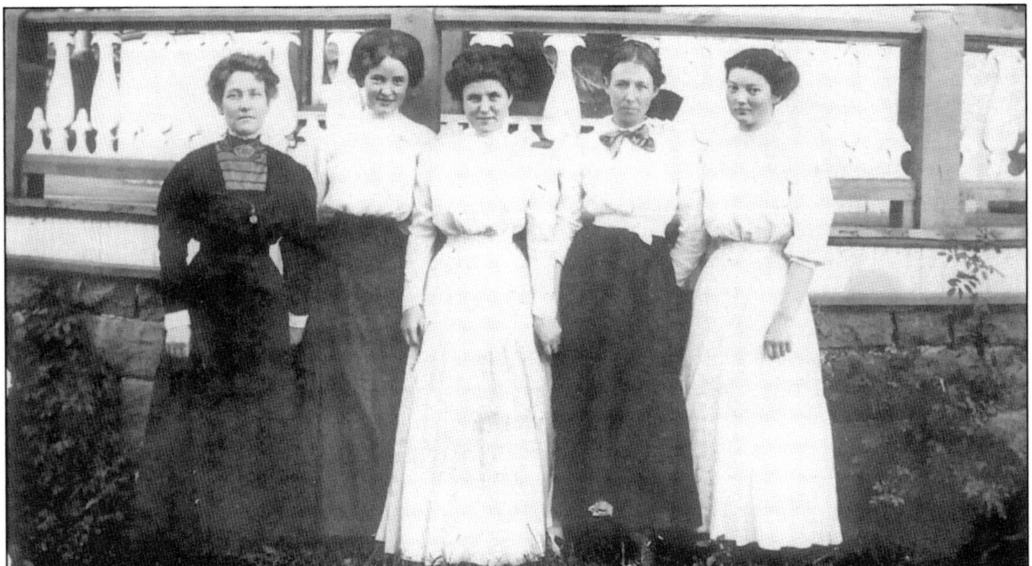

Pictured, from left to right, are Myrtle Salyer, Lulu Taylor, Lola Taylor, Lucy O'Neill, and Laura Furley, as they pose in front of the Riverside Home in this 1910 photo. A tragic fire destroyed this beautiful, complete, and costly home on January 12, 1912. The Salyer's daughter, Myrtle, and a friend, Miss Rosa Sullivan, were in the building when the fire broke out at about 2:00 a.m. Mr. Salyer was awakened by the crackling of the fire and set off the alarm. They all got out safely and with the help of two neighbors were able to save furnishing from the dining room and the two front rooms, including the piano. (Courtesy of Fred Frahm.)

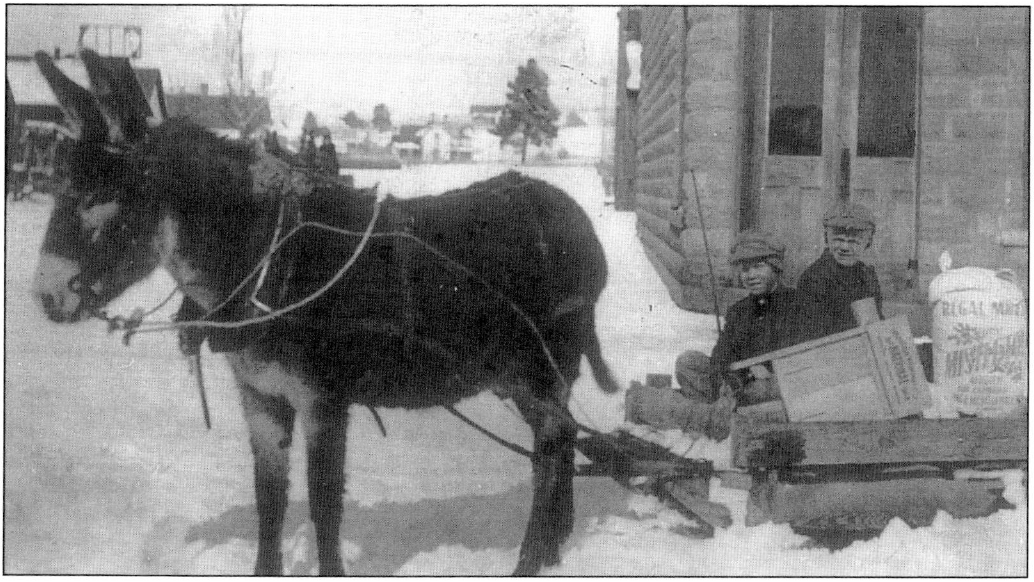

Mr. Barney Wiseman and his son, Lawrence, sit on their sled with supplies behind their mule, Smoke, *c.* 1912 or 1913. Notice the large washboard. They are in front of the Farmers and Merchants Bank on Mill Street. This building was built out of material ordered from the Sears & Roebuck Catalogue. The cement blocks, using the Sears' Block Machine, were made on site. (Courtesy of Tom Wiseman.)

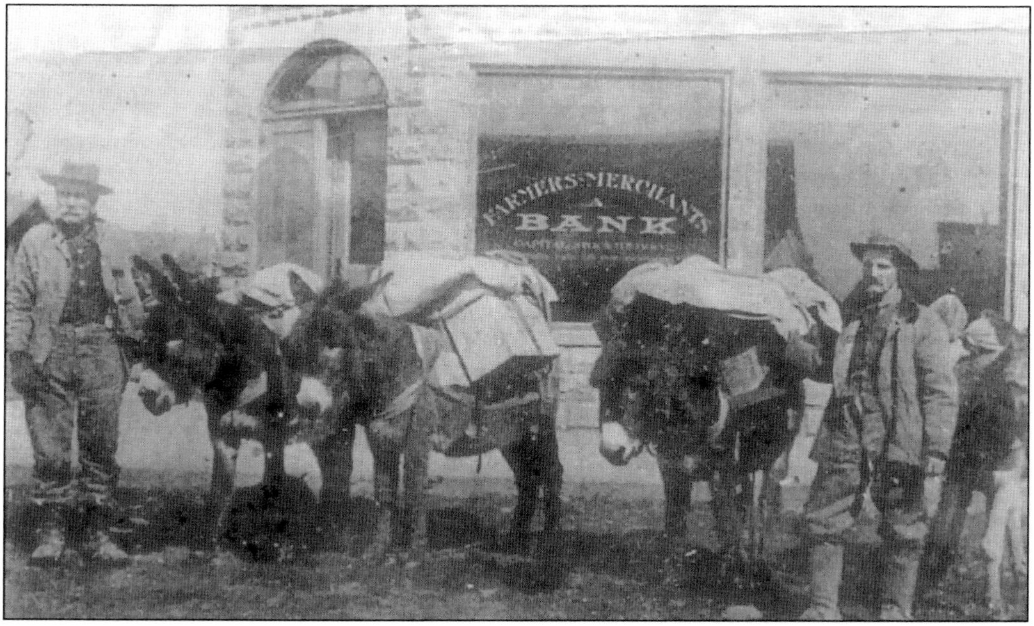

John Graves (left) and Sammy Dowell (right) stand with their packed mules in front of the Farmers and Merchants Bank, ready for their trip to Cave Basin. Bayfield was the major town for the miners to get supplies. The Farmers and Merchants Bank opened its doors in September 1910, and closed them in the early 1930s. This building was later the post office, with the Bayfield Reading Group meeting in the back. It now houses the public library. (Courtesy of Earl Jack.)

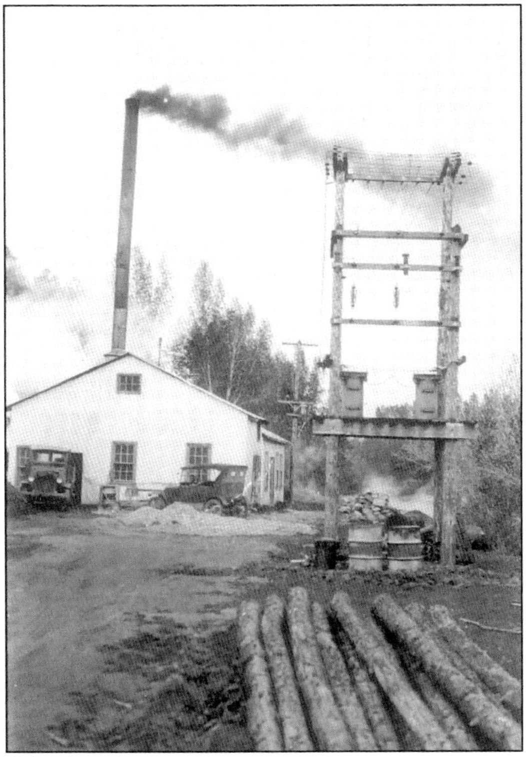

Bayfield got its first electricity from the Soens Hydro-electric Power Plant, built by Mr. W.L. Soens in 1939. The plant was built on the west side of the Pine River, west of Bayfield, below the King Ditch, from which it got its water. After the water went through the turbines it was returned to the river. The plant only ran from dusk until about 11 p.m., so repair work could be done if necessary. When the lights were going to be turned off, the plant would blink them a few times to warn residents of the impending darkness. One day, due to heavy rains, the ditch bank broke and the hillside, with all the mud and trees, slid into the west side of the building, damaging one of the large turbines. (Courtesy of Center of Southwest Studies, Catherine Conrad,, Todd Ellison.)

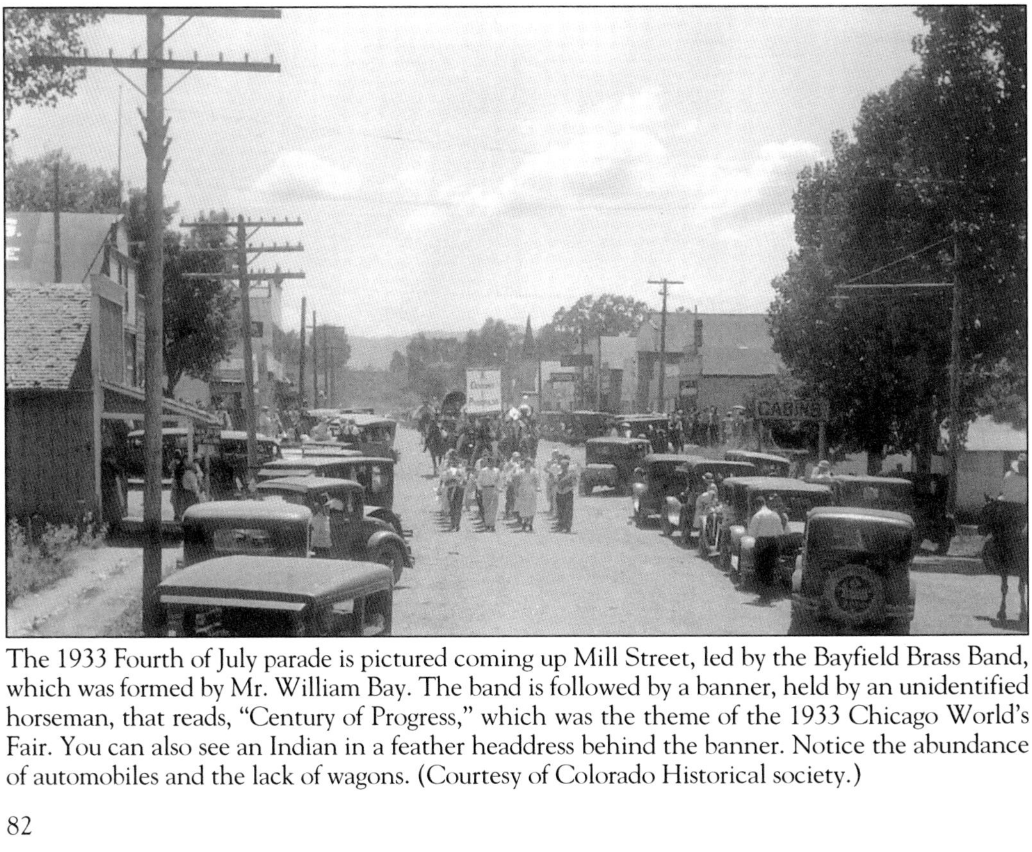

The 1933 Fourth of July parade is pictured coming up Mill Street, led by the Bayfield Brass Band, which was formed by Mr. William Bay. The band is followed by a banner, held by an unidentified horseman, that reads, "Century of Progress," which was the theme of the 1933 Chicago World's Fair. You can also see an Indian in a feather headdress behind the banner. Notice the abundance of automobiles and the lack of wagons. (Courtesy of Colorado Historical society.)

This is the back end, east side, of the Woodmen of the World (WOW) Hall when it was a two-story building. (Courtesy of Merle James.)

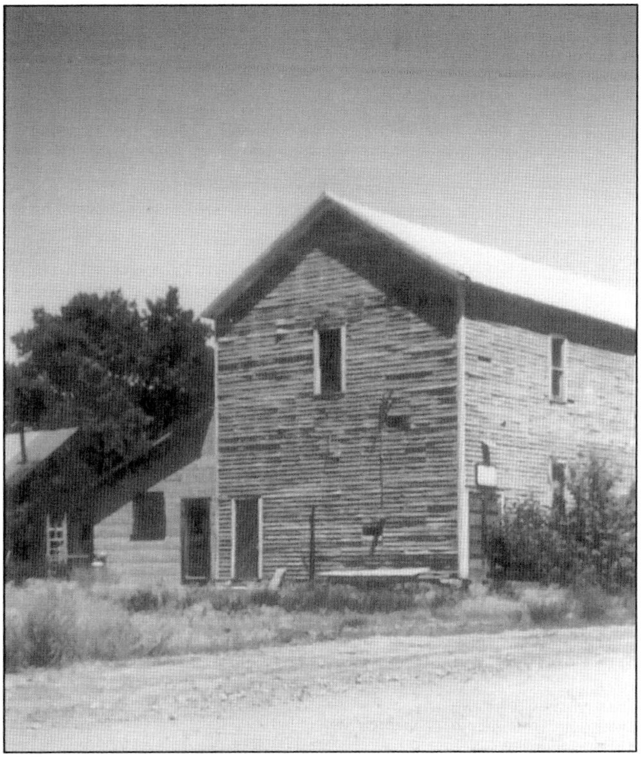

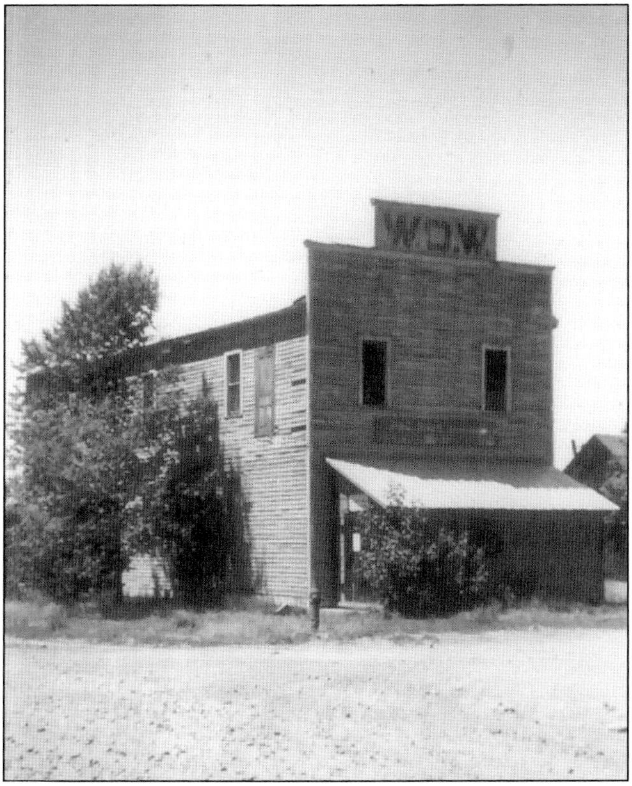

Here is the front side of WOW Hall. The streets were not paved but the town did have fireplugs. (Courtesy of Merle James.)

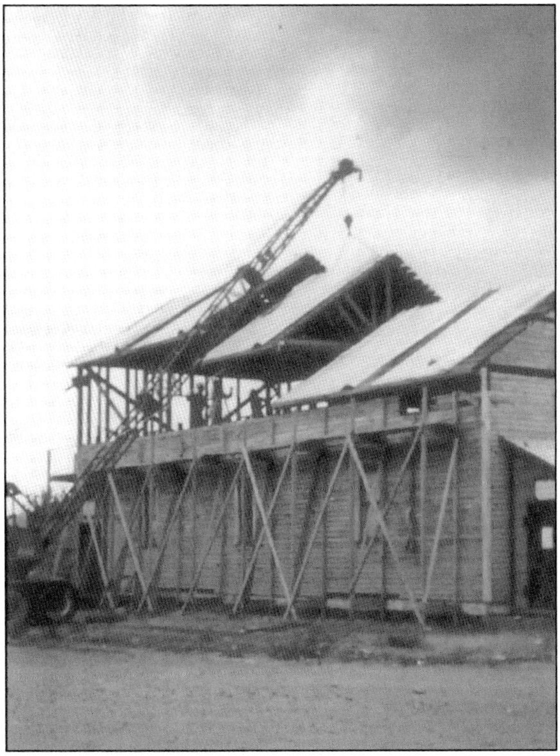

The Pine River Grange bought the building and later decided to cut off the second story. They cut the roof into five sections, hooked each section with the crane, lifted them up separately while carpenters cut the walls off, and then just lowered them down again to have the carpenters reattach them. (Courtesy of Merle James.)

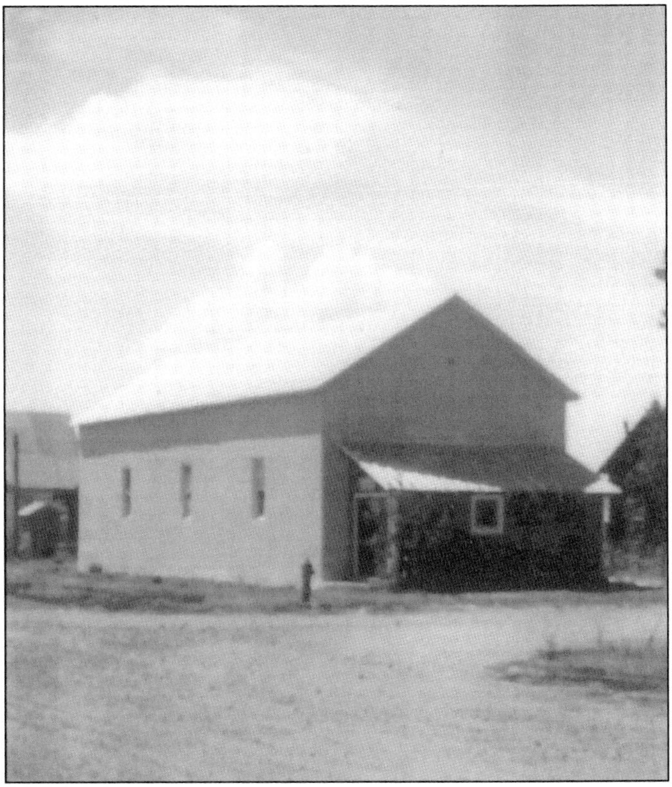

This photo shows the result of making the Woodmen of the World Hall into a single story. The building owned by the Pine River Grange is used by the Lions Club of Bayfield and for other social functions. (Courtesy of Merle James.)

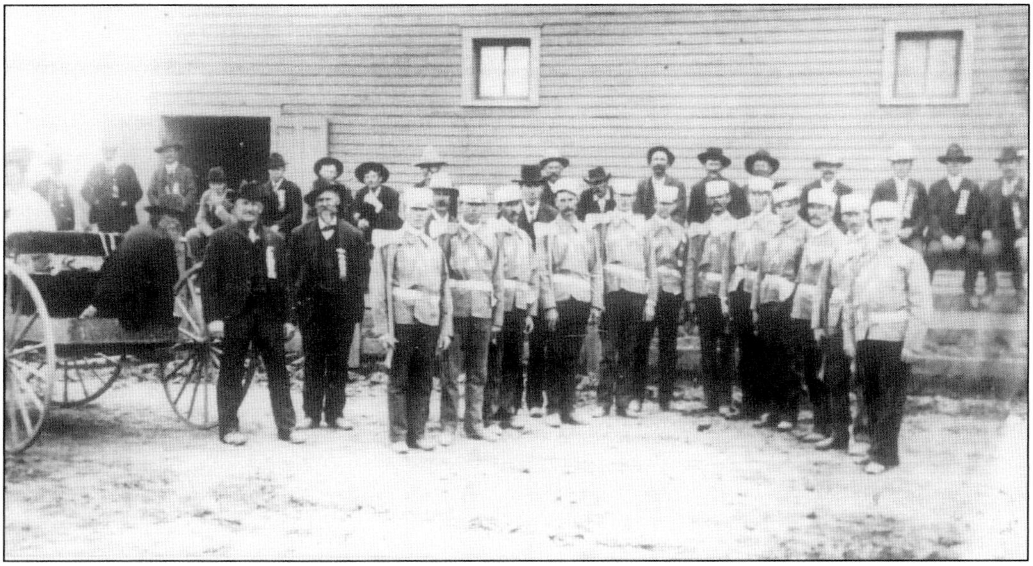

Woodmen of the World gather on the east side of their building in this 1916 photo. The Woodmen of the World are in the dark clothes, and Modern Woodmen of America in the light uniforms. Pictured, from left to right, are (front row) John Usher, Marion Drury, Gene Strawn, two unidentified men, John Parks, two unidentified men, Lyle DeWault, Kels Darnell, Bert Armstrong, Ed Dodson, Fred Jephcott, unidentified, and Pat McGary; (back row) unidentified, Bell Worrell, unidentified, Henry Wommer, unidentified, Clyde Harrond, Earl Smith, John Shelhammer, John Williams, Harve Severn, Lee Shelhamer, Lloyd Armstrong, (?) Underhill, George Black, George Wheeler, John Ong, John Everett, William Brink, Lester Shelhamer, Bob Maloy, and Wellis Wells. (Courtesy of L.T. Ostwald Collection.)

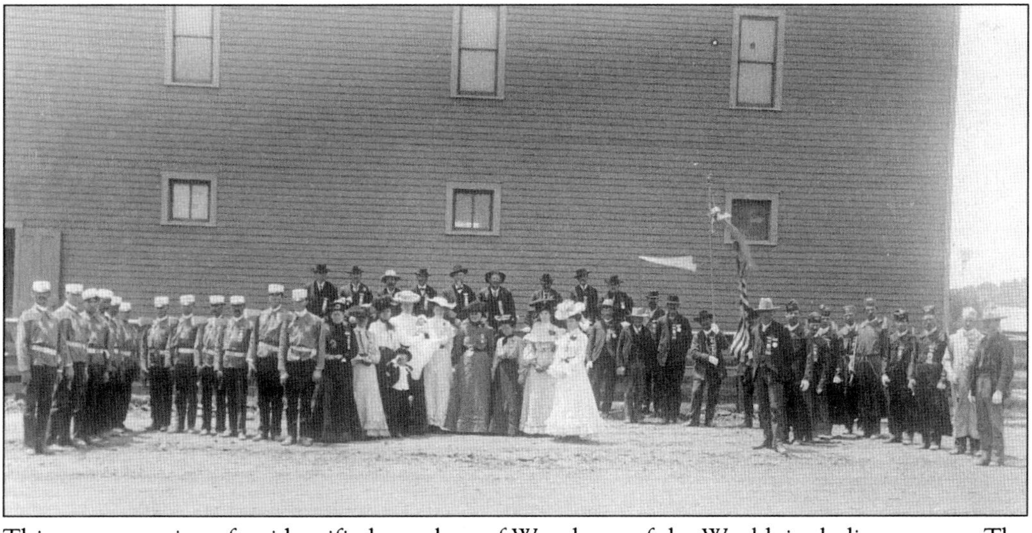

This group consists of unidentified members of Woodmen of the World, including women. The women are more than likely the wives or girlfriends of the members. The 12 men in light uniforms could be the same men as in the above photo. Some of the men in black have medals on, and one man is holding the American flag on a staff, while another holds the flag itself. (Courtesy of Center of Southwest Studies, Fort Lewis College, Catherine Conrad, and Todd Ellison.)

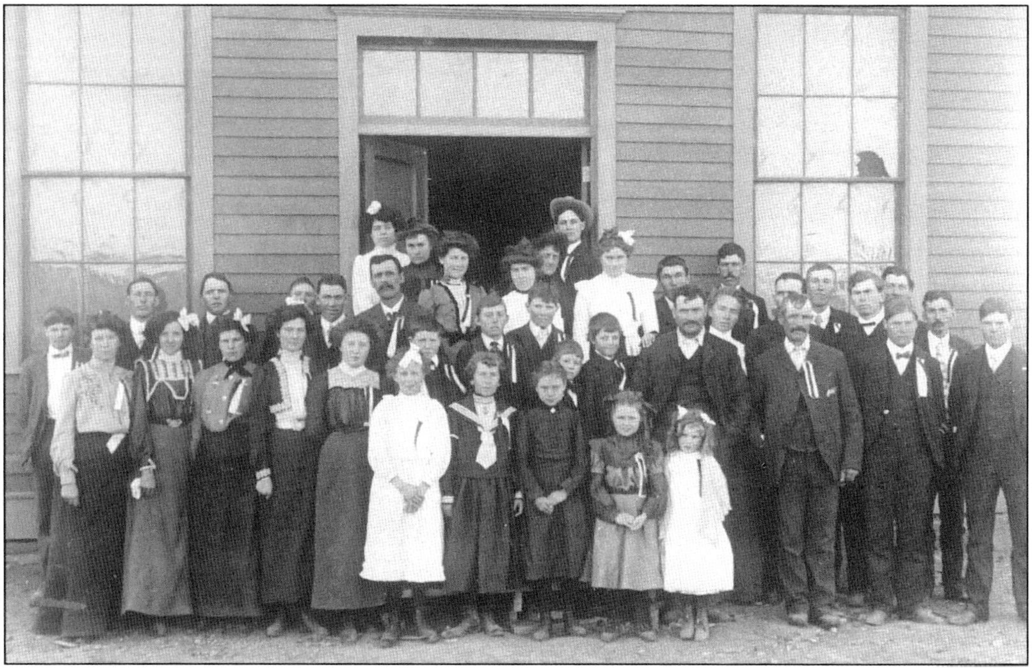

This is an unidentified community musical group on the east side of the Woodmen of the World Hall. (Courtesy of L.T. Ostwald Collection.)

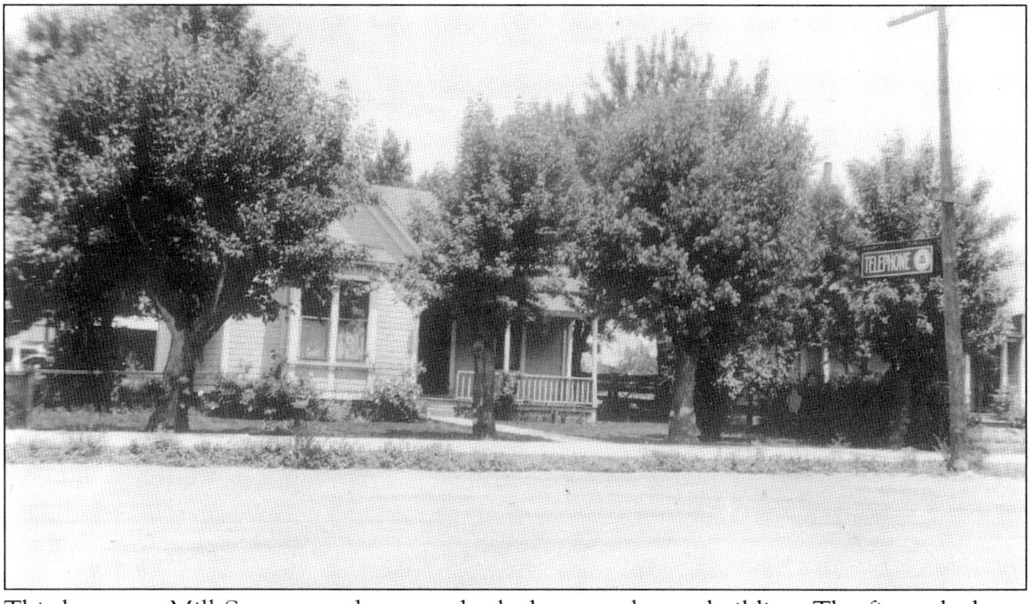

This house on Mill Street was the second telephone exchange building. The first telephone exchange was in the building that was Coulson Brothers first store. Telephones came to Bayfield in 1905. (Courtesy of Telecommunication History Group, Inc., Denver.)

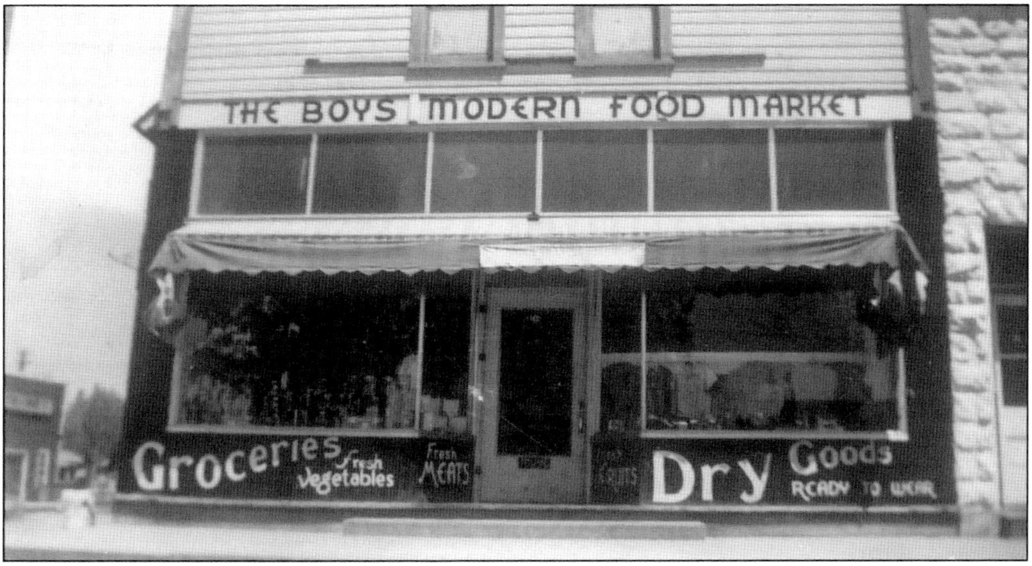

Mr. Coulson owned the Boys Modern Food Market. This was his second store and was bought from Mr. Arnold. Mr. Coulson also started a bank, but it went under soon after it opened. (Courtesy of Glade Stowell.)

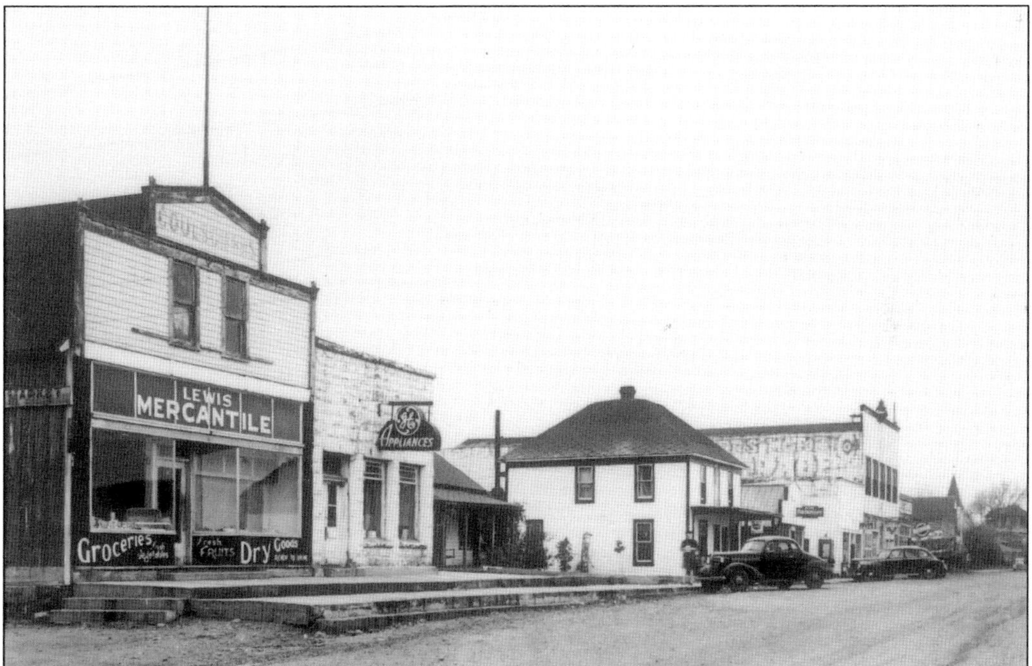

Henry J. Arnold built this frame building in 1889. He eventually sold it to the Coulson Brothers. The attached building was a hardware store built in 1904. Cecil Lewis bought the store and business from the Coulson Brothers and changed the name to Lewis Mercantile. Little did he know that the name would carry on for years. Today, Lewis Mercantile is located on the north side of the U.S. Highway and is owned by the Sower brothers, who still keep the Lewis Mercantile name. (Courtesy of Grade Stowell.)

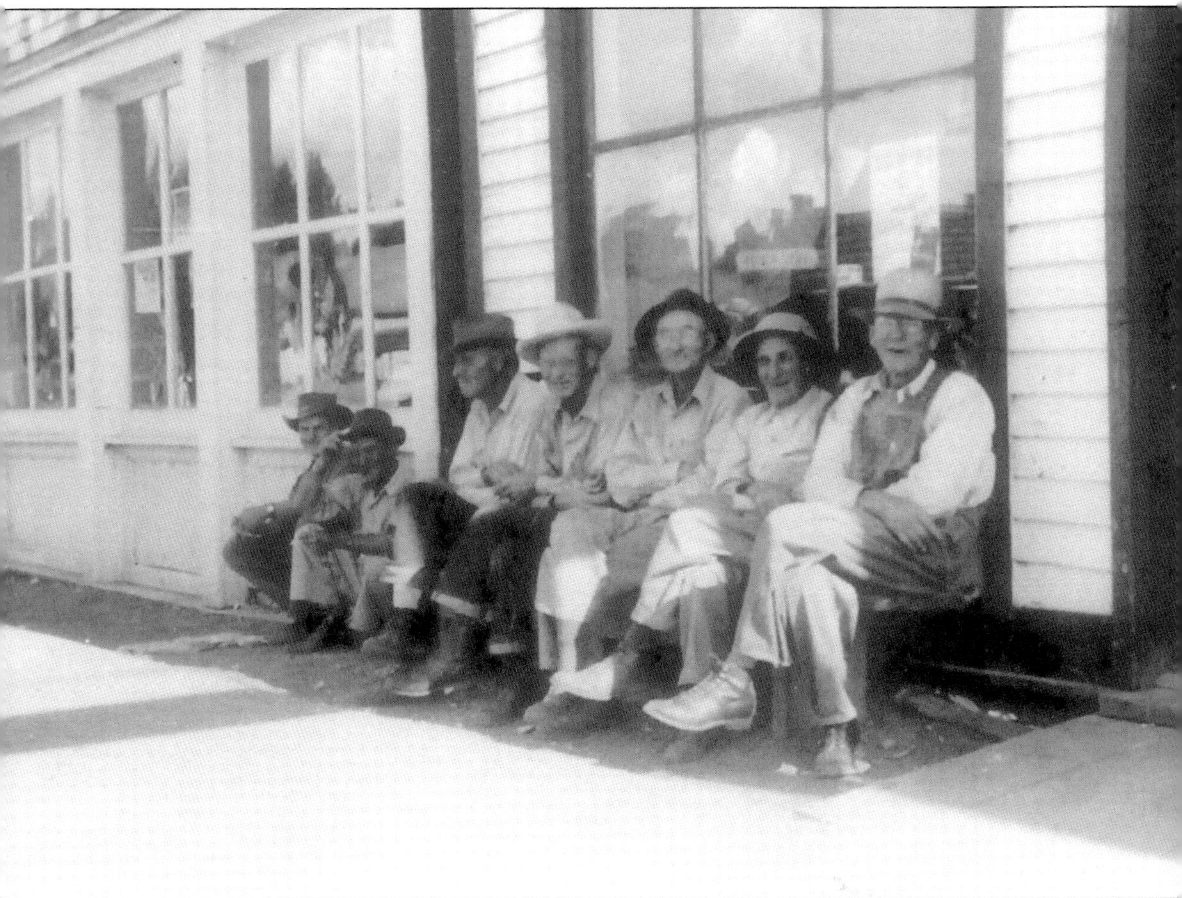

These men spent quite a lot of their time either sitting in front of the Town Hall or, when it got warm and they needed shade, across the street in front of the liquor store next to James Hardware Store. They were known as "The Spit and Whittle Club." Pictured, from left to right, are Roy Binder, unidentified, Tad Morrison, Floyd (?), Walter Carmack, George Williams, and Luther Lea. (Courtesy of Debra Janus.)

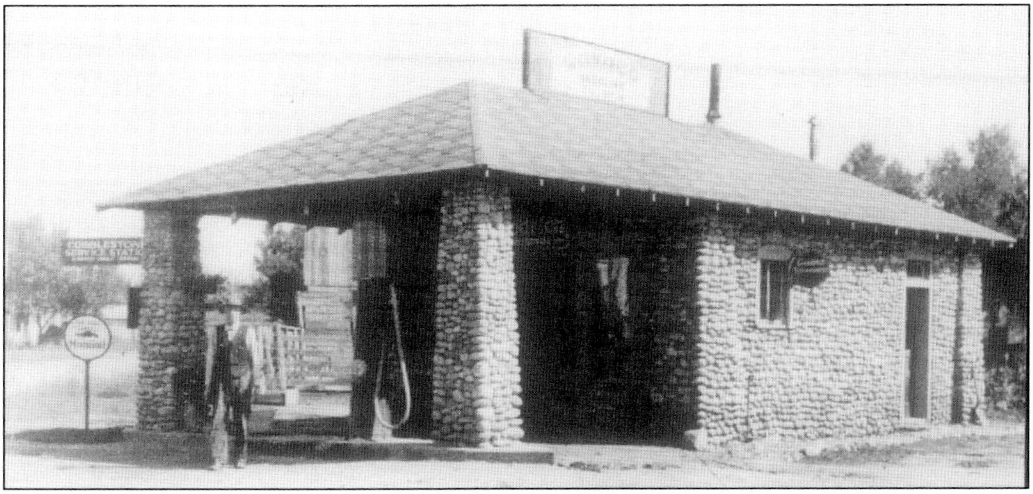

This filling station was located on the northeast corner of Mill and Church Streets, because this is where the early road through Bayfield turned off Mill Street. The station was built in the early 1920s. The small river rocks used on the outside of the building and the columns in front have been used throughout Bayfield. Many porches, chimneys, and foundations used these small rocks. After this building was torn down, a new building was built in 1955 for a post office. In 1985, a larger post office was built, at a different location, and the old one now houses the Mill Street Drug Store. (Courtesy of Mary O'Donnell Mill Street Drug.)

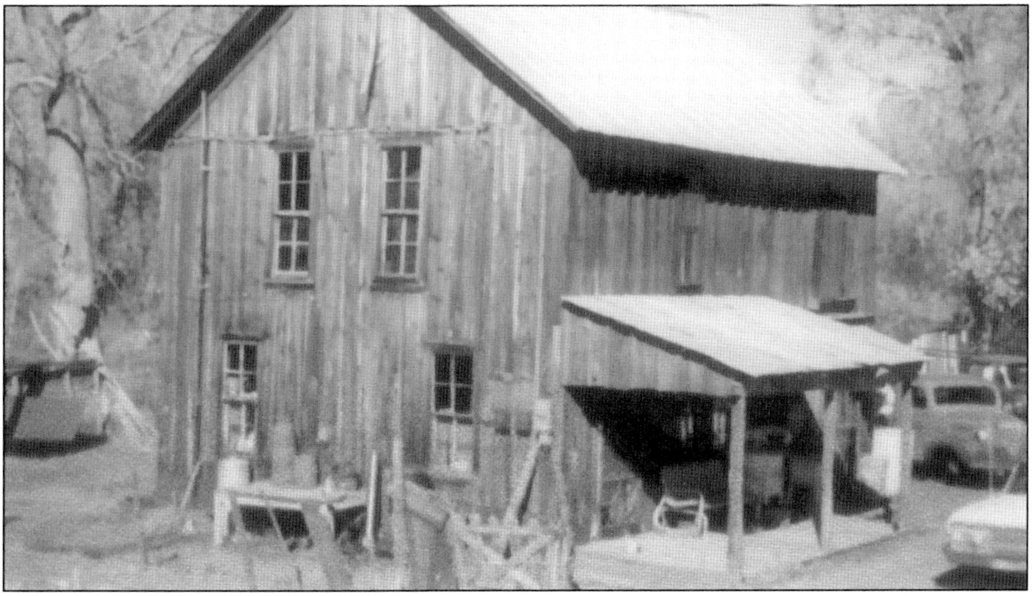

This two-story house used to sit on Church Street south of Mill Street, and was owned by Dee Dee Wells. It was moved to a location just west of town, and placed by an old slaughterhouse between the two Pine River bridges. A movie company bought it in the 1960s. The company, filming *When the Legends Die*, burned the house down for a scene in the movie. Unfortunately, when the house burned, the white Cadillac in front of the house (leased from Morehart Chevrolet in Durango) was damaged as well, and the movie company was forced to buy it. *When the Legions Die* is the story of a small Ute Indian boy growing up in this area and his rise to fame as a rodeo star. (Courtesy of Ray Wells.)

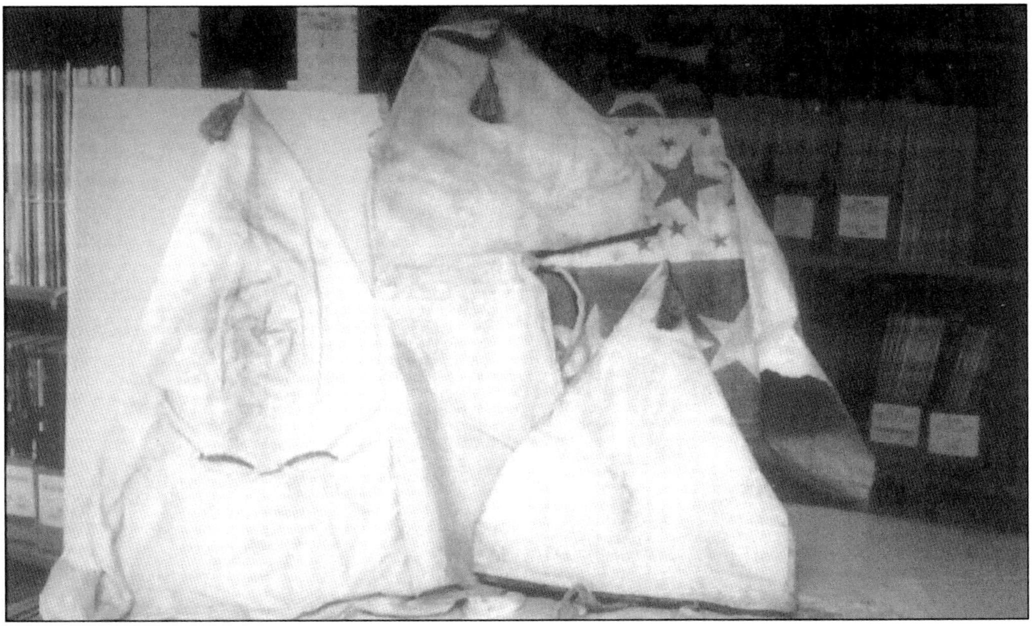

Pictured are three types of Ku Klux Klan hoods and red, white, and blue patriotic bunting with stars. In 1984, Mr. Jeff Bryson bought the Stocks Garage building, and during a remodeling of the second floor into apartments, builders came across two boxes hidden in the walls. The boxes contained the minutes and membership records of the KKK in Bayfield and other KKK propaganda. The boxes were turned over to the Center of Southwest Studies, Fort Lewis College, and the box with the minutes and membership was sealed for 98 years. The KKK was active as a social club in the 1920s. In 1988, an anonymous benefactor donated a robe, wooden cross, caps, hoods, sacks, and fabric swatches seen in these two photos. (Courtesy of Center of Southwest Studies, Fort Lewis College, Catherine Conrad, and Todd Ellison.)

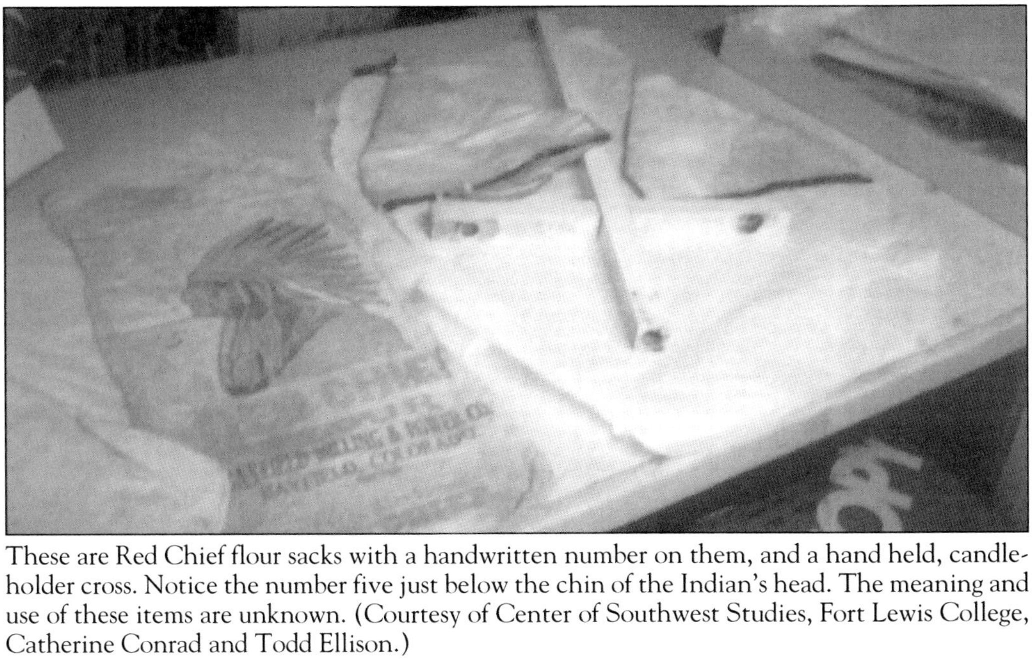

These are Red Chief flour sacks with a handwritten number on them, and a hand held, candle-holder cross. Notice the number five just below the chin of the Indian's head. The meaning and use of these items are unknown. (Courtesy of Center of Southwest Studies, Fort Lewis College, Catherine Conrad and Todd Ellison.)

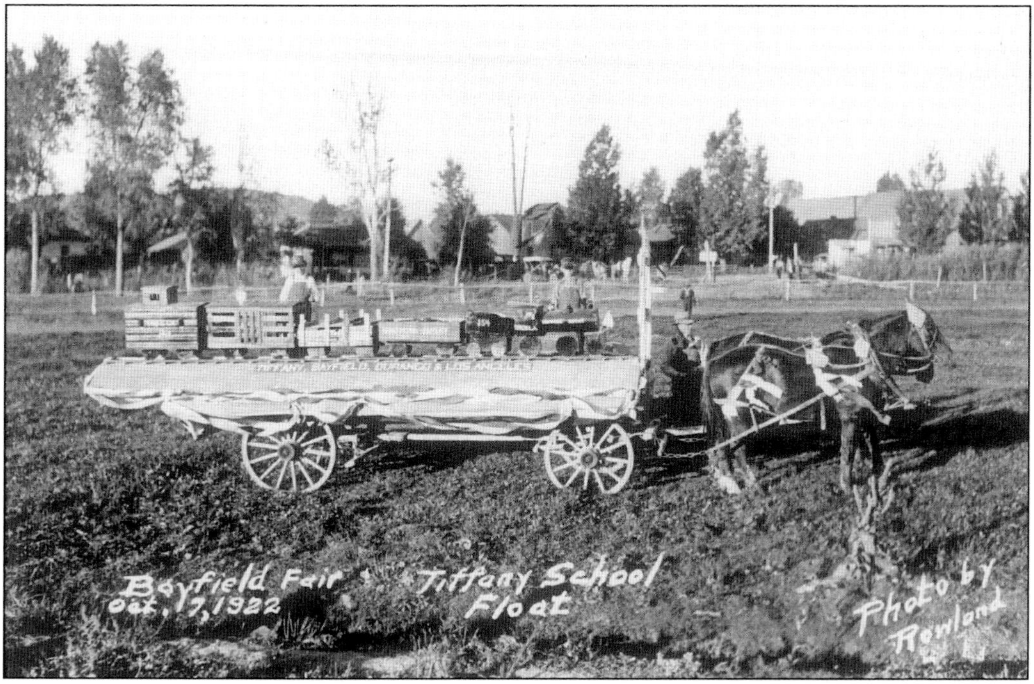

Pictured here is a Tiffany School float entered in the October 17, 1922, Bayfield Fair. Tiffany is a small rural community south of Bayfield. (Courtesy of Center of Southwest Studies, Fort Lewis College, Catherine Conrad, and Todd Ellison.)

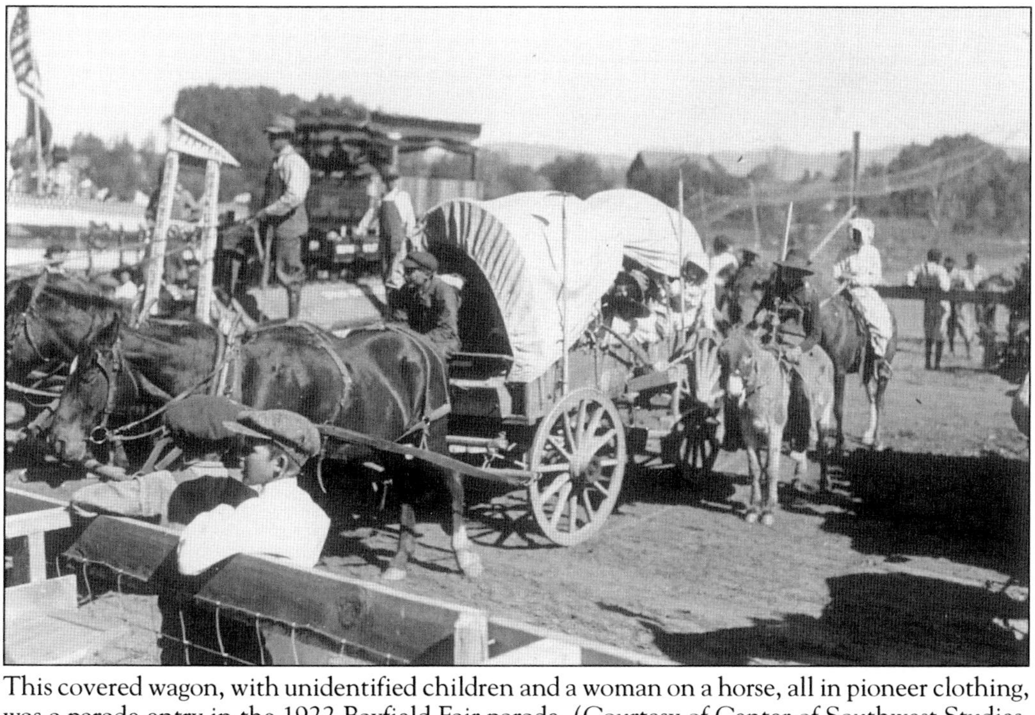

This covered wagon, with unidentified children and a woman on a horse, all in pioneer clothing, was a parade entry in the 1922 Bayfield Fair parade. (Courtesy of Center of Southwest Studies, Fort Lewis College, Catherine Conrad, and Todd Ellison.)

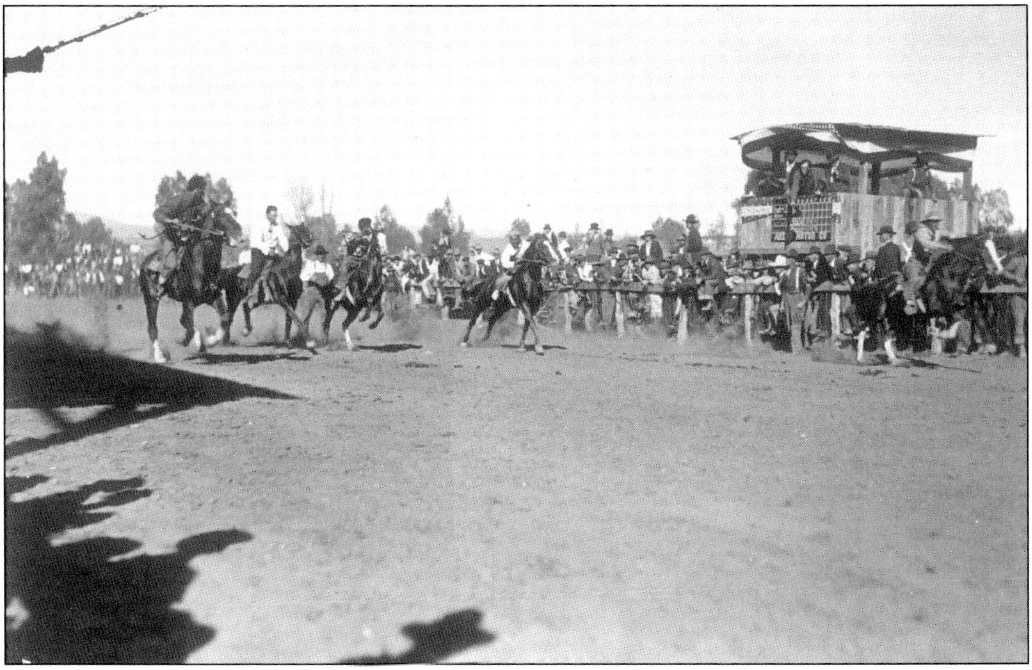

Horse racing at the rodeo was held in conjunction with the 1922 Bayfield Fair. (Courtesy of Center of Southwest Studies, Fort Lewis College, Catherine Conrad, and Todd Ellison.)

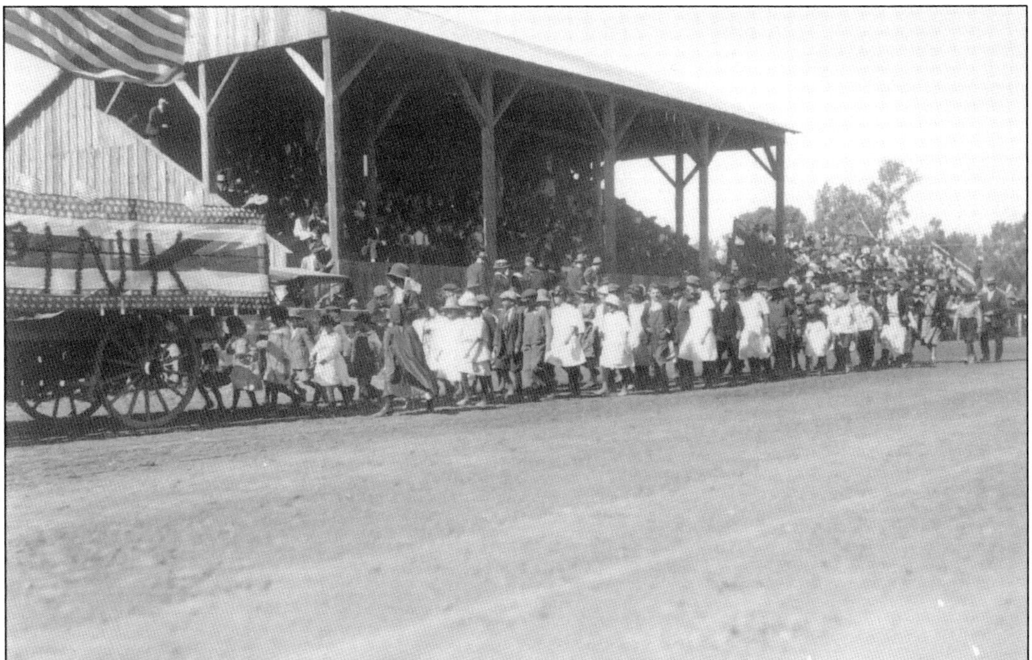

Bayfield school children and adults follow a wagon past the fairground grandstands at the 1922 Bayfield Fair. The grandstands were later torn down, but it is unclear as to when. (Courtesy of Center of Southwest Studies, Fort Lewis College, Catherine Conrad, and Todd Ellison.)

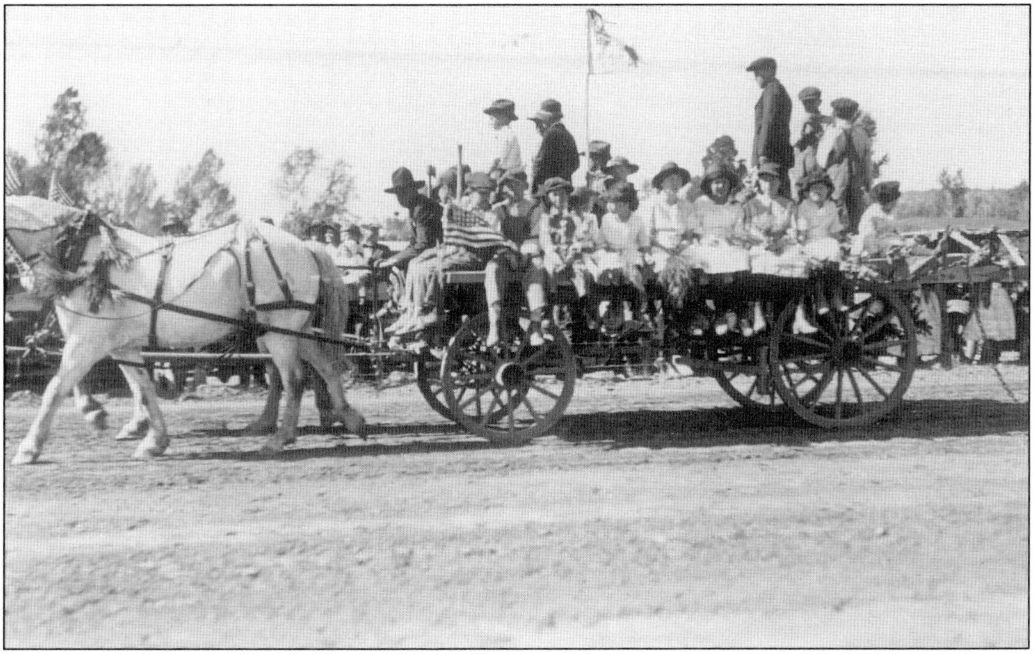

A matched pair of white draft horses pulls a hay wagon loaded with people in the 1922 Bayfield Fair parade. (Courtesy of Center of Southwest Studies, Fort Lewis College, Catherine Conrad, and Todd Ellison.)

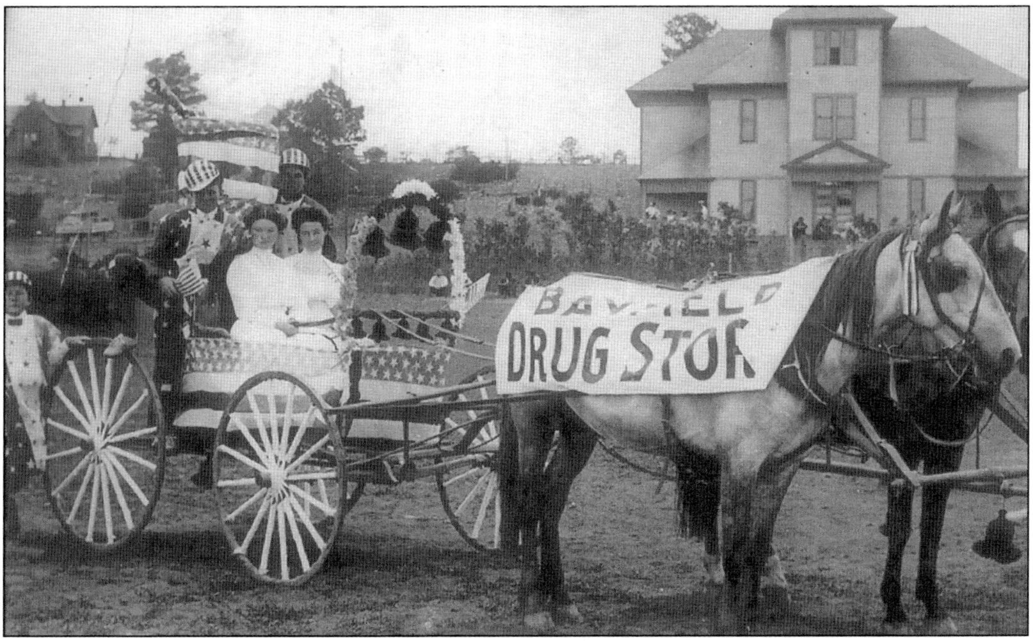

Unidentified men and women sit in this 1911 Bayfield Drug Store parade entry for the Fourth of July parade. The Old Yellow School, built in 1906, is in the right background. Bayfield celebrated the Fourth of July with parades, ball games, and rodeos from 1906 until the beginning of World War II, when it was discontinued until the early 1970s. (Courtesy of Center of Southwest Studies, Fort Lewis College, Catherine Conrad, and Todd Ellison.)

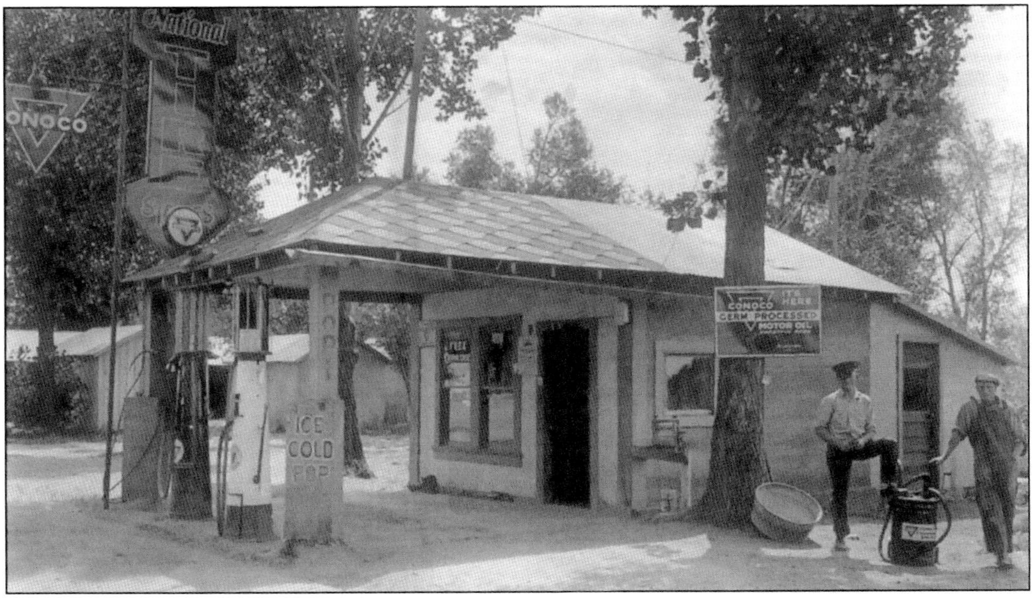

Pictured is Dee Dee Wells' service station at west end, south side of Mill Street. Pictured are Dee Dee Wells, with his foot up on a barrel, and Homer Wells, his older brother. The station sold Conoco Gas with hand-pump gas pumps. One was for regular gas and the other for supreme. (Courtesy of Nobel Wells.)

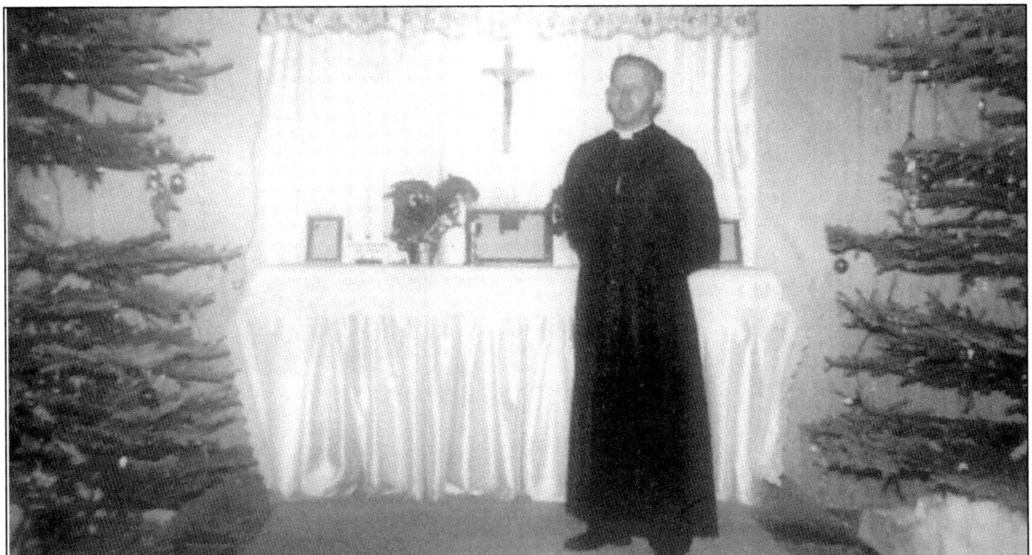

Father Bernard Casper conducted the first mass held in the newly built Catholic church on Christmas Eve, 1957. The congregation met in the Union Church until they could get permission to build their own building. Helen and Minette MacDonald donated the land to the church. They started construction of the building in 1956 and completed it in 1958. The cross, which stands in front of the church, was put up before the walls were started. The Ralph Martinez family worked all one day and into the night, in the rain, to get the cross ready to be put up the next day. The church was built by Catholic members and volunteers. (Courtesy of Ralph Martinez.)

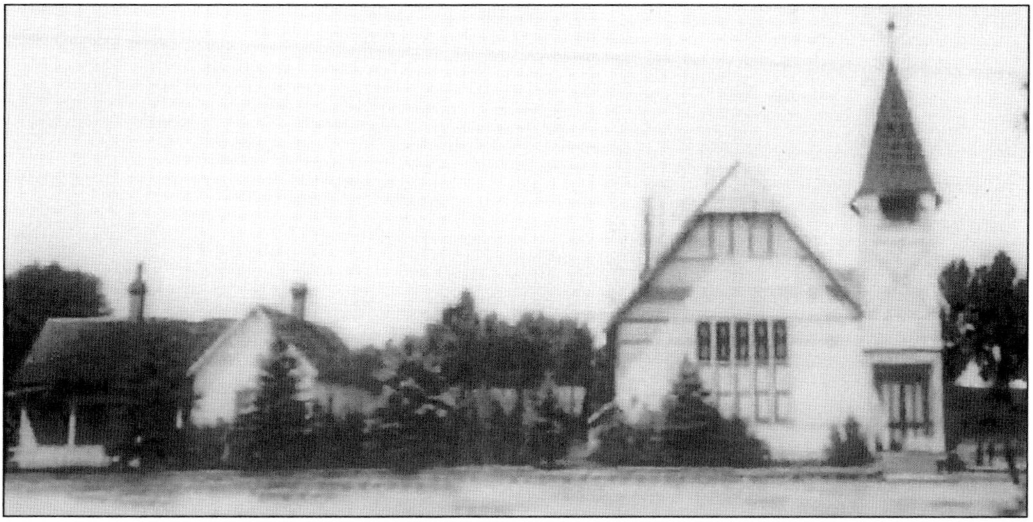

The Calvary Presbyterian Church was built in 1898–99, on land donated by William A. Bay. The first service was March 15, 1899, and was presided over by the Rev. L.R. Smith. The church was dedicated on June 7, 1899. The bell for the tower was purchased for $40 in 1906. They did not get water into the manse until 1917. They celebrated their 100th anniversary in June, 1998. (Courtesy of the Calvary Presbyterian Church.)

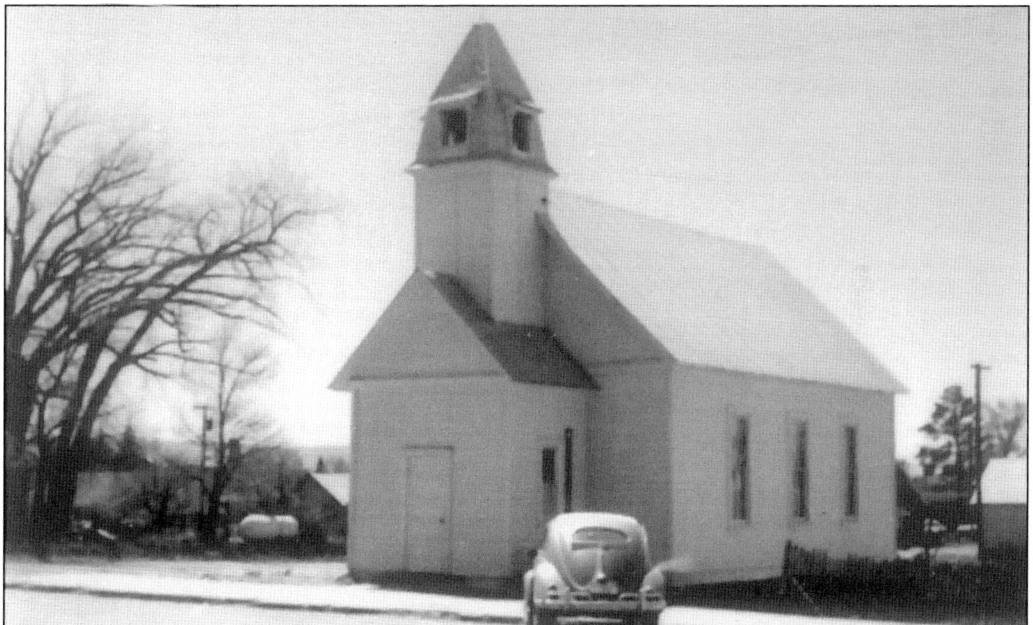

The Union Church was built *c.*1901, across Mill Street, on the south side, across the street from the Calvary Presbyterian Church. The land was donated by Warren A. Schiller and was built by donations from many people. It later became known as the Community Church and was used by various denominations including Catholics, the Church of Jesus Christ of Latter-Day Saints (Mormons), Church of Christ, and Methodists. Today it is occupied by another branch of the Church of Christ. The bell tower was taken off in 1999, and the bell was given to the town of Bayfield. (Courtesy of the Church of Jesus Christ of Latter-Day Saints.)

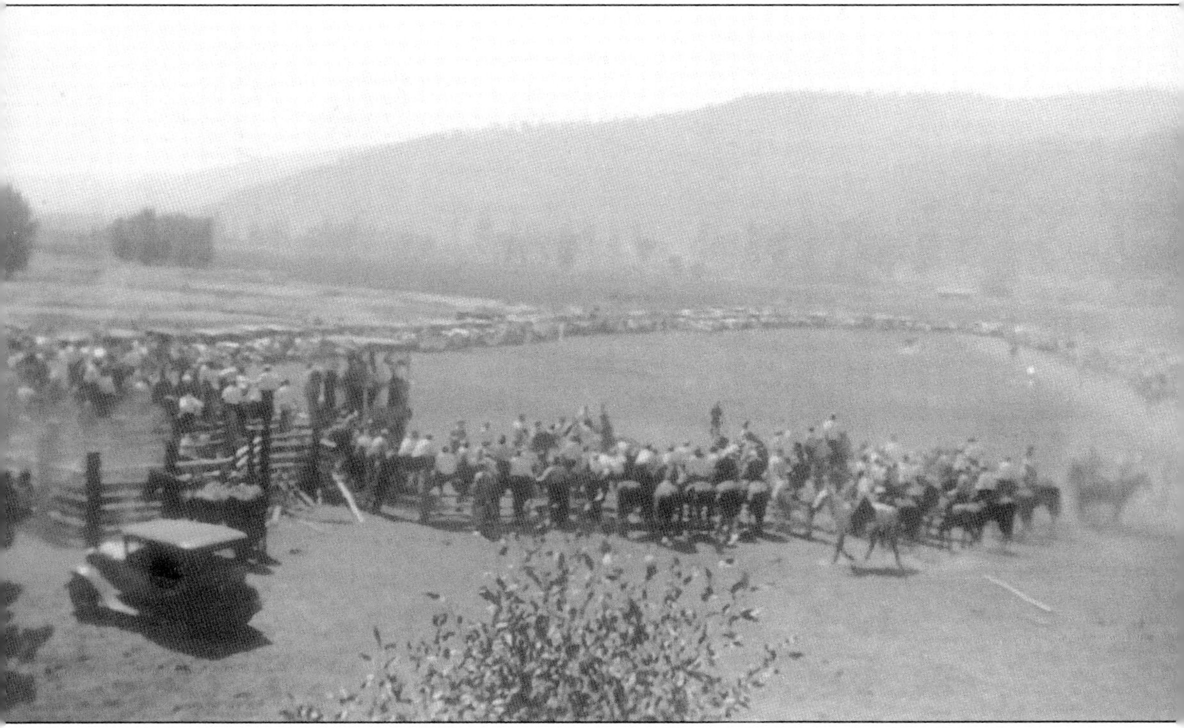

Bruce Sullivan owned a big ranch above the confluence of the Pine and Vallecito Rivers. He held rodeos almost every weekend, but on Labor Day they held a larger one, and people came from all over for the event. They had to cross over a small bridge, across the Vallecito, to get to the ranch. Someone would stand at the bridge and charge 25 cents per person to cross. This fee included camping, fishing, the rodeo, and the big barbecue. The barbecue usually included both barbecued lamb and beef. Model-T's and Model-A's were used to form the arena. When the dam was built, Mr. Sullivan moved the ranch house up on the hill, built some cabins, and it became known as Bruce's on the Pine. The original ranch house today is a store called Elk Point Lodge. (Courtesy of Kenny Montgomery.)

Five

Farming and Ranching

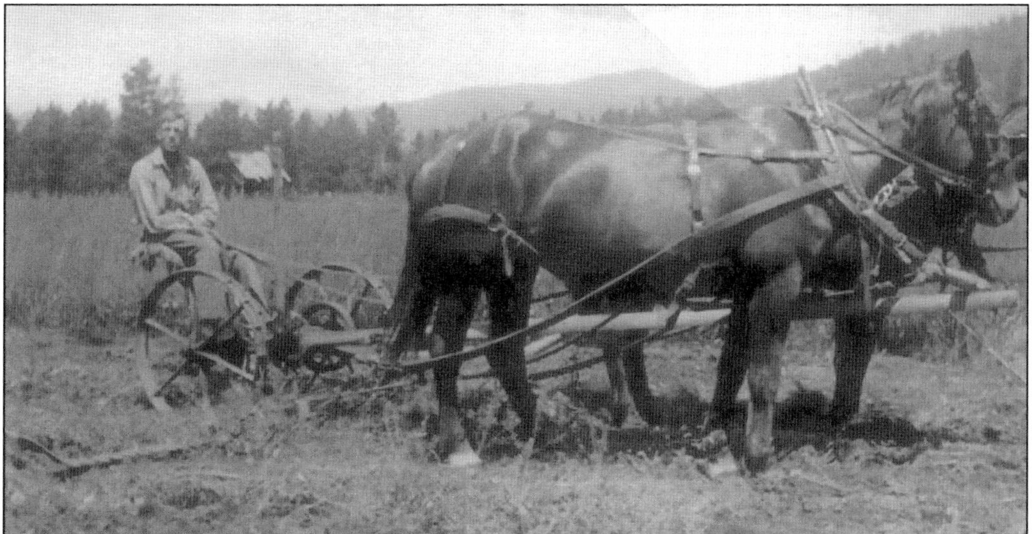

Elmer Shelhamer lets his horse take a rest before finishing cutting his hay. Native hay is still raised in abundance in the Pine River Valley. (Courtesy of Poncho McNew Collection.)

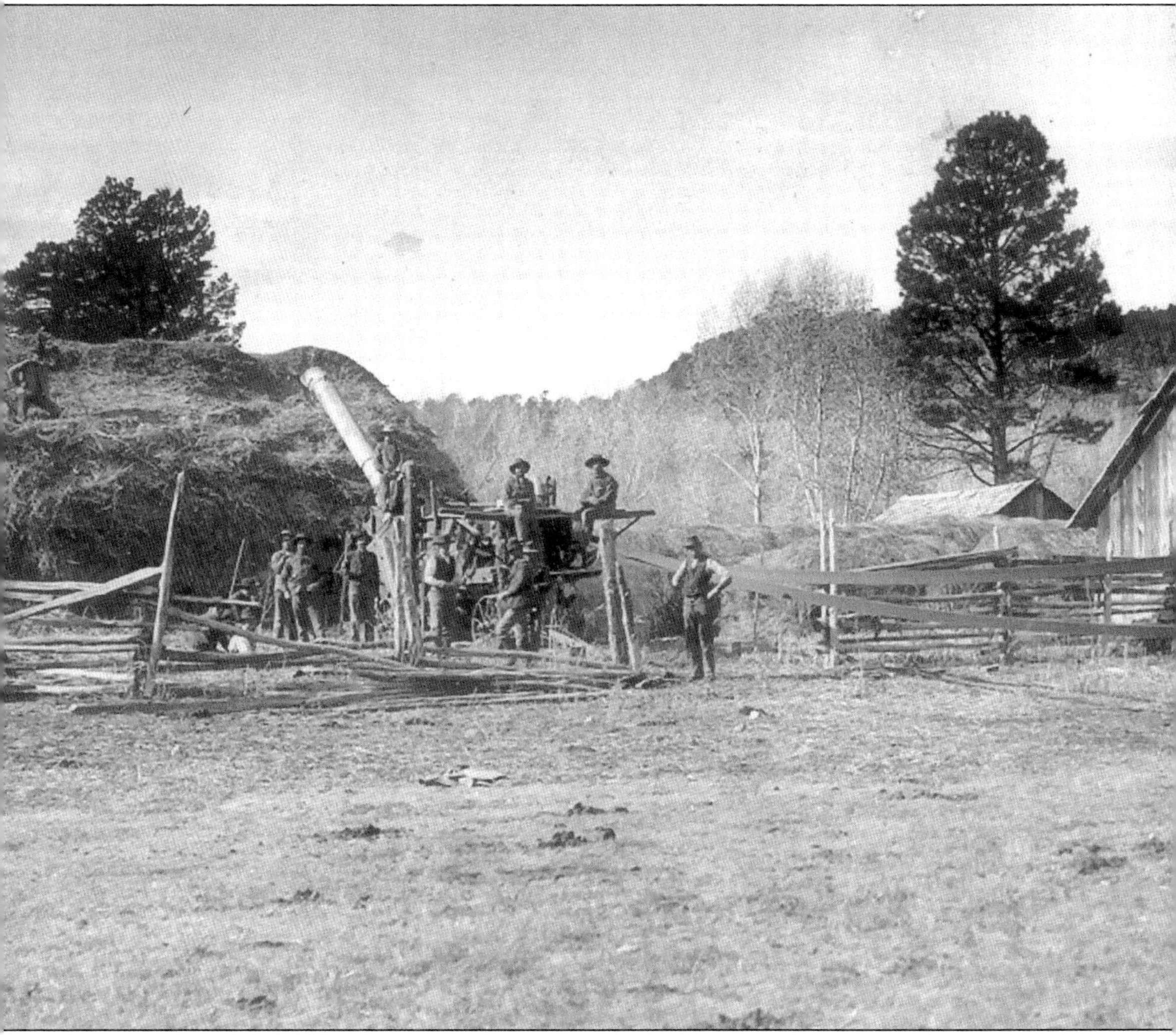

Mr. Herman Schroeder brought the first steam-powered threshing machine to the Pine River Valley. It could be run by burning wood or coal. The valley was known for its quality and quantity of wheat, barley, and oats. When other threshing machines began to come into the

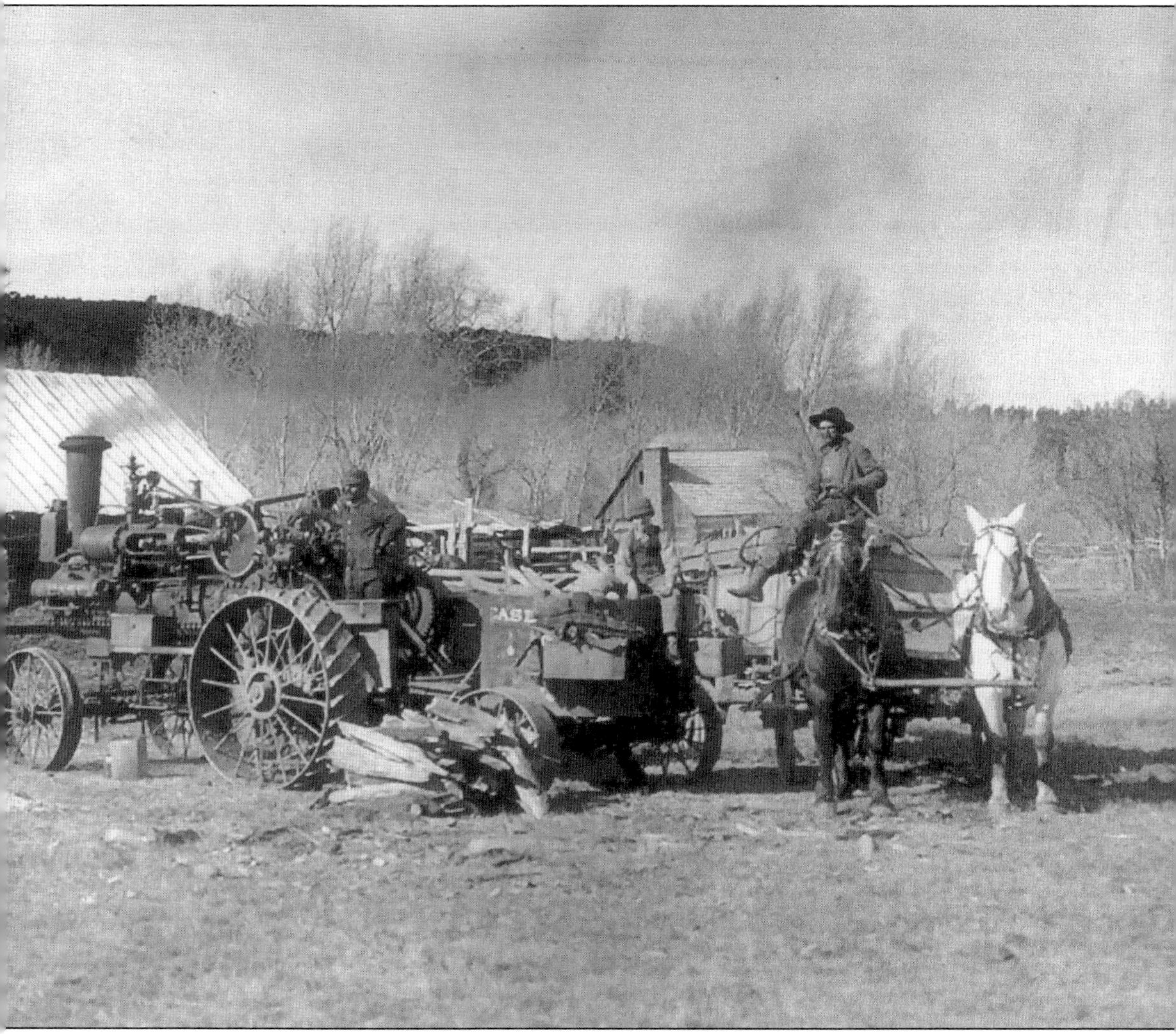

valley, they would go to different farms and thresh their grains. The farmers would help one another by going with the machines from farm to farm. (Courtesy of Betty Fahrion.)

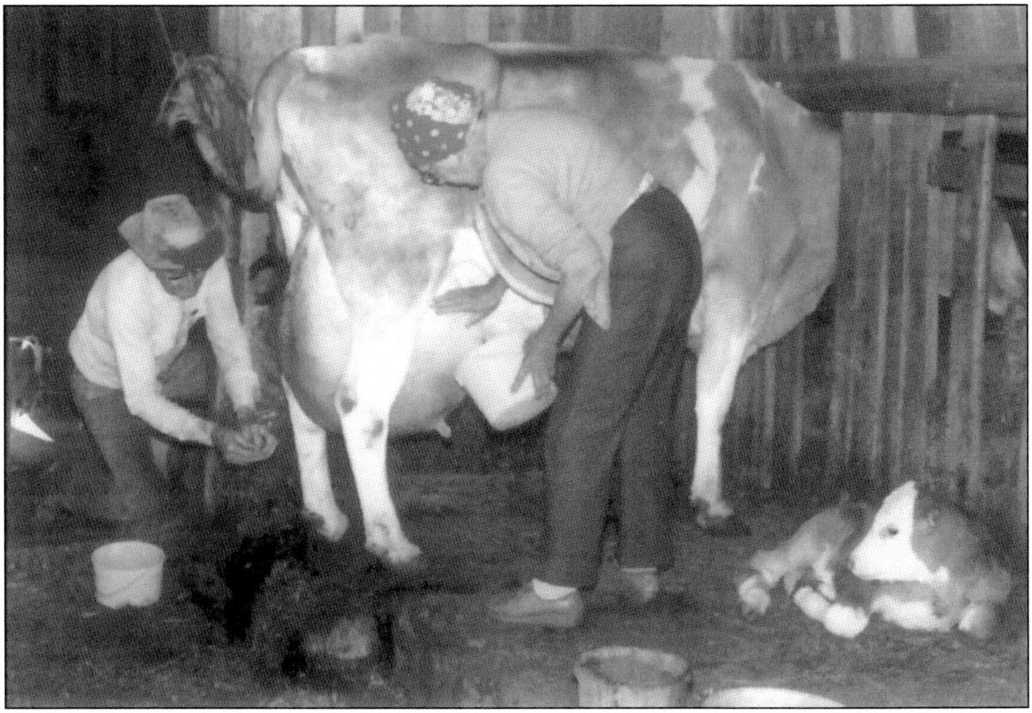

Melba McCoy and her husband Chet clean their milking cow's udder while she stands in the stanchion and peacefully eats her hay—that in itself looks like quite a cleaning job. Notice how the tail has been tied up, so the milker will not get swished in the face. Also, her new calf patiently waits for his share. (Courtesy of Melba McCoy.)

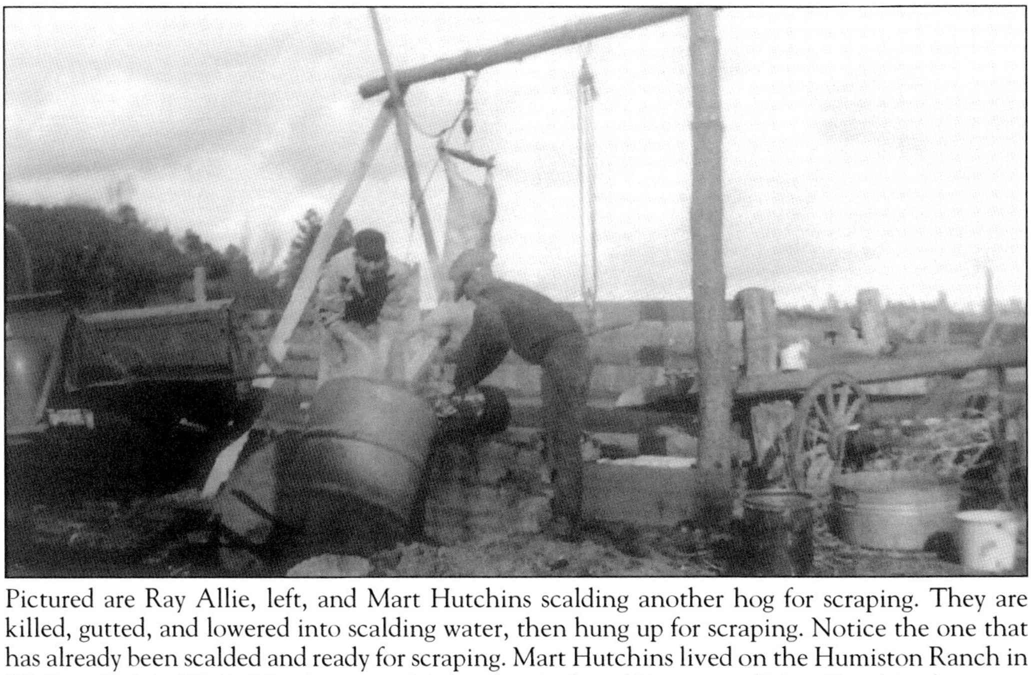

Pictured are Ray Allie, left, and Mart Hutchins scalding another hog for scraping. They are killed, gutted, and lowered into scalding water, then hung up for scraping. Notice the one that has already been scalded and ready for scraping. Mart Hutchins lived on the Humiston Ranch in Wallace Gulch; Wylie Humiston was his brother-in-law. (Courtesy of Mart Hutchins.)

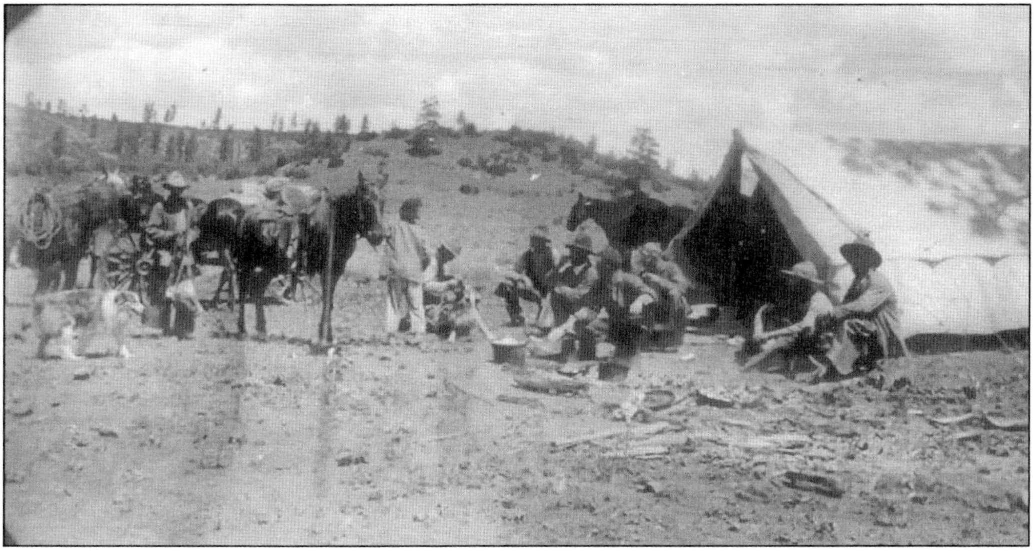

Unidentified cowhands relax after their meal at the Montgomery cow camp on Sauls Creek in this 1918 photo. The Montgomerys have been in the valley for six generations. (Courtesy of Kenny Montgomery Collection.)

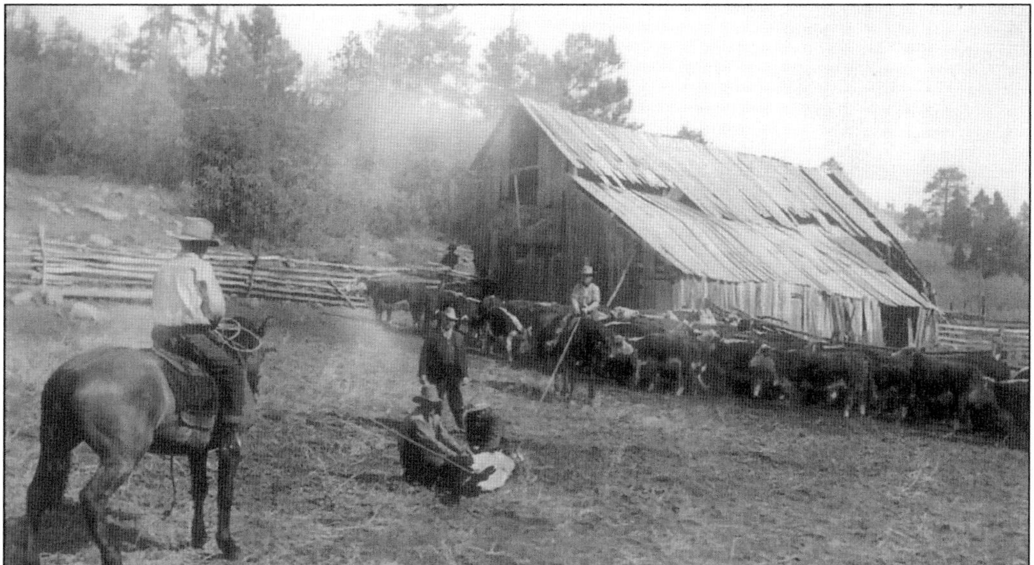

It's branding time at Elmer Shelhamer's ranch on Beaver Creek, east of Bayfield. One cowboy ropes the head, and another ropes the hind legs. This way they could stretch the calf and immobilize it so the branders could do their job. Besides branding their cattle, earmarks were also used by some ranchers. (Courtesy of Kenny Montgomery Collection.)

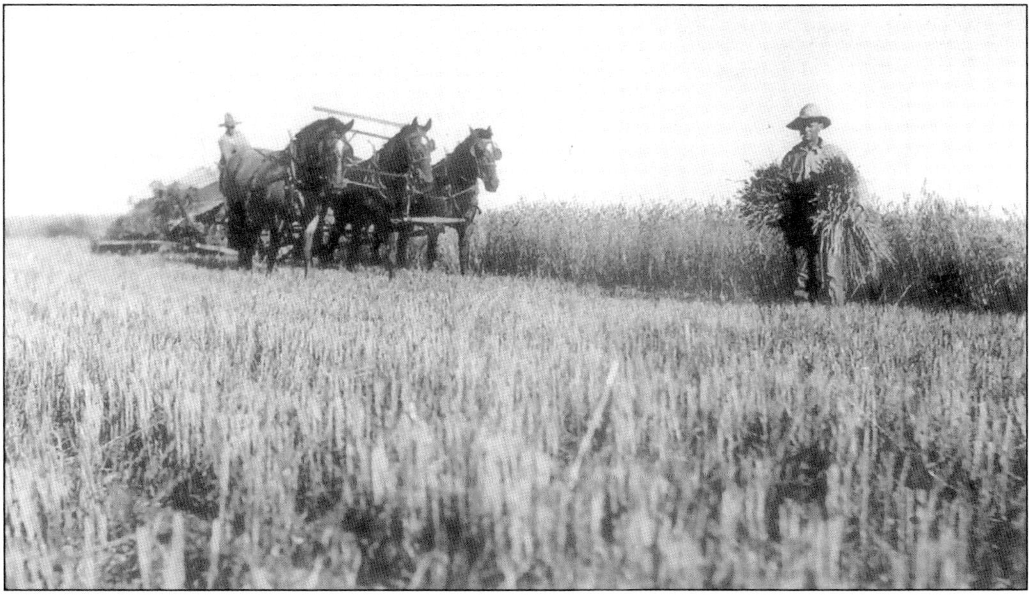

Elmer Shelhamer is cutting his grain, and Bert Montgomery is doing the sheathing at the Shelhamer Farm on Dry Creek. Many farmers raised prime wheat, oats, and barley in the valley. They also saved and sold their prime seed all over the country. (Courtesy of Kenny Montgomery Collection.)

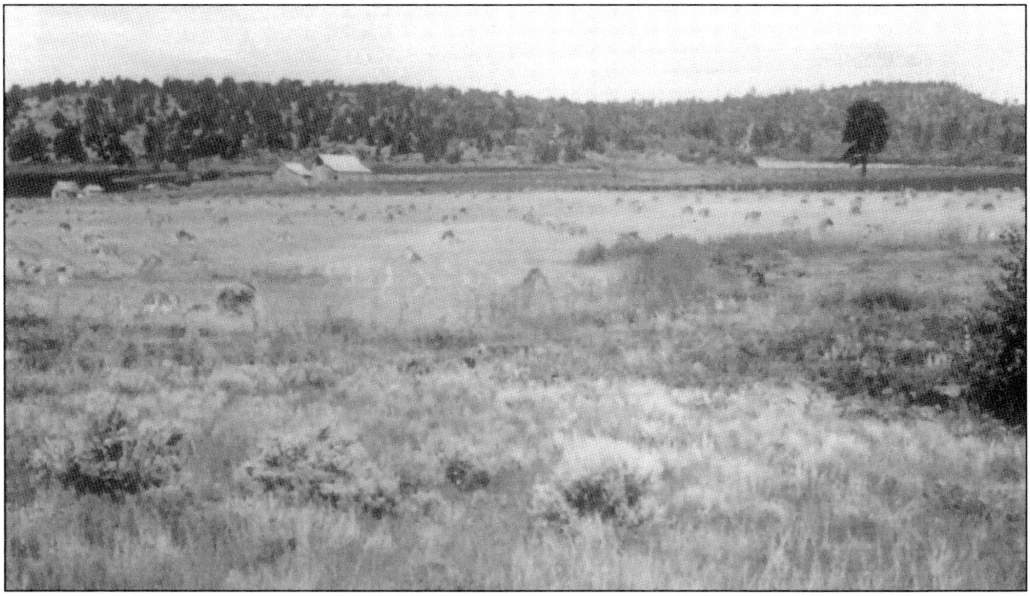

Grain, already cut and shocked, is waiting for the threshing machine to come and finish the job at the Shelhamer Farm on Dry Creek. (Courtesy of Poncho McNew Collection.)

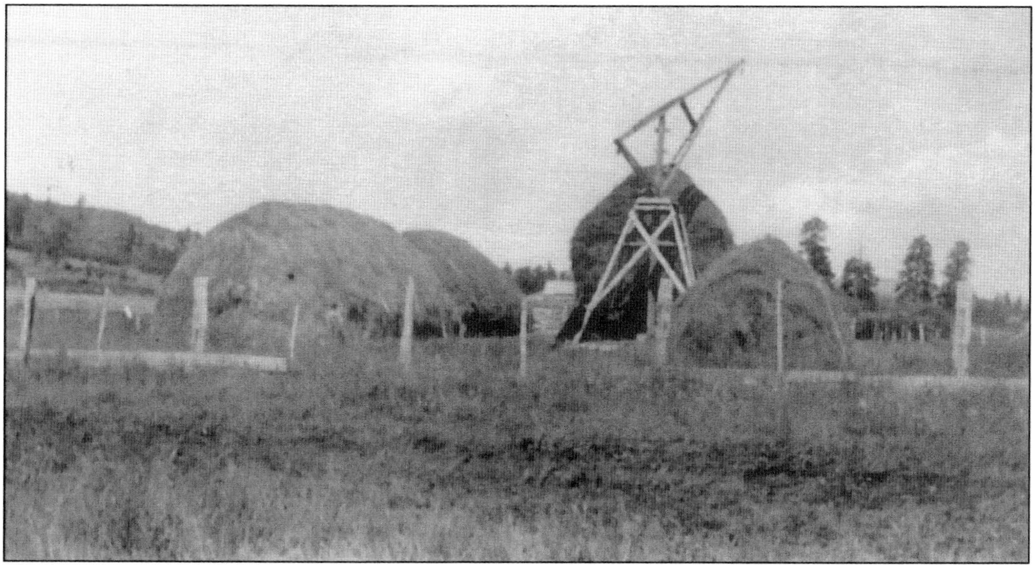

A hay derrick sits in the middle of the stacks of hay that have been put up for the winter at the Lyons Ranch in Wallace Gulch. (Courtesy of Roberta Barr Collection.)

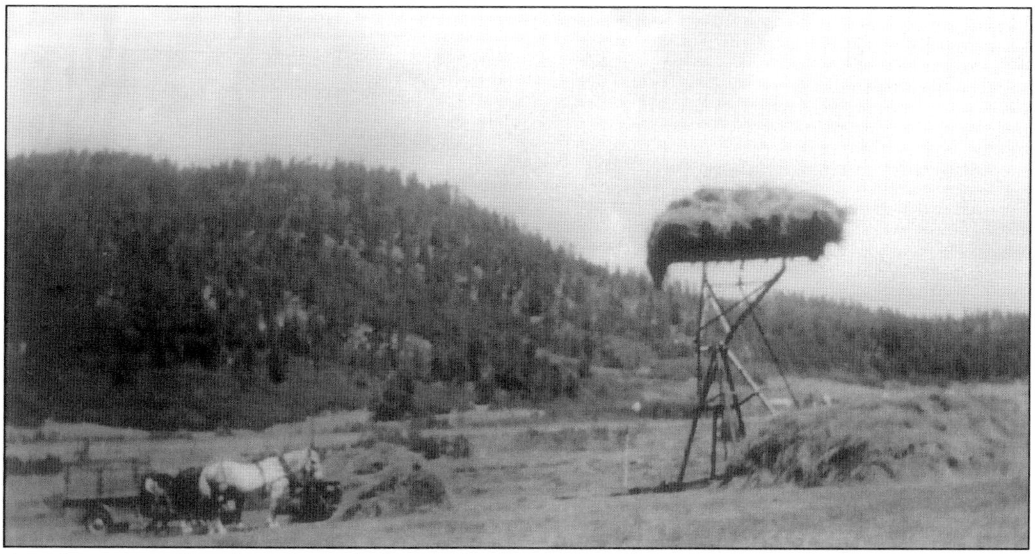

Another type of hay derrick stacks hay at the Buton Ranch in the Pine River Valley. (Courtesy of Freda Brown.)

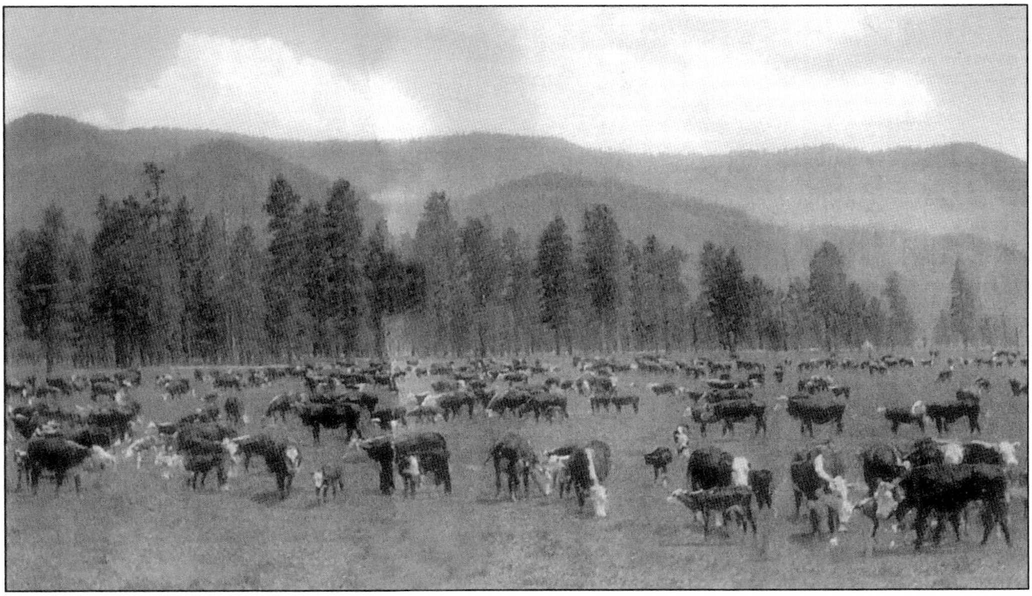

Claude Decker's cattle, *c.* 1920, graze in the bottom of the valley, between the Pine River and Vallecito Creek. The Decker Ranch was up Vallecito Creek, and they also ran sheep. The Decker Ranch moved to Florida Mesa, about 10 miles west of Bayfield. Now it is just across the Colorado state line in New Mexico, below Arboles, Colorado. They still take their cows, by truck, to the upper end of Vallecito Lake and summer them on Middle Mountain. (Courtesy of Kennon Decker.)

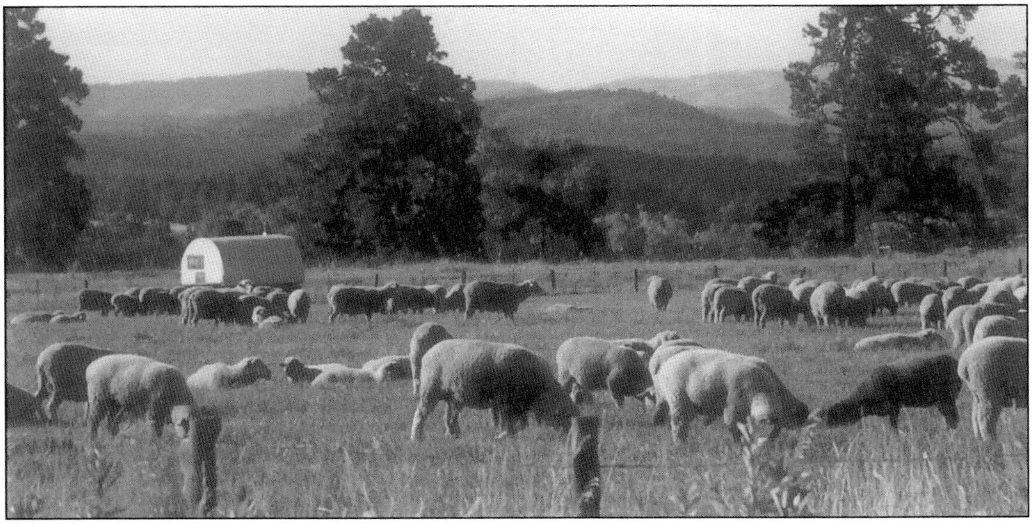

Houston Lasater, a new sheep rancher in the valley, rests his sheep overnight at the Harold Wilmer Ranch, about 2 miles north of Bayfield, on the road from Vallecito Lake. Mr. Lasater runs his sheep above Lemon Dam, which is on the Florida River in the San Juan Mountains. It usually takes the sheep five days to get to his ranch, which is about 2 miles south of Bayfield. However, for the past two years they have stopped them at Wilmers, so they could be turned up Mill Street for Bayfield's annual Sheep Trailing and Heritage Days. September 2001 was the second annual festival. Usually, the sheep just go down the Buck Highway that goes by the east edge of town. (Courtesy of Carole McWilliams.)

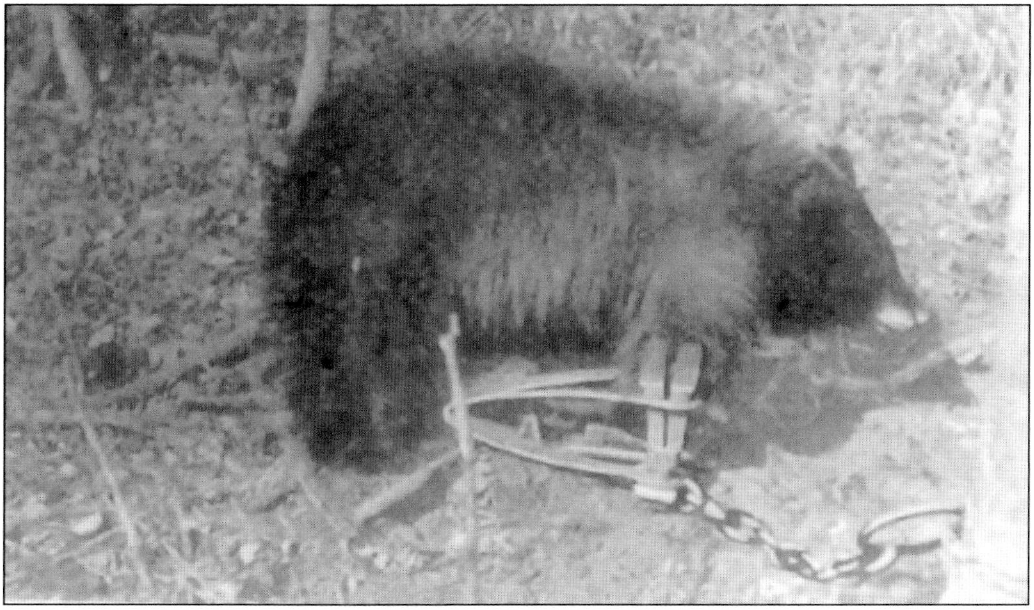

A yearling bear stands in a trap, with his front leg caught, in this early photo of bear trapping in the Pine River Valley. Bears are a real problem for sheep ranchers when they take their sheep to their summer range in the San Juan Mountains. Some ranchers lose as many as 100 sheep, especially lambs, to bears nearly every year. (Courtesy of Melba McCoy.)

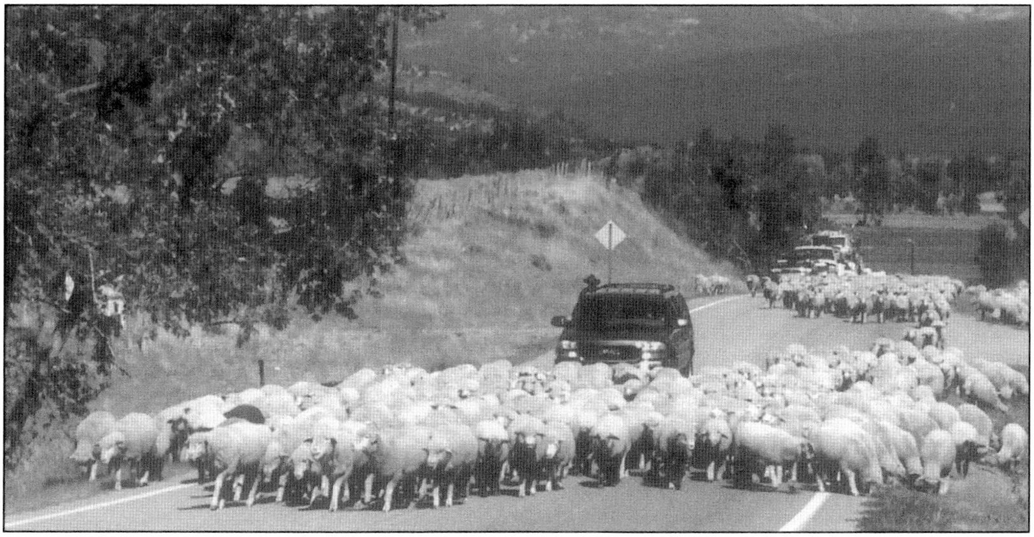

Houston Lasater's sheep cause a New Zealand-like traffic jam as he brings them down County Road 501, from the high country. This familiar scene can be seen twice a year: once when the sheep are taken to their summer pasture high in the San Juan Mountains, and again when they return to their ranches below Bayfield in the fall. There are still two ranchers who drive their sheep on the Buck Highway that comes through the east side of Bayfield, and on up the valley on County Road 501. They have to cross U.S. Highway 160 that goes through Bayfield, and highway traffic comes to a halt. This, however, gives tourists a brief look into the past as they sit at the intersection waiting for anywhere from 1,000 to 2,000 sheep to cross the highway. (Courtesy of Carole McWilliams.)

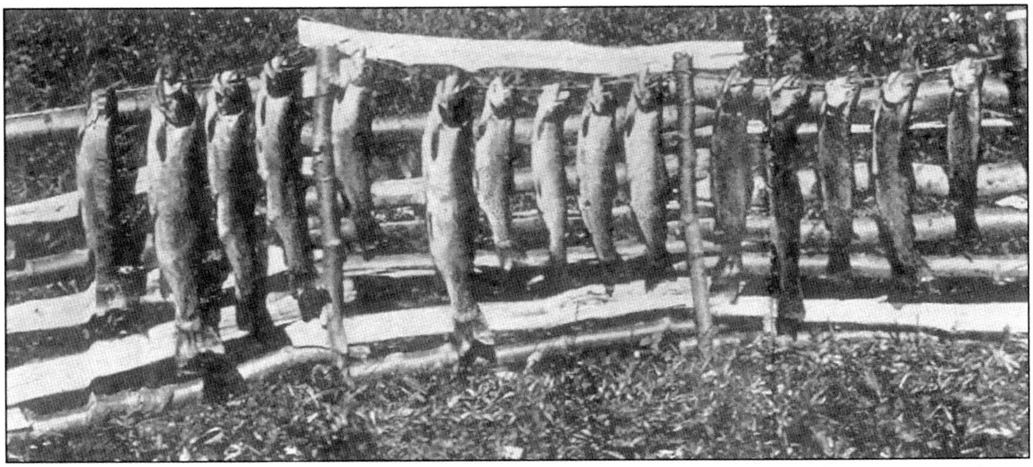

Fishing on the Pine River was very profitable, as this early picture of trout hanging on a fence testifies. This picture was taken before the dam was built. (Courtesy of Melba McCoy.)

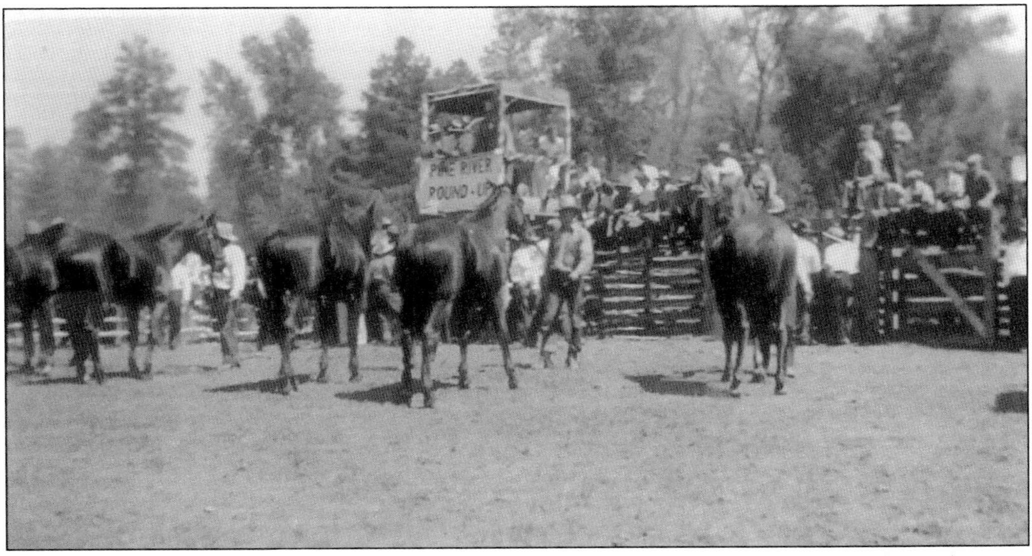

Cowboys and spectators wait for action at the 1932 Pine River Round-Up. The rodeo was held in conjunction with the Pine River Fair. Rodeos were also held on the Fourth of July and other weekends. (Courtesy of Center of Southwest Studies, Fort Lewis, Catherine Conrad, and Todd Ellison.)

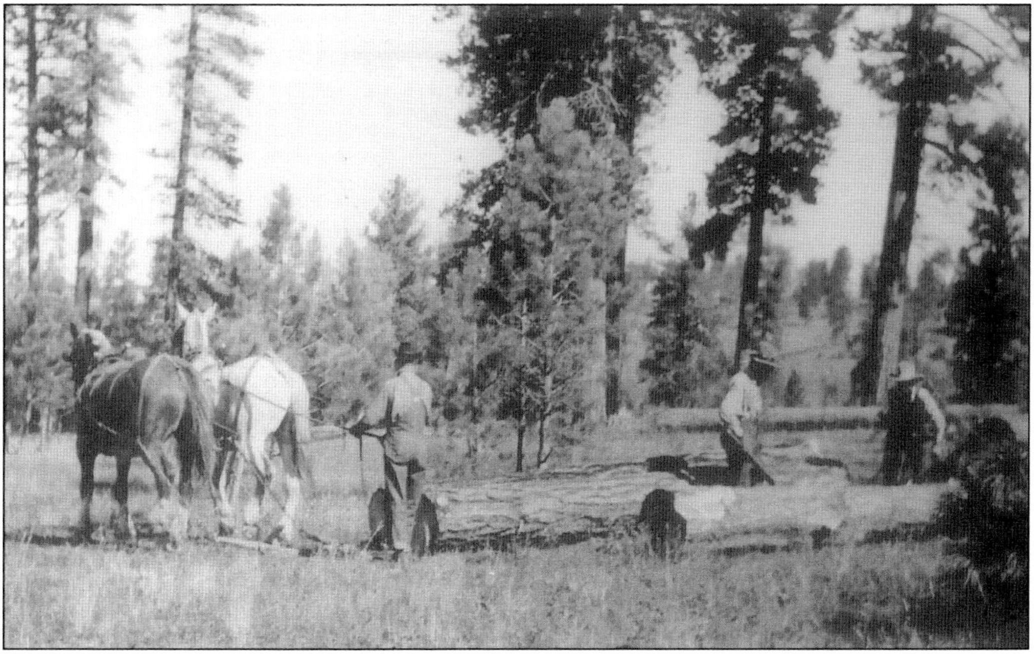

A team skids logs, getting them ready to load and be taken to the saw mill. When settlers began to come into the valley, many saw mills began to spring up because of the need for lumber. (Courtesy of Faye Culp.)

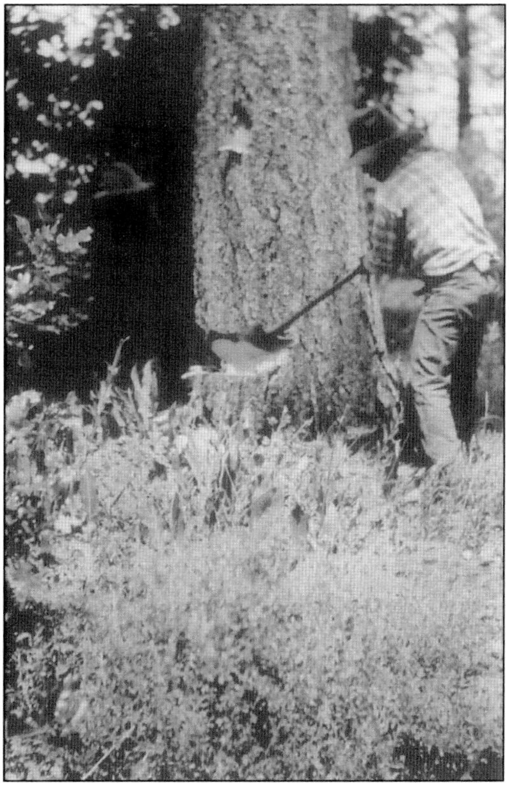

An unidentified lumber-jack notches a large pine to be felled and taken to a saw mill. (Courtesy of U.S. Forest Service.)

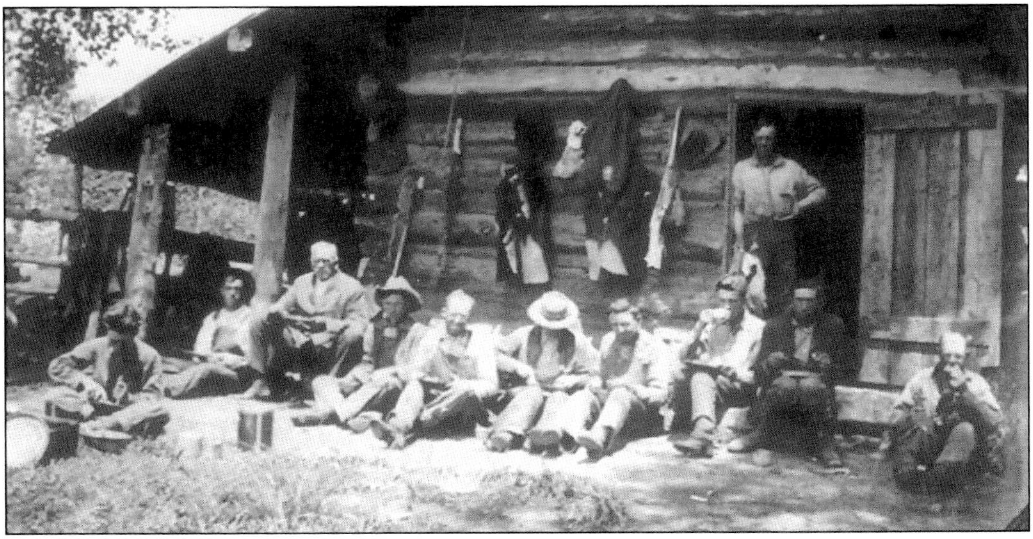

These unidentified cowhands enjoy their meal at a Beaver Creek cow camp east of Bayfield. (Courtesy of Henry Montgomery Collection.)

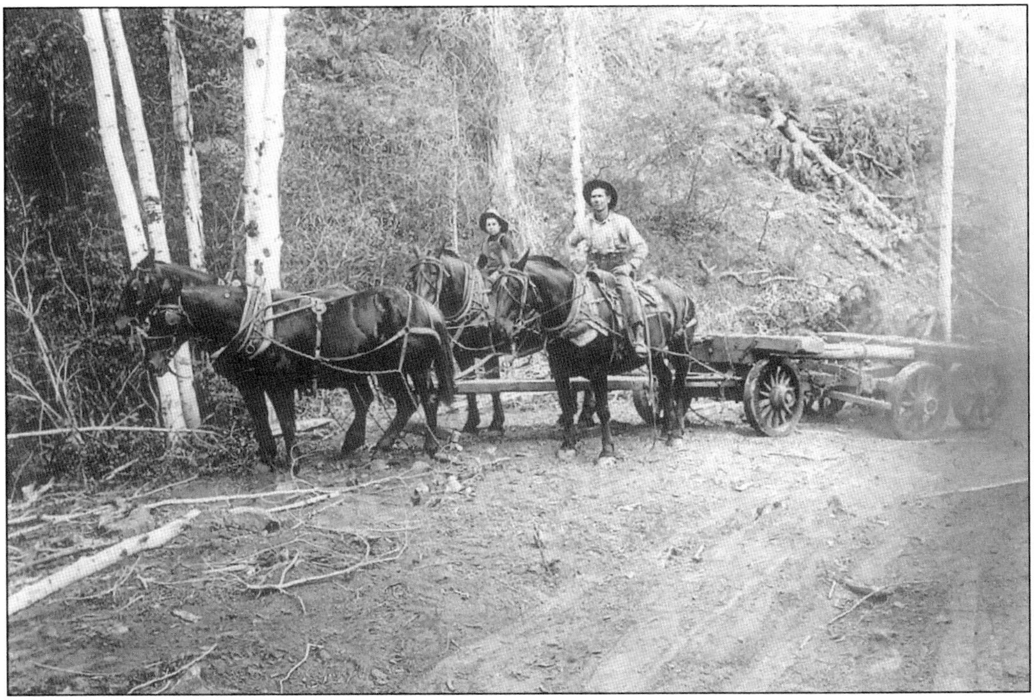

Pictured with their wheeler team at their 1925 horse camp are Mart Hutchins, shown left riding on Dover, and Bye Hutchins, on the right riding Darling. The lead teams names are Dick and Star. A horse camp is what they called their logging crew: they cut timber and built logging roads. This was on Middle Mountain between the Pine and Vallecito Rivers. (Courtesy of Mart Hutchins.)

Six

Emerald Lakes, Cave Basin, and Tuckerville

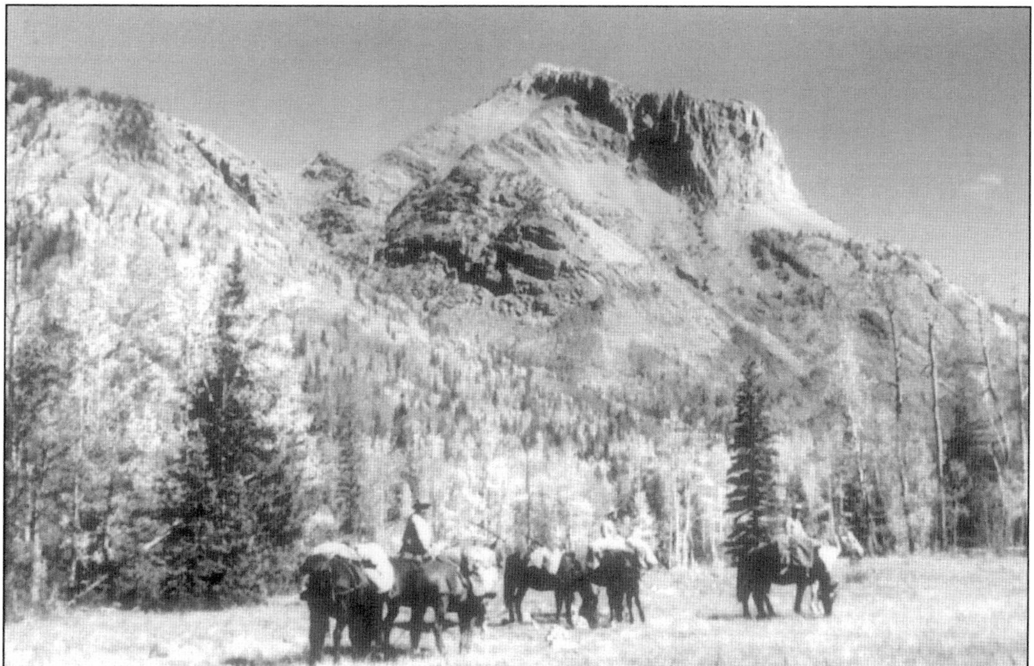

Packers on their way to Cave Basin pause in a small mountain park on the Pine River, below the Guardian, a prominent land mark. (Courtesy of U.S. Forest Service.)

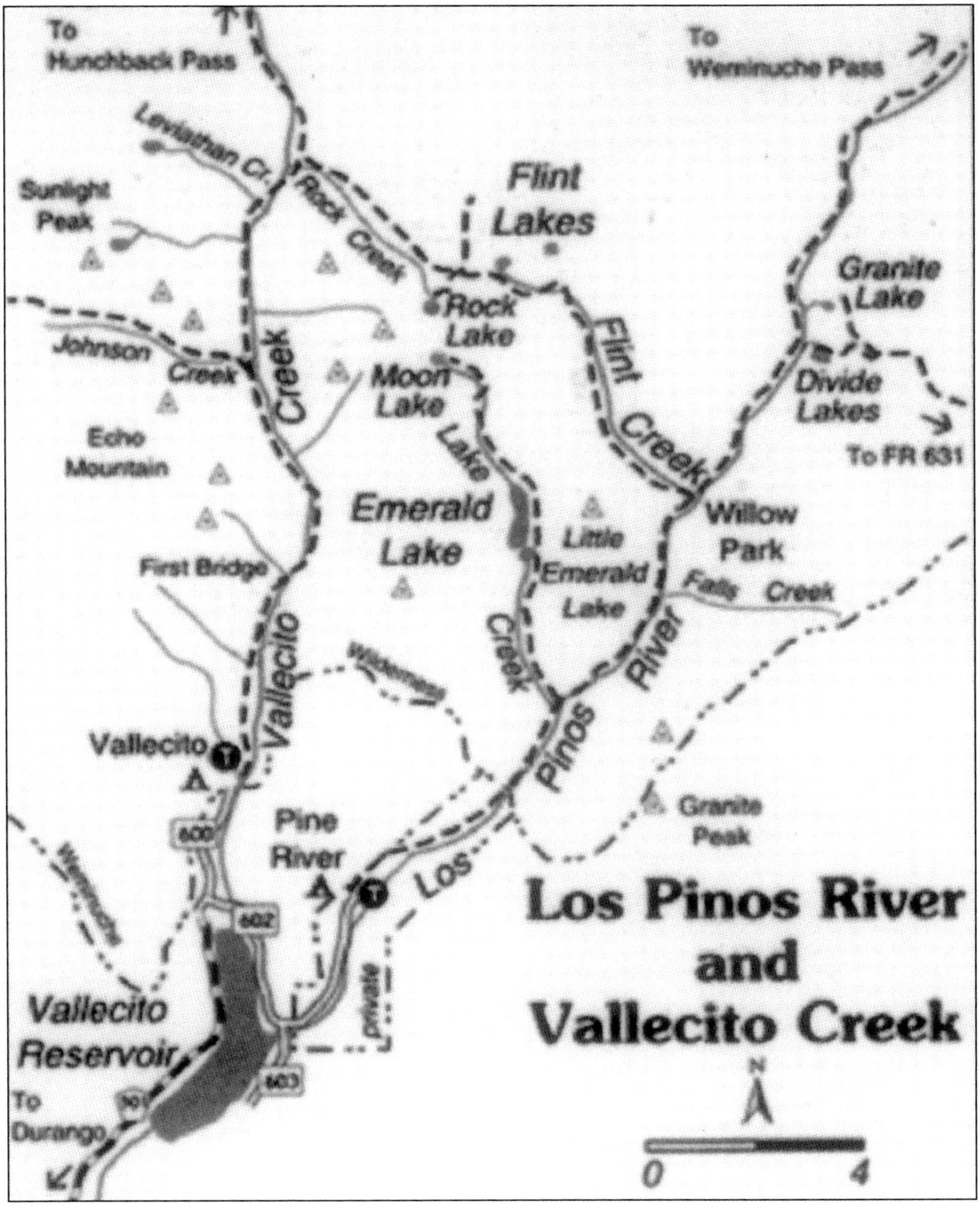

This is an identification map of the Los Pinos River and Vallecito (River) Creek, showing both Emerald Lakes and the Weminuche Wilderness boundary. This does not show Cave Basin or Tuckerville, but both are in this area. (Courtesy of Bayfield Area Chamber of Commerce.)

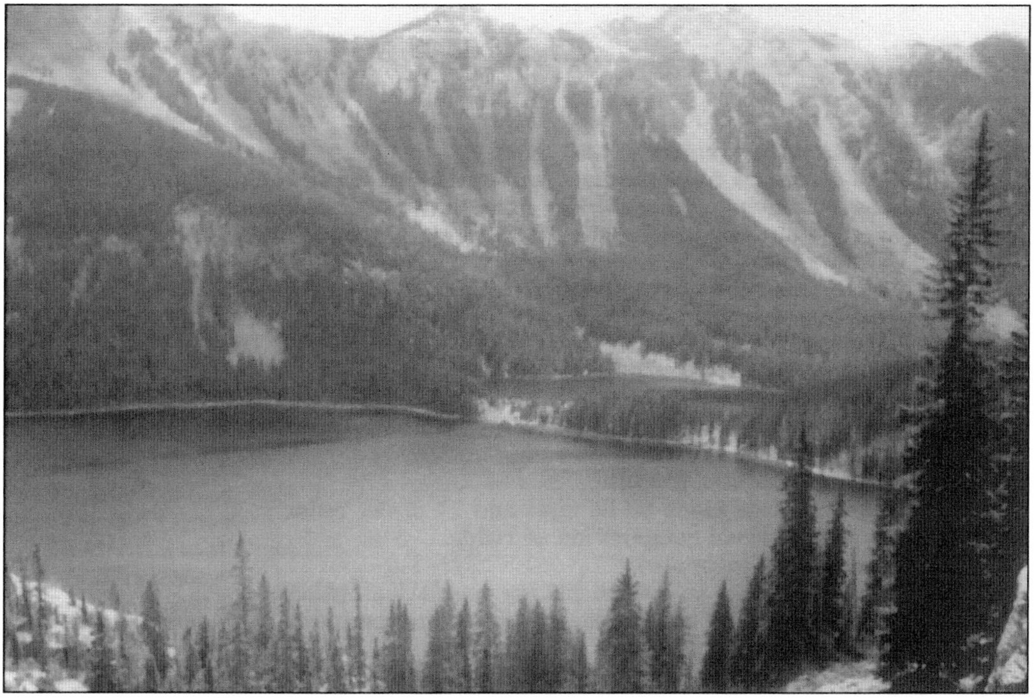

Pictured are Upper Emerald Lake and Little Emerald Lake, as viewed from a ridge below Dollar Lake, another high mountain lake in the San Juan Mountains between the Pine and Vallecito Rivers. Emerald Lake is one of Colorado's largest natural lakes. In 1899, the Emerald Lakes were privately owned by W.T. Kirkpatrick. He stocked the barren lake with trout caught out of the Pine River and carried in cream cans loaded on mules or horses. (Courtesy of Gene Bassett.)

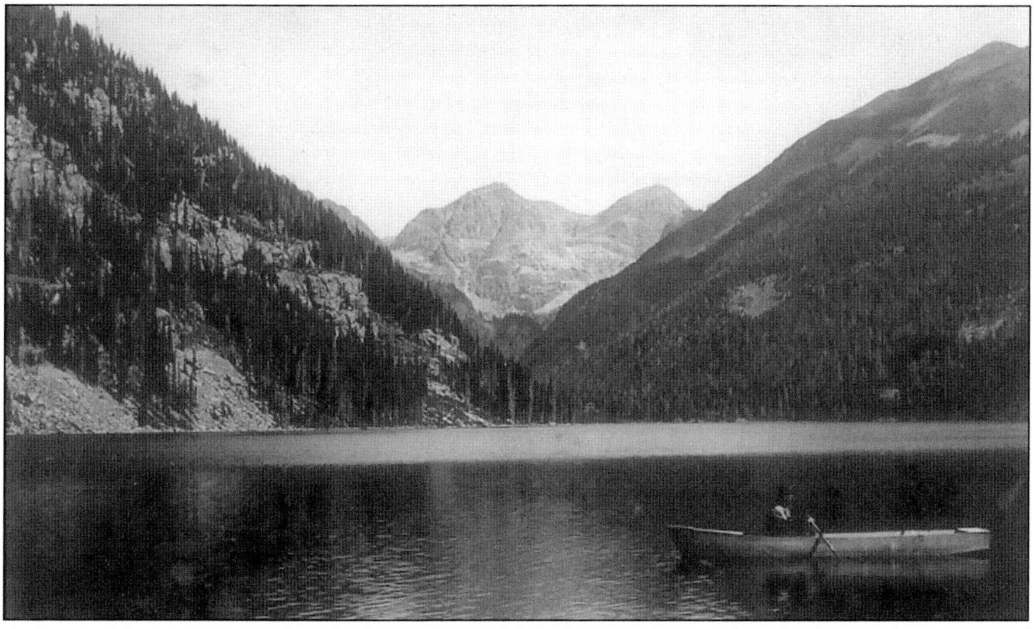

A lone fisherman tries his luck in Emerald Lake in this undated photo. (Courtesy of U.S. Forest Service.)

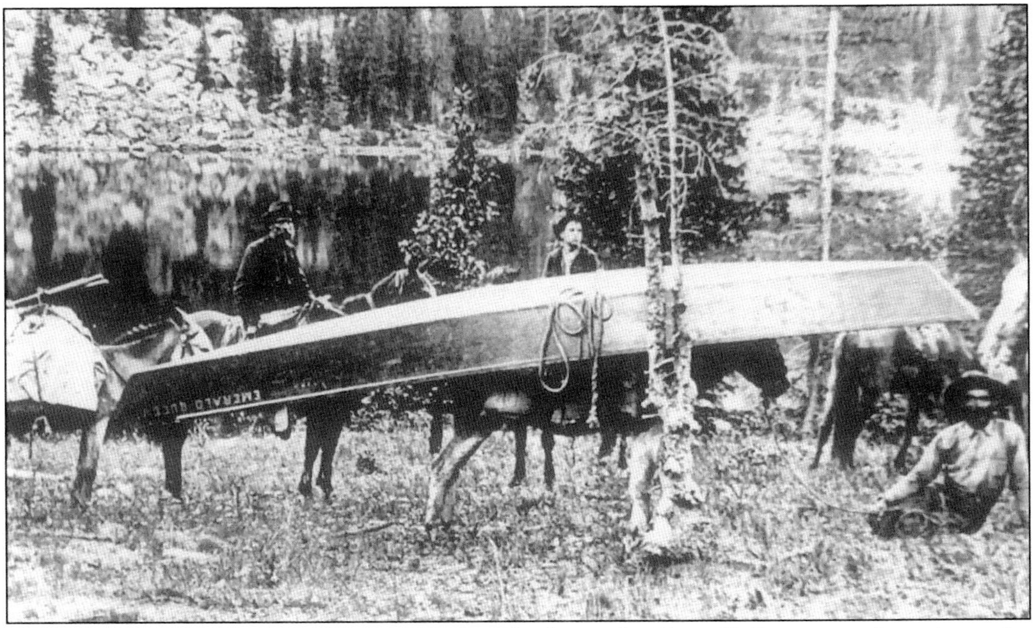

Men stand around the edge of Emerald Lake. The boat, the *Emerald Queen*, was brought to the lake on the back of the mule. The boat was used to catch trout to milk them for their spawn. (Courtesy of Gene Bassett, photo from *Outdoor Life*, June 1902.)

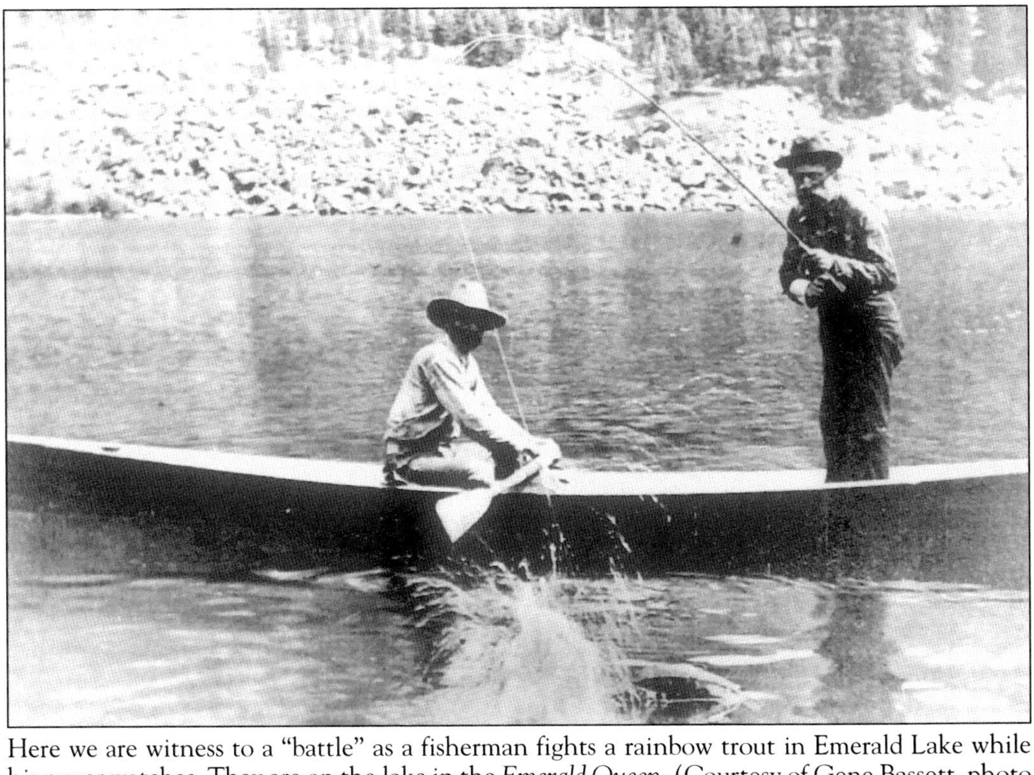

Here we are witness to a "battle" as a fisherman fights a rainbow trout in Emerald Lake while his rower watches. They are on the lake in the *Emerald Queen*. (Courtesy of Gene Bassett, photo from *Outdoor Life*, June 1902.)

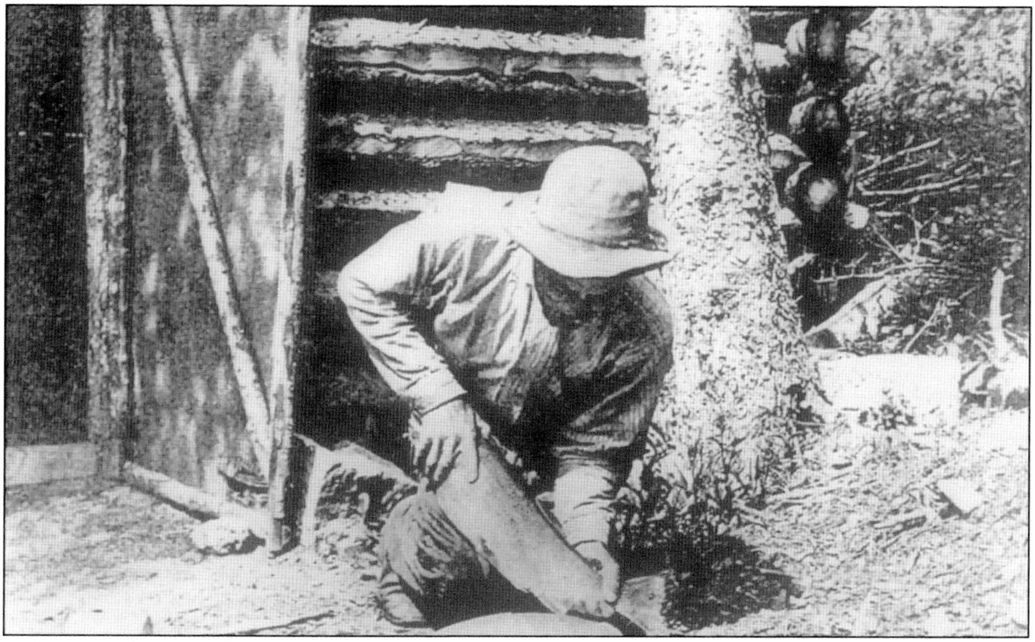

W.F. Patrick sits in front of a cabin at Emerald Lake, milking (stripping) a female rainbow trout for her eggs that will be packed in snow, and taken to a fish hatchery at Wits End, a ranch on the Vallecito River. Mr. Kirkpatrick, owner of Emerald Lakes, also supplied other fish hatcheries in Colorado. He later built his own hatchery at Emerald Lake and not only supplied fish hatcheries with fingerlings, but also stocked other high mountain lakes in the area. (Courtesy of Gene Bassett, photo from *Outdoor Life*, June 1902.)

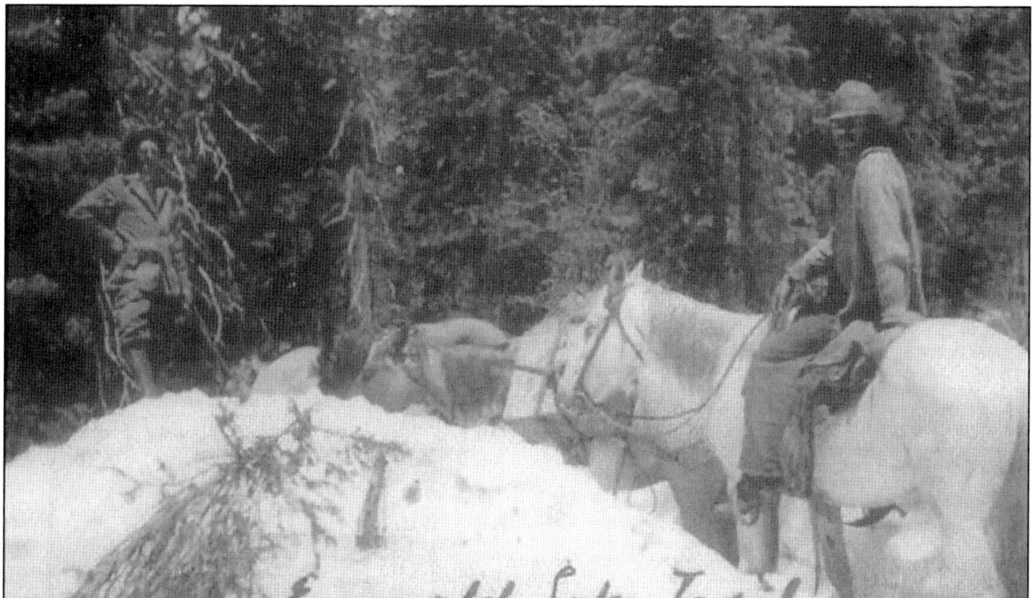

Trout spawn being taken out of Emerald Lake on the Emerald Lake Trail, in June of 1902, by pack animals. The riders are unidentified. (Courtesy of Colorado Game and Fish Department, photo by R.G. Parvin.)

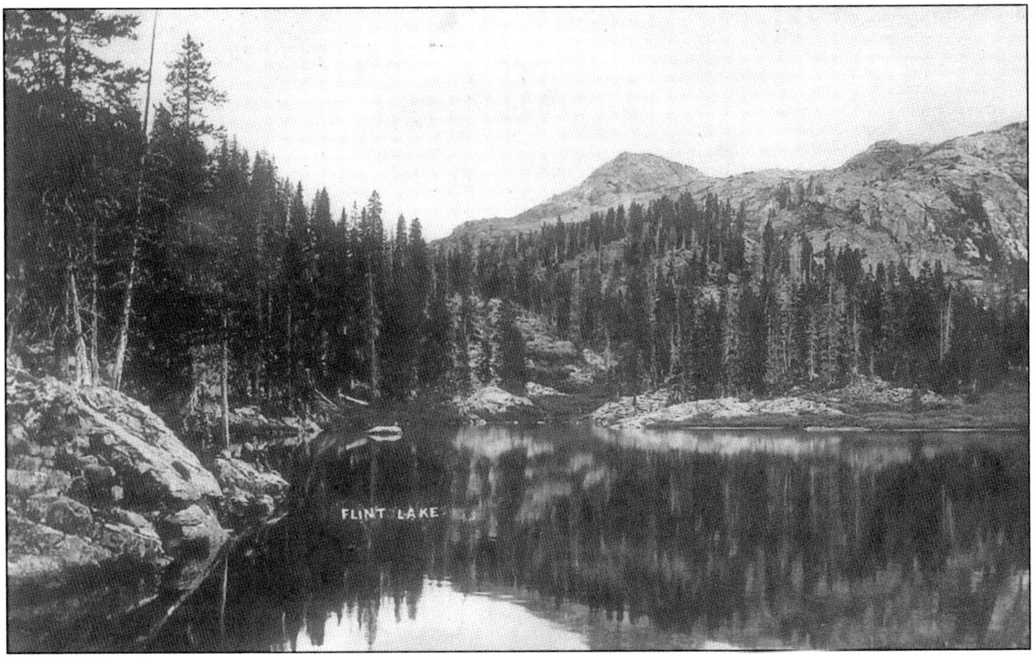

Pictured is Flint Lake, another high 10,000-foot lake in the Weminuche Wilderness. This is an area where many sheep were taken for summer pasture. (Courtesy of U.S. Forest Service.)

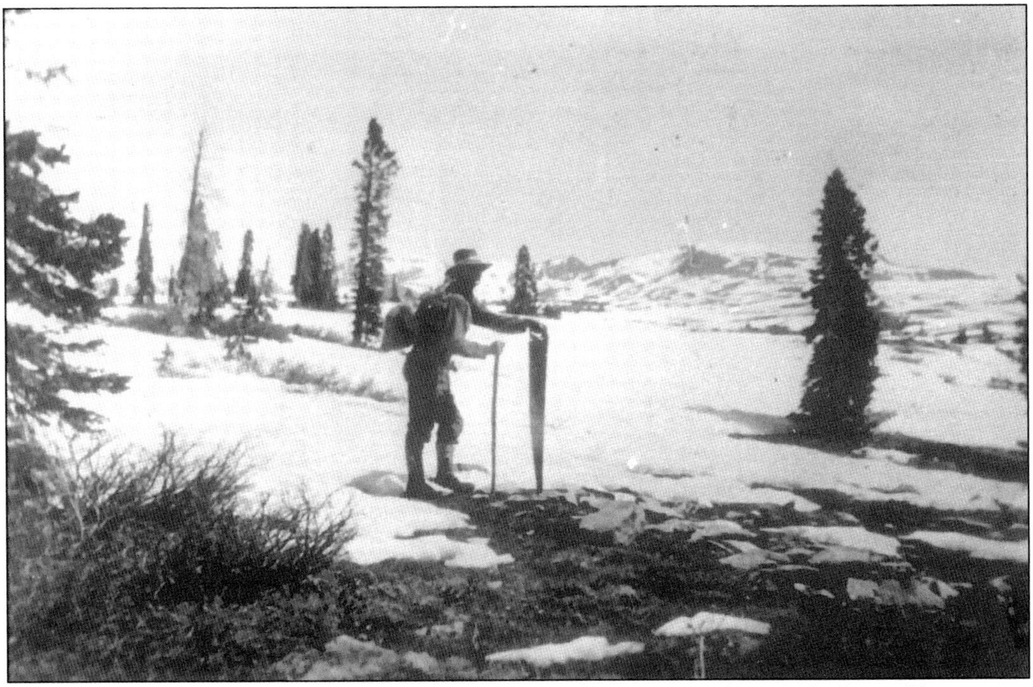

A miner stops for a breather close to the Mary Murphy Mine in this 1920 photo. He rests on his walking stick and a long, one-man, cross-cut saw. Miners usually waited until the snow was almost gone before returning to their claims. (Courtesy of U.S. Forest Service.)

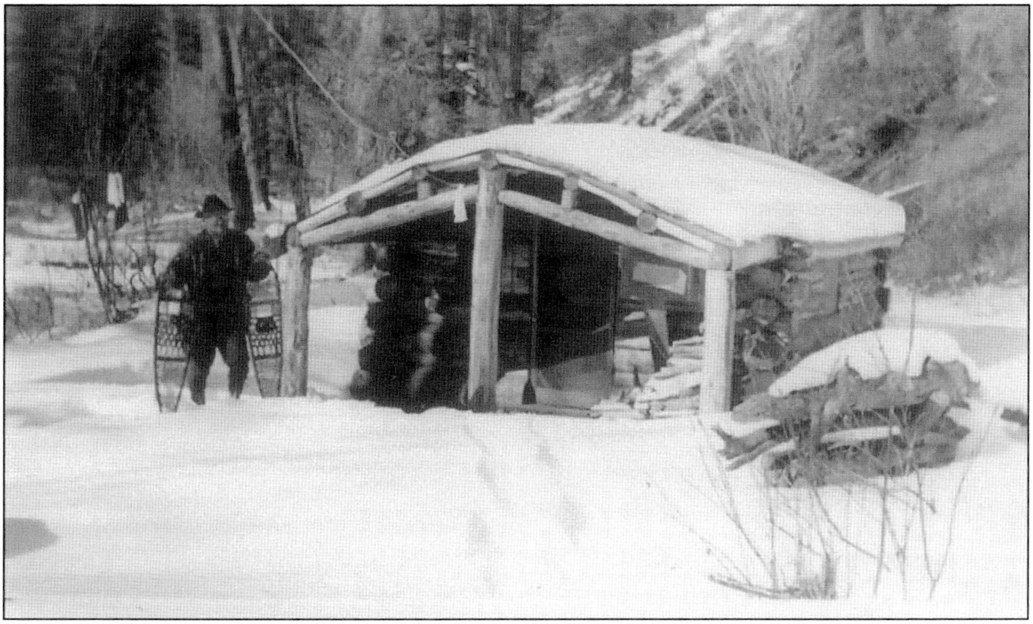

An unidentified man stands by his cabin in Cave Basin. (Courtesy of U.S. Forest Service.)

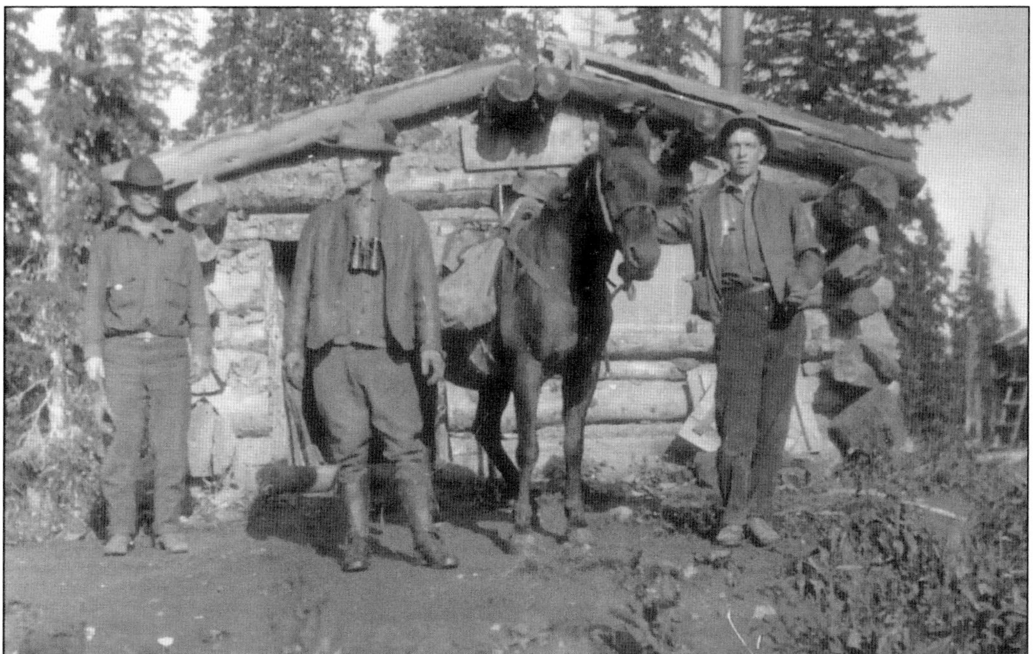

Pictured, from left to right, are Arch H. Campbell, Harold Payne, and Buster Ong, standing in front of their cabin in Cave Basin near the Mary Murphy Mine. (Courtesy of Orrel Brewer Collection.)

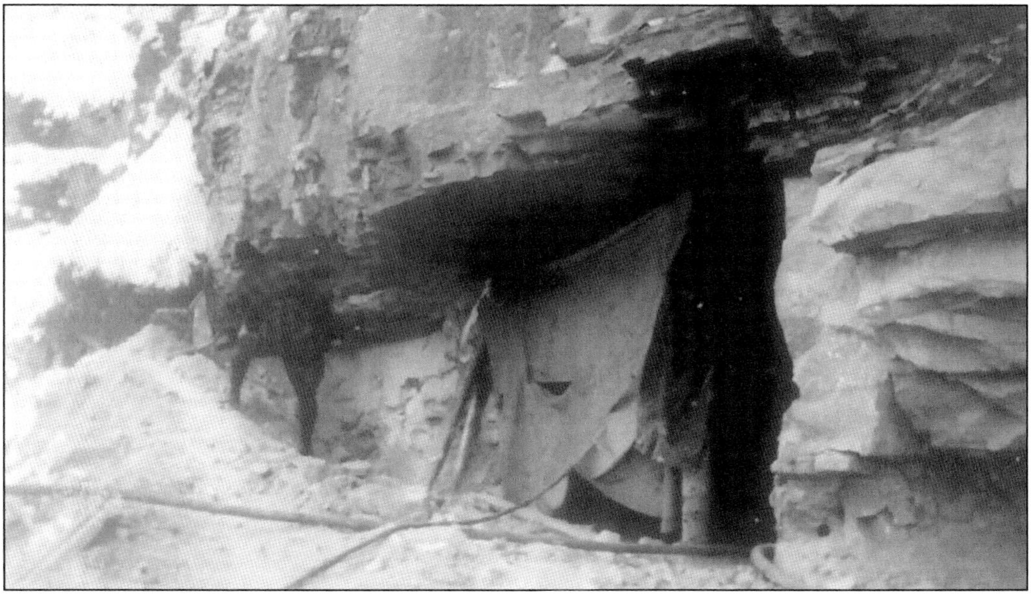

Tillman Brewer looks at an ore vein at his mine claim in Cave Basin in this early 1900 photo. (Courtesy of Orrel Brewer Collection.)

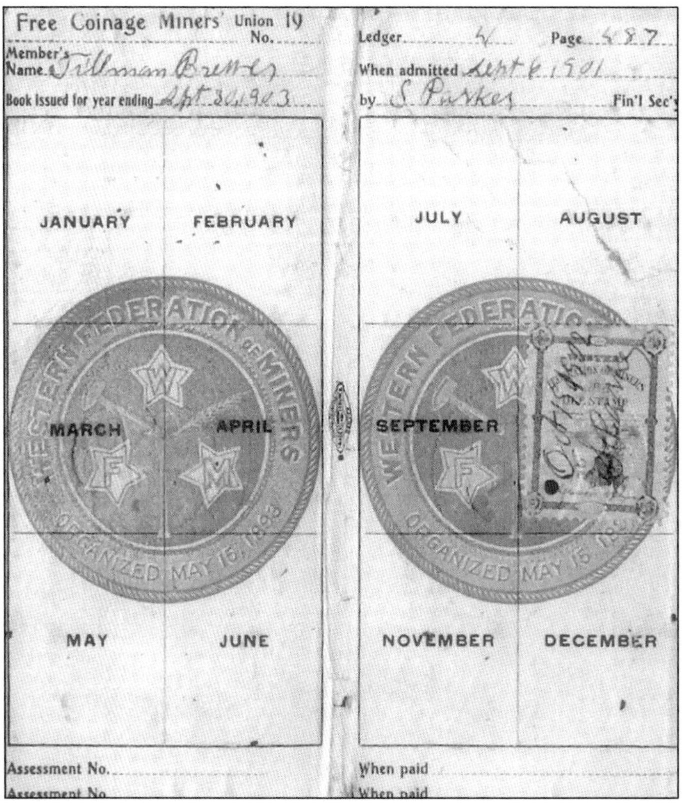

Free Coinage Miners' Union No. 19

Member's Name Tillman Brewer

Book issued for year ending Sept 30, 1903

Ledger 4 Page 487

When admitted Sept 6, 1901

by S. Parkes Fin'l Sec'y

JANUARY FEBRUARY

MARCH APRIL

MAY JUNE

JULY AUGUST

SEPTEMBER

NOVEMBER DECEMBER

WESTERN FEDERATION OF MINERS

ORGANIZED MAY 15, 1893

Assessment No.

When paid

This is a Free Coinage Miners Card, Union 19, issued to Tillman Brewer and Sam Parks. The dates indicate when they were admitted. (Courtesy of Orrel Brewer Collection.)

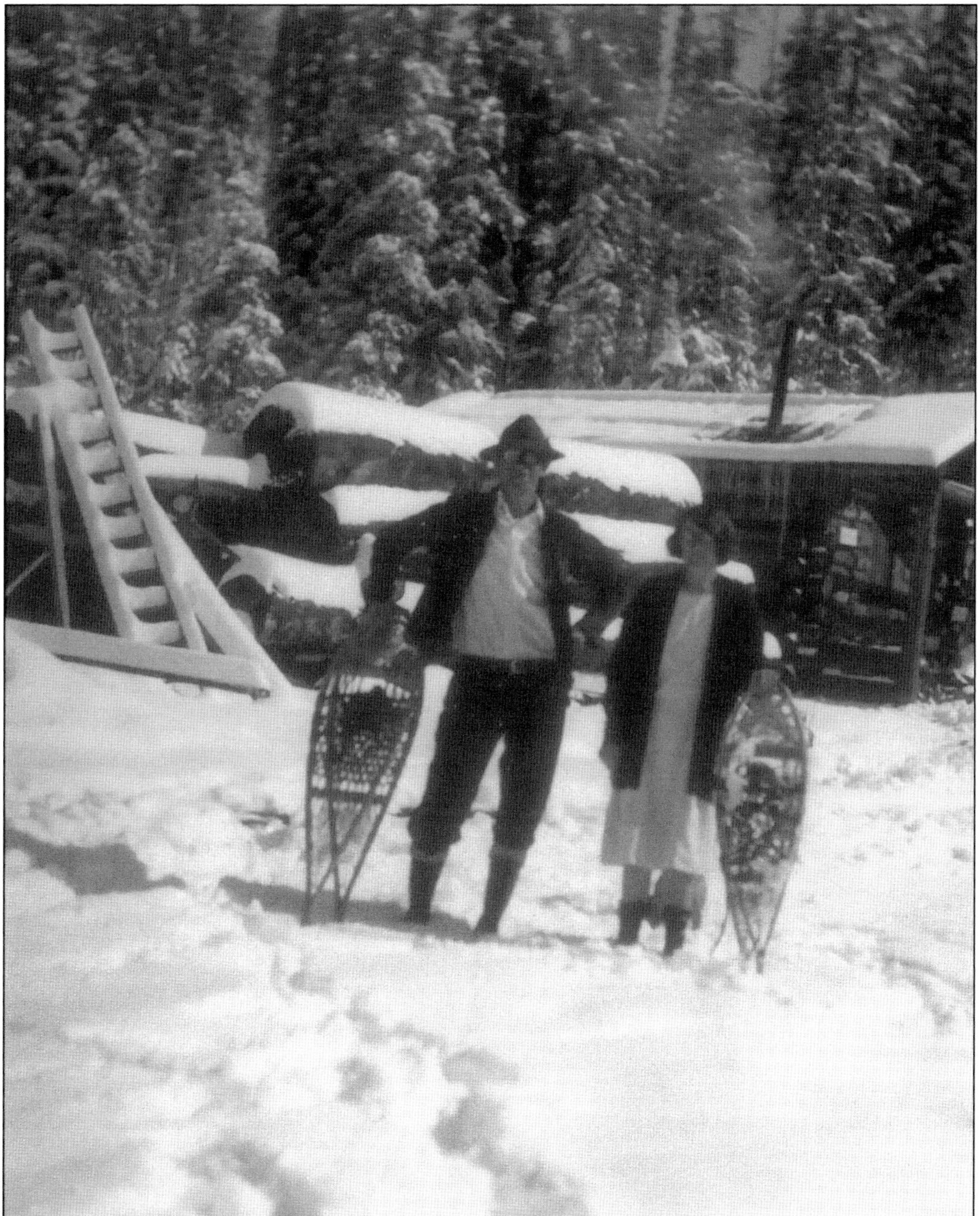

A man and woman stand with their snowshoes in front of their cabin in Cave Basin. (Courtesy of U.S. Forest Service.)

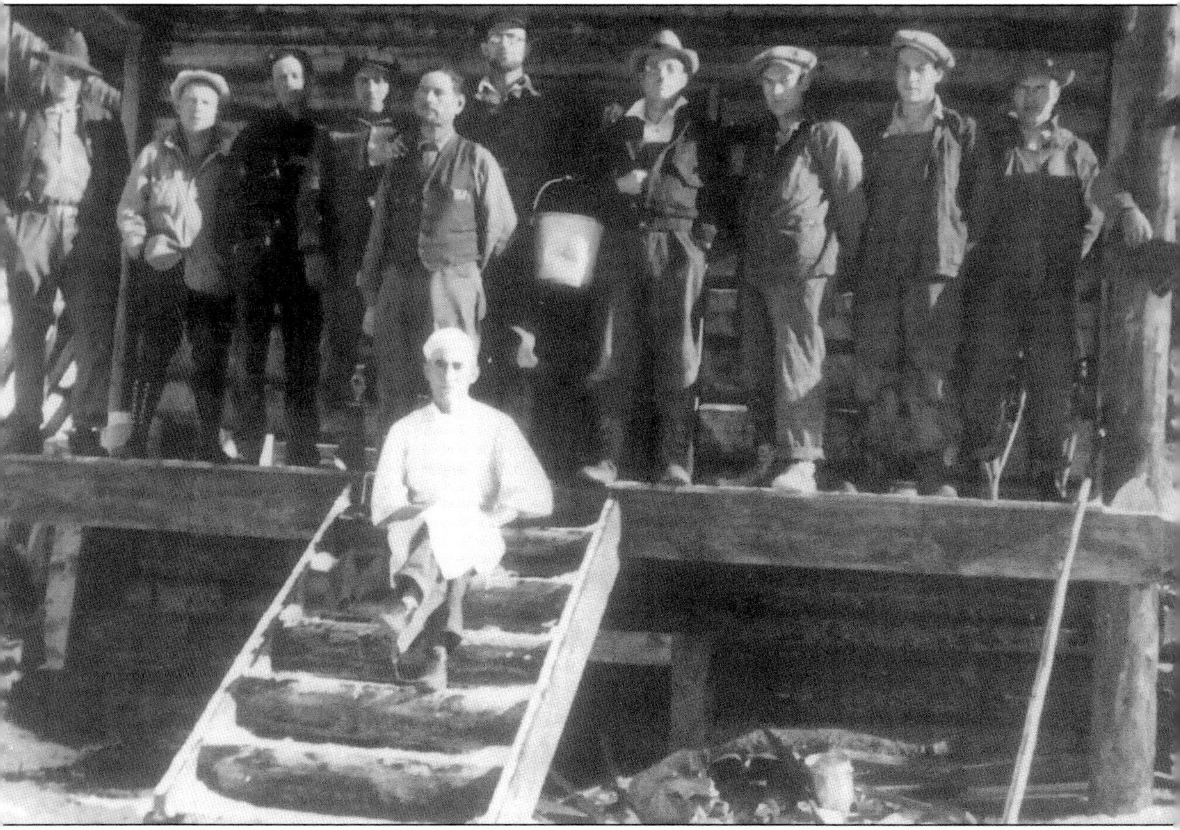

The entire population of Tuckerville poses on the front porch of the dining hall in 1928. Although Mr. Addington built a road up to Tuckerville on the Pine River side, you now have to go up Middle Mountain road on the Vallecito River side to get there. (Courtesy of U.S. Forest Service.)

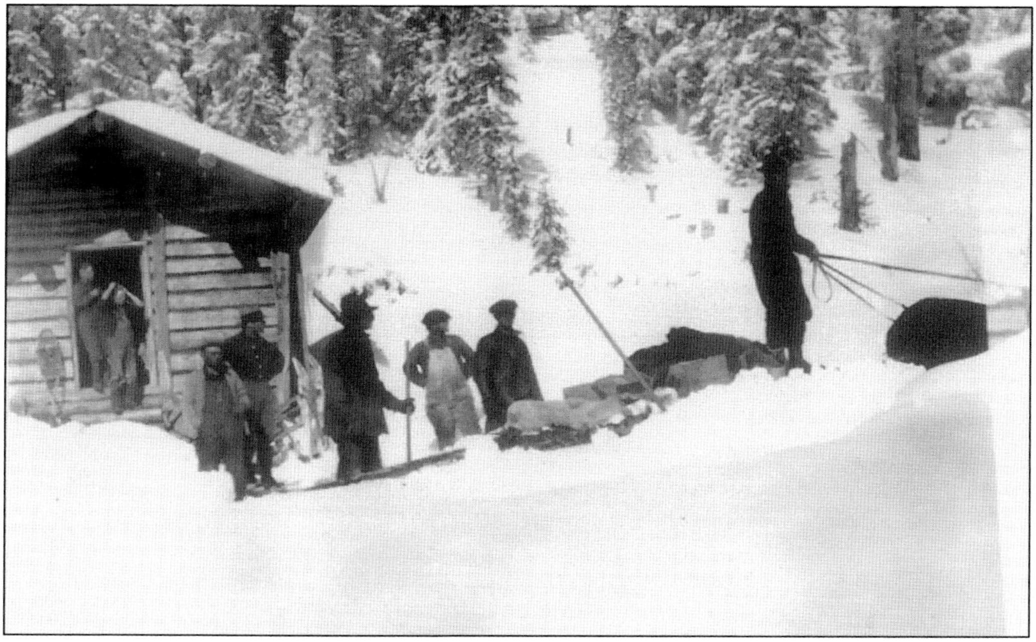

Supplies arrive at Tuckerville by a horse-drawn sled. (Courtesy of Orrel Brewer Collection.)

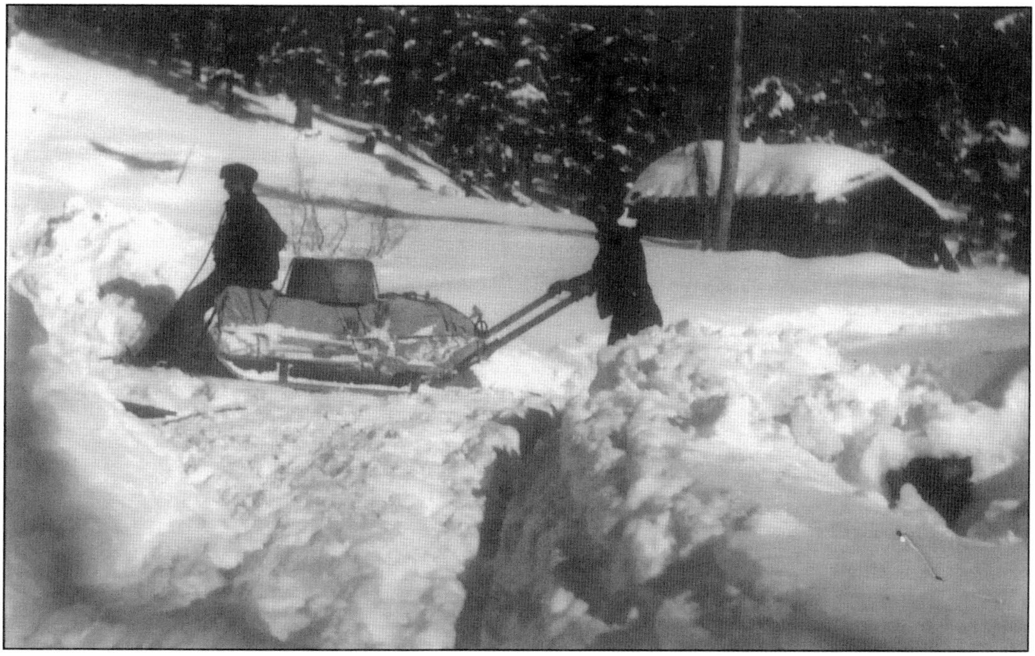

Unidentified individuals taking their supplies by sled are shown taking a rest. The man sitting on the sled pulls while the one in the back pushes. (Courtesy of U.S. Forest Service.)

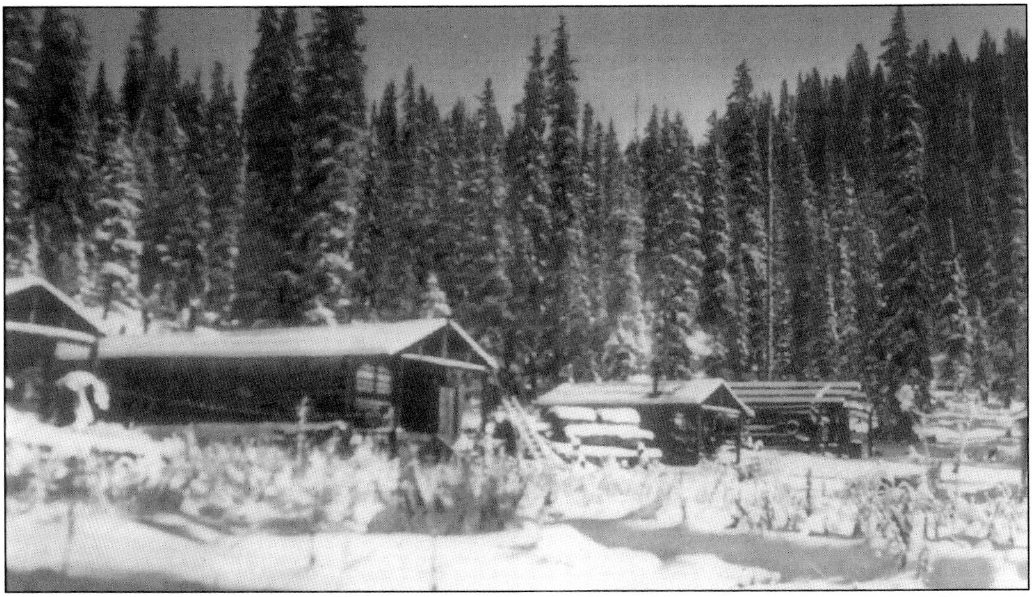

This photo of Tuckerville in the winter of 1929 shows the mess hall and other cabins. The town was abandoned, almost overnight, when the workers found out that Mr. Addington was not going to pay them. In 1986, the Forest Service put a historical marker on the remains of a cabin in Cave Basin. This attracted sightseers, who took pieces of the cabins for souvenirs. Today, all that is left of Tuckerville are the cement foundations. (Courtesy of Orrel Brewer Collection.)

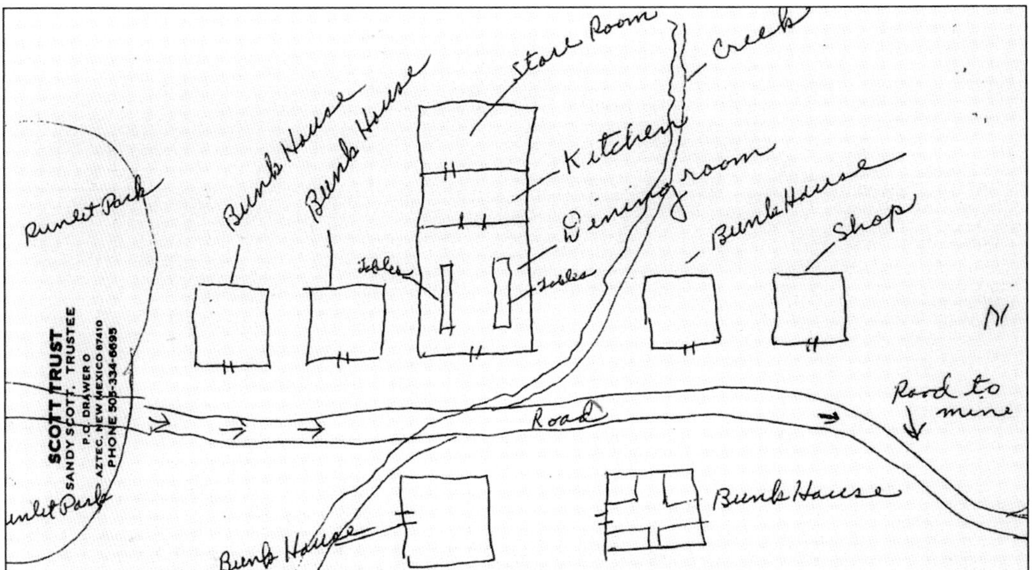

This hand-drawn map of Tuckerville correlates with the above photo of Tuckerville. (Courtesy of Orrel Brewer Collection.)

Seven

Floods and Vallecito Dam

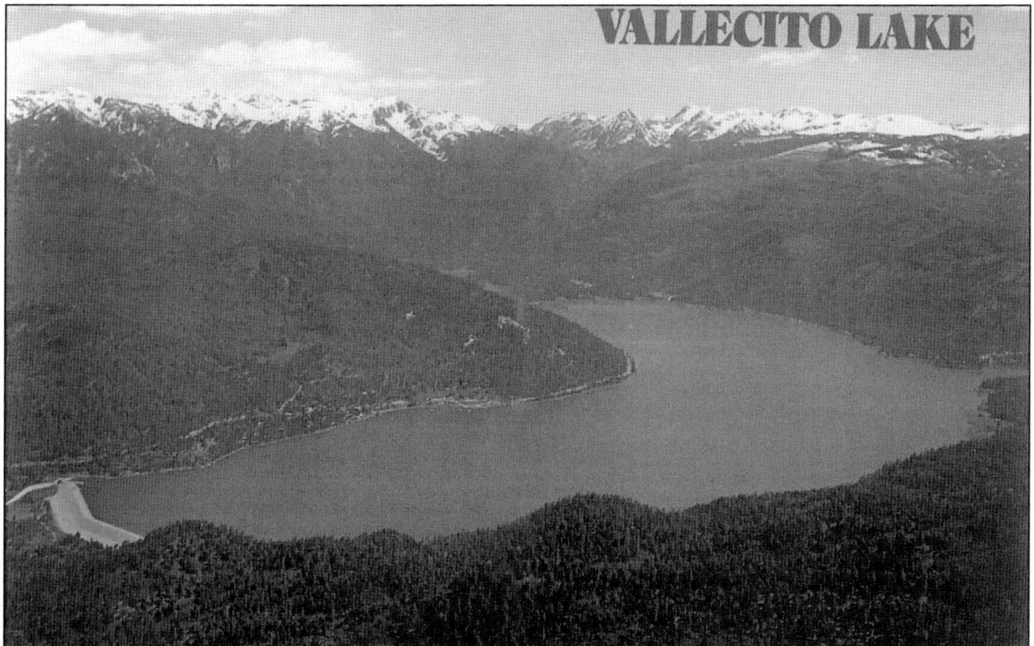

This is an aerial view of Vallecito Lake, Bayfield, Colorado, with the beautiful San Juan Mountains in the background. Vallecito Creek (River) and the Pine River both flow into the Vallecito Lake. (Courtesy of Pine River Lodge, Ermalee Atchinson.)

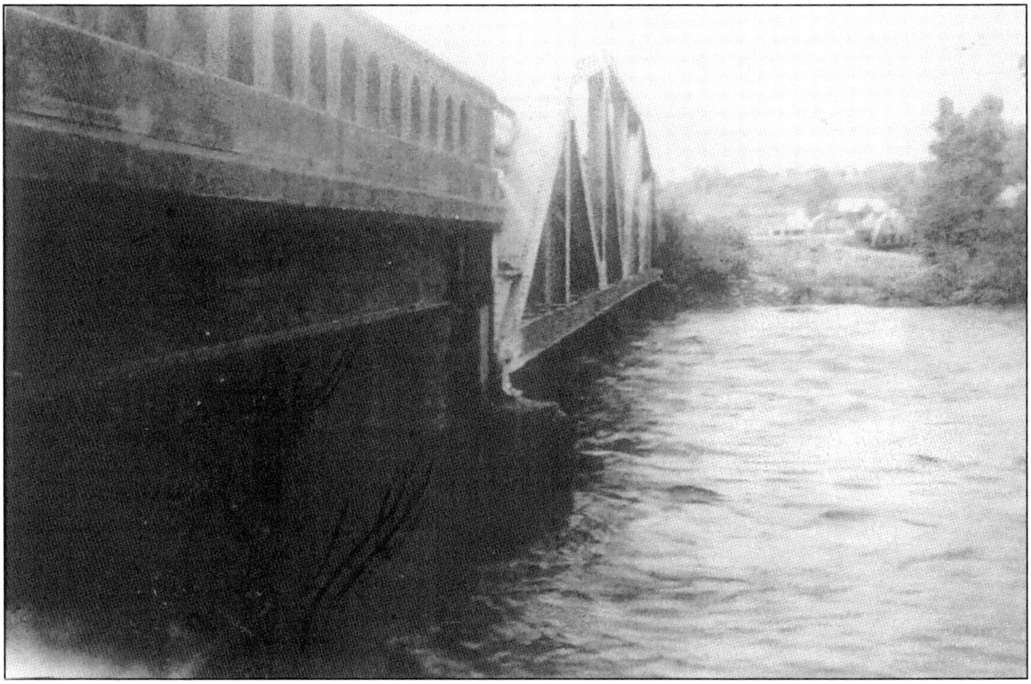

The first bridge on what is now U.S. Highway 160-B, over the Pine River, east of Bayfield, was knocked off its pier in the flood of 1957. The second bridge, in the background, was undamaged. (Courtesy of Louise LeGill Parks.)

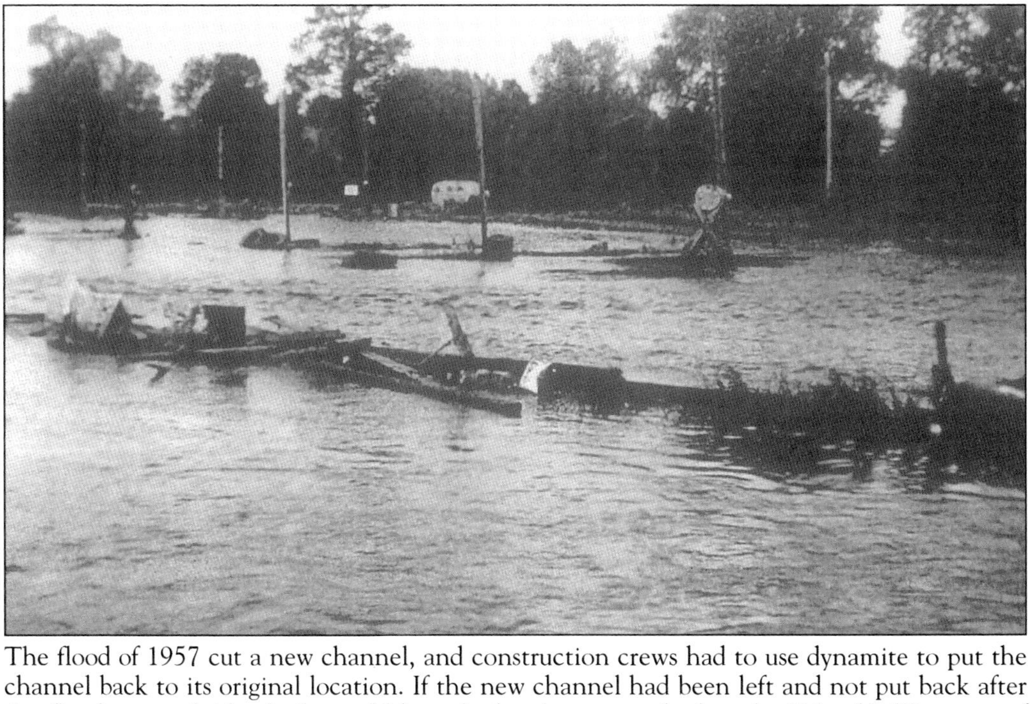

The flood of 1957 cut a new channel, and construction crews had to use dynamite to put the channel back to its original location. If the new channel had been left and not put back after the flood, a new bridge built would have had to have stretched to the "island." (Courtesy of Louise LeGill Parks.)

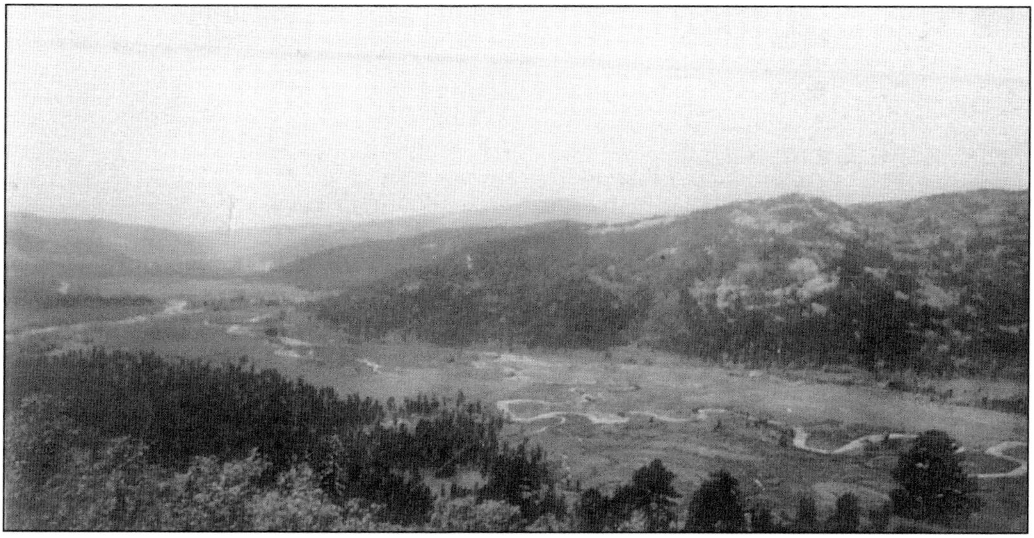

Vallecito Creek (River) winds its way through the Pine River Valley before flowing into the Pine River. This part of Vallecito Creek, due to the building of the dam, is now under water. The Ute Indians called Vallecito Creek *Shu-ah-guche*, which means "crooked water." (Courtesy of Kennon Decker.)

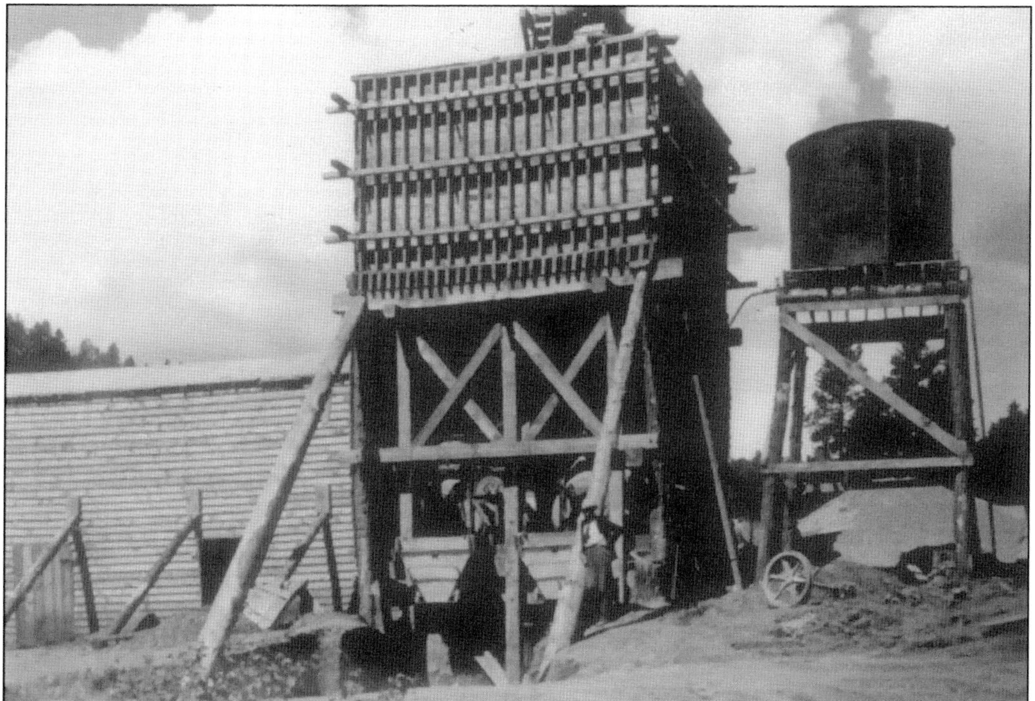

The cement plant was built after the timber had been cleared, above where the dam was to be built. (Courtesy of Bureau of Reclamation.)

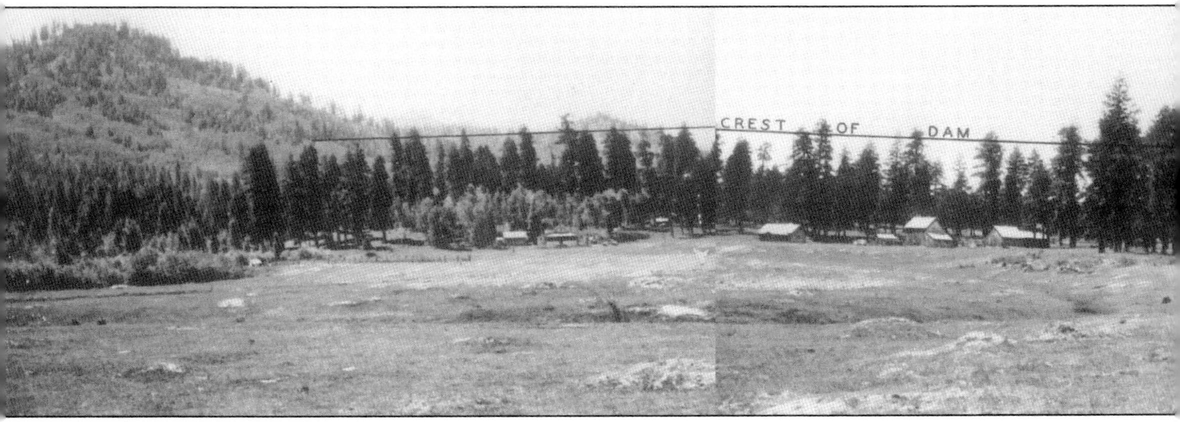

This photo, showing the proposed crest of the dam, was taken about 1936, before the dam was built. The dam was started in 1937 and completed in 1940, just below the confluence of the Pine and Vallecito Rivers. Most of the ranch houses, barns, and out buildings were moved. Those that were not moved were either torn down for the lumber or just burned. One dude

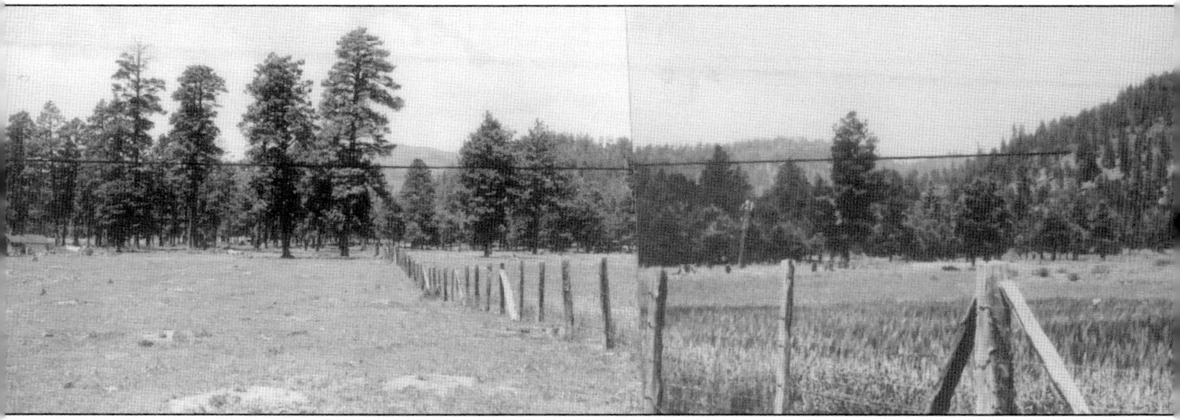

ranch moved up on the hill to be above the level of the water after the dam was built. The clearing of timber from the bottom of the to-be-formed lake was contracted out. Now, when the reservoir is low, you can see the stumps that are left. People walk out to retrieve fishing tackle that has gotten hooked on the old stumps. (Courtesy of Bureau of Reclamation.)

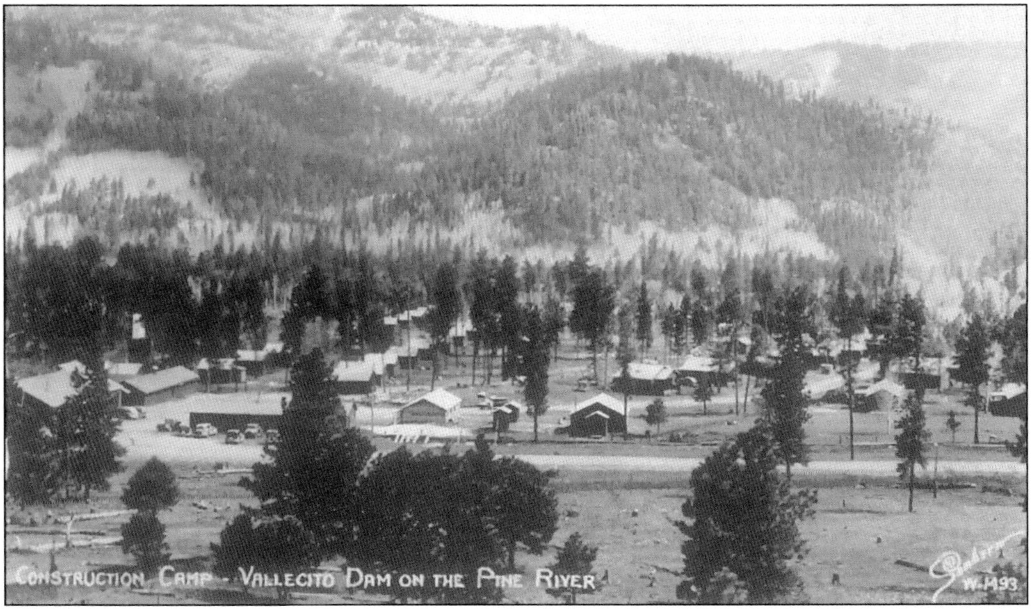

This camp was built by the government for the construction workers below the dam site. Some of the buildings are still in use today as the Vallecito Resort. The majority were either torn down or moved away. The government staff houses, not shown, were up on the hillside across the road from the camp. Almost all of the government houses are homes today, except the office building and superintendent's house, which are still used by the Pine River Irrigation District. The building at the far left is the commissary and the mess hall is next. The water tower is next to the mess hall. (Courtesy of Bureau of Reclamation.)

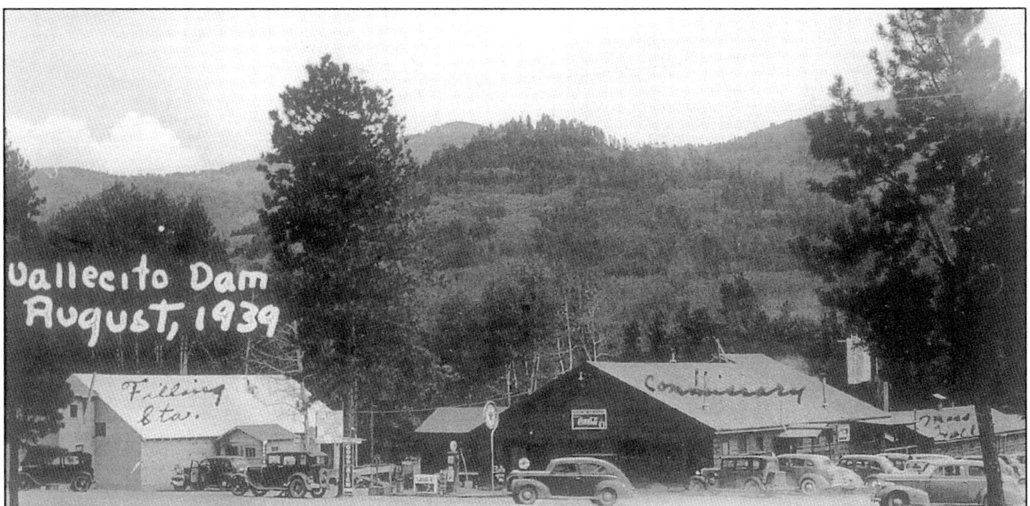

This 1939 photo shows a closer look at the construction camp's commissary, mess hall, and filling station. This photo was made into a postcard, as were many of the photos used in this book. Most of the cabins were town down. The campground today is a trailer park resort called Vallecito Resort. Most of the trailers are permanently set up, and the people come up from Texas, New Mexico, and Arizona for the summers. The commissary, one of the few existing buildings, is the store and office for the resort. (Courtesy of Rex Hornbaker.)

One of the Last Best Places

Laddie John has produced a labor of love. This small book on the Pine River Valley and the town of Bayfield, Colorado has consumed him for several years as he has sought out historic photographs, interviewed old-timers (though he himself is long past 65), and tried to assemble bits and pieces of local history to create this meaningful mosaic of time and place. It is always a pleasure working with dedicated amateur historians who bring to their work a love of the landscape and a deep understanding of those who have gone before.

I have learned much from Laddie as he wrote this book, and I am looking forward to long hikes into the San Juan Mountains and the Weminuche Wilderness, which is the vast mountain massif to the north of the Pine River Valley. Wilderness is vital and important to us, and it is the one natural resource that can be lost but never recovered. Wallace Stegner, Edward Abbey, and a host of eloquent writers have written about wilderness and its meaning.

Southwestern Colorado and the Pine River Valley remains unique in the history of the American West because it was settled so late after being carved out of lands traditionally reserved by Ute Indian bands. While much of America has been plowed or paved or built upon, the Pine River Valley exists as an intact cultural landscape, though equity émigrés from other states are building expensive summer homes, and the pioneer families Laddie writes about can no longer survive on ranch incomes alone.

Irrevocable change is occurring in the valley as farms and fields give way to part-time residences, yet the mountains remain and dominate the landscape at the north end of the Pine River Valley. Some of the finest hiking and fishing in the Rocky Mountains can be found between Bayfield to the south and Twilight Peak and the Needles Mountains to the North. And then there are the high altitude lakes like Emerald Lake, Little Emerald Lake, Four Mile Lake, Flint Lake, Crater Lake, Lake Eileen, and others.

The Conservation Congress drafted many significant pieces of federal legislation in 1964, in part to commemorate the death of John F. Kennedy. With that, Congress gave us the Clean Air Act, the Clean Water Act, and Wild and Scenic Rivers, but most importantly they gave us wilderness. Pioneers into the Pine River Valley in the 1880s and 1890s would have had plenty of wilderness, but by the 1960s, very little roadless public land remained. The Wilderness Act preserves roadless areas in national forests like the San Juan National Forest. Humans are only visitors into wilderness areas, and we must travel on foot or on horseback. Mechanized travel is not permitted and helicopters can land in emergencies only with special permission of the Secretary of Agriculture.

The 500,000 acre Weminuche Wilderness north of the Pine River Valley is the largest wilderness area in Colorado, and one of the main trails follows Vallecito Creek, which is a tributary of the Pine River. Mountains have deep meaning for those of us in southwestern Colorado who have chosen to live here, because we value landscape and isolation. We live four-and-a-half hours from the nearest interstate highway system, and we are rewarded with some of the cleanest air in the United States.

We value these high mountain valleys just as the pioneers did before us, and the Moache and Capote bands of Ute Indians before them. The poet Robinson Jeffers wrote, "But for my children, I would have them keep their distance from the thickening center; corruption never has been compulsory; when the cities lie at the monster's feet there are left the mountains."

Laddie John has written and edited this photography book because he believes in the spirit of place, and he believes that the architecture of the pioneers must be remembered. Yes, they would still recognize the valley, but they would not believe the boats on Vallecito Lake or the many hikers or fishermen. Pioneers fought hard to live off the land. They had little time for recreation. T.K. Whipple understood their generation and our generation perfectly. He wrote:

All America lies at the end of the wilderness road,
And our past is not a dead past, but still
lives in us.

Our forefathers had civilization inside themselves,
The wild outside. We live in the civilization
They created, but within us
the wilderness still lingers.

What they dreamed, we live, and what they lived,
We dream.

Enjoy this book by Laddie John and visit the Pine River Valley. Hike the trails around Vallecito Lake and breathe deeply when you cross the boundary into the Weminuche Wilderness.

Our forefathers, the families that Laddie writes about, had three things we have lost in the 21st century. They had silence, solitude, and darkness at night under a canopy of stars. Enter the Weminuche Wilderness at the upper end of the Pine River Valley and experience a pristine mountain landscape. Listen to Vallecito Creek as it tumbles through the rocks hundreds of feet below and think about nature as it was meant to be.

Andrew Gulliford
Director
Center of Southwest Studies
Professor of Southwest Studies and history
Fort Lewis College, Durango

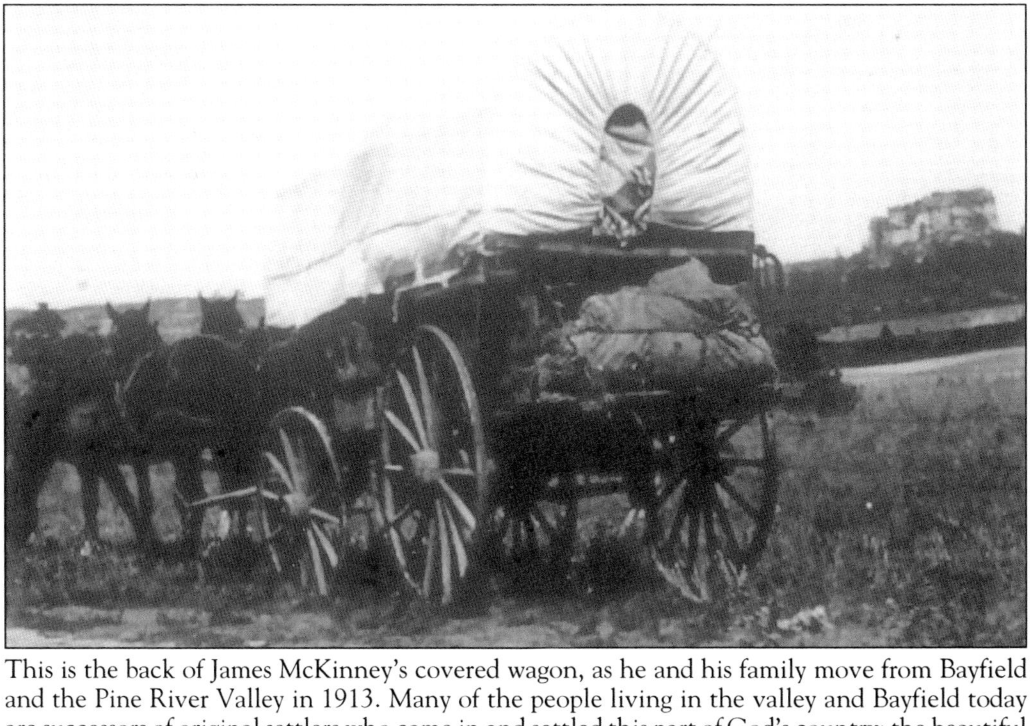

This is the back of James McKinney's covered wagon, as he and his family move from Bayfield and the Pine River Valley in 1913. Many of the people living in the valley and Bayfield today are successors of original settlers who came in and settled this part of God's country: the beautiful Pine River Valley. (Courtesy of Barb Fjerstad.)